POLICY ANALYSIS AND RESEARCH TECHNOLOGY

Political and Ethical Considerations

Also available from Lyceum Books, Inc.

POLICY ANALYSIS AND RESEARCH TECHNOLOGY

Political and Ethical Considerations

Thomas M. Meenaghan
Keith M. Kilty

LYCEUM
BOOKS, INC.

5758 S. Blackstone Ave.
Chicago, Illinois 60637

© Lyceum Books, Inc. 1993

Published in the United States by
LYCEUM BOOKS, INC.
5758 S. Blackstone Avenue
Chicago, Illinois 60637
Phone: 312/643-1902
FAX: 312/643-1903

Library of Congress Cataloging-in-Publication Data

Meenaghan, Thomas M.
    Policy and methods : political and ethical considerations / Thomas
M. Meenaghan and Keith M. Kilty.
        p.   cm.
    Includes bibliographical references and index.
    ISBN 0-925065-46-3
    1. Social service.   2. Human services.   3. Policy sciences.
I. Kilty, Keith M. (Keith Michael), 1946–   . II. Title.
HV40.M4567   1993
361.6—dc20   93-30524
                                                        CIP

CONTENTS

The Book is Dedicated to

Kathleen, Christopher, Mary
Peter, and Rose

Christina, Kenneth and Sheila

PREFACE

This book was written with a specific point in mind: that as a result of the explosion of information and the increased demands for accountability in human service programs, society in general and human service professionals have tended to lose sight of the "big picture." The result has been a focus on individuals and specific needs rather than on prevention and the overall political and ethical considerations that interact with and shape policy and research.

Over the past several years the helping professions, especially social work, have seen an expansion of literature related to social work research. Major works by authors such as Grinnell, Rubin, Babbie, Fischer, Bloom, and Powers, to name a few, have greatly contributed to this expansion and have helped the social work profession in its development and its quest for more validated knowledge concerning practice.

Although the research literature has expanded and become increasingly inter-related with practice, there also has been some fragmentation between research and critical analysis in social policy. Further, although research, theory, and practice interventions have developed, there has been some contraction in the awareness of the larger social world within which that development has occurred.

This book examines the relations among interventions, inquiry, and the larger social/political context. This larger context involves such elements as culture, political and economic interests, and professional concerns. The interplay of the larger social world and practice and research requires analysis of issues that transcend research methodology. Such analysis can explicate some of the choices, even alternative normative structures, facing social service professionals.

This book also interrelates aspects of policy and research within the context of our political structure. Thus it goes beyond conventional policy or research texts to consider these topics within a particular focus. This focus recognizes that research methodology is important but contextually contaminated. The book integrates content that is required in social work programs—policy and research. It also focuses on groups at risk, society, and the helping professions' emerging concern with prevention. Thus we have attempted to follow the Council on Social Work Education's mandates to include curriculum integration, emphasis on groups at risk, and the stress on values and ethics.

Both of the authors have taught policy and research for several years. We are not arguing against scientific inquiry; rather, we are urging competency in inquiry and in the analysis of the interactions of the larger world with the profession in action.

To develop this focus, we have divided the book into five parts. The first part, which comprises one chapter, stresses political and rational developments within social work and the human service fields. (Some of the ideas in Chapter 1 are also expressed in a forthcoming article in *Social Work*.) The second part of the book has four chapters that trace how science and policy get contaminated within the world of politics and practicality. The realities of agencies, organizational policy and inquiry are all stressed. The third part of the book, which consists of two chapters, reviews the critical concepts of, as well as the choices associated with, need, risk, and populations and groups at risk. These critical concepts, reviewed at length in chapters 6 and 7, reflect both policy and research concerns. They also tend to set up the boundaries within which programs ultimately get created.

The fourth part of the book is a specification and critique of two major ways in which research technology is tied to policy and programs. Chapter 8 reviews the technology of needs assessment, and chapter 10 reviews the technology of program evaluation. Chapters 9 and 11 discuss crucial issues, many of them ethical, that can and do affect the research technology.

The book concludes with a short chapter on broad, even philosophical, observations concerning the book's focus on the larger social, political, and economic context interacting with research and policy.

We would like to thank several people for their involvement in this manuscript. David Follmer accepted the premise of this book. A number of people helped in preparing and assembling the manuscript: Joan Frazier, Sherri Bell, Helen Beapré, Julie Hanson and Catherine Washington. A very special thanks to Mary Schiltz for her wisdom, degree of organization, and most of all her sense of humor as she solves problems. Kenneth Kilty deserves special thanks for his help in preparing some of the computer graphics. Nancy Helmick and Jennifer Kuehn, from the Ohio State University College of Social Work Library, were especially helpful in developing the literature search, and Michael Coconis provided invaluable aid in tracking down materials. Richard Dietz deserves attention simply because he is Richard. Last, but most of all, we thank Gina Bart for her work, her critique, and her interest in our work.

Tom Meenaghan
Keith M. Kilty

PART 1

The Helping Professions: Inquiry and Political Influences

Part One develops several points that are central to the study of policy and scientific inquiry as they relate to the helping professions. Among the topics raised are:

- The convergence of a conservative political climate in the larger society.
- The contraction of the welfare state.
- The theoretical and scientific developments within the helping professions, especially social work.
- The functional relations between political imperatives emanating from the larger society and use of scientific inquiry within the helping professions.

We argue that the development and needs of social work may have inadvertently contributed to, and have reflected, society's preoccupation with scientific justification for its lack of commitment to addressing adequately certain problems and issues in the American welfare state. Overall, the significant consequence of this process is that although certain at-risk groups have been overlooked, the quest for scientific credibility has proceeded.

CHAPTER 1

The Helping Professions and the Convergence of Politics and Science

The helping professions relate to and are affected by scientific inquiry, technology, and values. Whereas academic disciplines are directed to understanding aspects of nature and environment, the helping professions normatively are obligated to engage the world, to understand selective aspects of it, and to attempt to change some features or facets of that world. Thus, whereas academic diciplines are concerned primarily with knowledge, the helping professions are concerned primarily with action—doing something to promote activity or change.[1]

Central both to the disciplines and the helping professions is the distinctive role of scientific inquiry. It is through scientific inquiry that many disciplines pursue their primary goals of seeking truth and understanding the world. In related fashion, the helping professions depend on scientific inquiry. Either the helping professions adapt and borrow insights from the relevant disciplines in an attempt to act and modify the environment, or they attempt to develop and then use their own body of scientific knowledge. In either instance, the helping professions use and apply scientific knowledge for a particular reason or purpose. In short, the helping professions are oriented to achieving a chosen goal or meeting a certain expectation. Within this context scientific inquiry is helpful.

In using science to extend understanding and knowledge of the world, the disciplines are not focused on "practical" implications. Rather, the relevant norms are accuracy, and what Merton has called "organized skepticism."[2] More specifically, the values attached to the scientific process affirm attitudes of objectivity, impersonality, disinterestedness, and political neutrality.

Distinct from science and the disciplines is the world of technology, the selective application of science. In a real sense, technology is the purposeful attempt to apply science to shape, maybe at times manage, the environment—or at least specific components of it. Technology is inherently driven by utilitarianism, that is, valuing something because it is functional.[3]

Professions, in some respects, are quite close to technology. For example, like technology professions are primarily directed to the application of knowledge. In this context the skills of professionals are central as they attempt to interact with and shape the environment. More specifically, human service professionals are coming to see that technology can be used in the context of working with people and communities. Use of the MMPI, the fruit of scientific inquiry concerning the personalities of human beings, can be positively applied in working with individual clients. Similarly, the technology of large-scale surveys can now be used by major agencies and funders in setting priorities.

Even though the helping professions are increasingly aware of the relevance of technology, they ultimately are distinct from technology in much the same manner as they are distinct from "pure" science and the disciplines. For example whereas the helping professions are linked to science in the goal of knowing, sharing a common utilitarian focus with technology, the helping professions, because of their values and norms, are dramatically different from both. The helping professions seek consequences—call them "effects"—that are value statements or value preferences. These values can be embodied in case goals for clients and broader professional standards. For example, the purpose of intervention with a client is not merely to study him or her but also to assess and to help that client relative to a preferred standard, such as, completing school or communicating better with parents. On a larger scale, the values can be embedded in expectations concerning the reduction of infant mortality rates or increasing the percentage of people with incomes above certain levels. Intervention by the helping professions is always framed by a desired state or goal.[4] In short, professional behavior is and should be value-oriented relative to a particular standard of functioning. Put another way, successful or effective professional intervention is consequential in that it produces and/or affirms a particular value.

Professional behavior also reflects values in terms of the people or populations served by helping professions and in terms of how those populations are served. In a period when human welfare resources are assumed to be fixed or contracting, the questions, increasingly seen as political in nature, of who should receive what and how are not answered automatically; nor are they easily determined. Nonetheless, some people or groups will receive more (or less) attention, and the attention will vary in terms of amount and intensity of professional interventions. For example, the amount and range of federal benefits and services for the elderly as a group far outstrip the responses that human service professionals give to low-income female heads of households. There is legitimate reason to infer that by design or not, the elderly currently are a more "special," more valued population than young mothers who are poor.[5]

In a similar vein, an examination of who receives the attention of helping professions shows that certain types of clients with certain needs often prevail. This value commitment overshadows a potential commitment to persons who, largely because of the status they occupy in society, share high rates of risk. Regardless of whether need or risk were to dominate, such domination—intended or not—would reflect a value commitment.

In looking at the implications of valuing groups with needs and groups at greater risk, we can begin to see the complexity of the situation. Not only would society become aware of the relation between and among certain groups and risk, there would be greater appreciation of how social position affects certain at-risk groups. This in turn could lead logically to the consideration of policy and program interventions that would transcend modification of individuals in need. Not only would prevention be pursued, but intervention would reflect the changing social structure and the prevailing configurations between and among groups. This very conclusion may be precisely why the larger society does not value certain at-risk groups and why policy and program interventions tend to move both in the direction of individuals and need. It also may be that, even when prevention is stressed, the prevention tends to focus mainly on the relationship between group characteristics and behavior patterns rather than on the interplay between the larger system and those group characteristics and behavior patterns.

In related fashion, selective use of scientific methodologies can and will occur within this political context of valuing certain populations and addressing certain problems. In this regard, scientific inquiry and the scientific methods applied cannot be fully divorced from the larger political and volitional context.

As we move further into the 1990s, it is important to be aware of the linkage between scientific inquiry and the helping professions, and between technology and the professions. In the former case the linkage is understanding and knowledge; in the latter it is the motivation for, and the application and usage of, knowledge. Ultimately, however, the values and norms of the helping professions are unique because they require the professional to orient his or her behavior to preferred standards and outcomes and to see whether doing so made a difference. These values include an individual's right not only to survival and maintenance, but to maximum human growth and development; to improved social functioning; and to the obligation of society and the professions to provide for just and fair responses to its members. Concern with practice effectiveness should not occur without a full continuing appreciation of the value context in which the practice occurs. Values and norms also require the human service professional to examine the broader questions of who does and does not receive services and what the focus of such interventions is. This last issue, because it is political, requires the professional to be aware of how the larger cultural and political context influences the human service professions as they address specific people, and in terms of what they offer them. Without appropriate attention to both issues—degree of effectiveness and role of the larger cultural and "political" context—the helping professions run the risk of losing their bearings and perhaps becoming accountable to forces and processes of which they are not even aware.

Political and Cultural Context and the Use of Inquiry

Outside forces can and will affect how human service professions operate. In turn, operations within the human service professions will reinforce larger cultural and political processes. This section examines how, over time, conservative themes in the larger society interact with the emerging emphasis on science and technology within the human service professions.

If one had to characterize the 1960s, one might say it was a decade of questioning. Questions were raised about basic values in American society, e.g., work, love and commitment, and the role of the military. Within the human service fields, similar questions were raised about opportunity structures in the society, and about the degree of inequality to be tolerated or encouraged.

Questions also were asked about the options for poor people, people of color, and women. The questions included:

- Why are so many people poor in a very wealthy society?
- Why is poverty routinely prevalent in certain groups?
- Why is poverty intergenerational, especially in a society that views itself as offering upward mobility?
- Why are so few women and racial and ethnic minorities represented in certain organizations?
- Why are women and minorities denied access to certain services and opportunities, e.g., education and employment?

Such questions reflected an increasing concern with the apparently limited options afforded members of certain groups, and the resulting inability of these groups' members to compete in the American system.[6]

The critical role of the education and economic institutions and the interaction between them was increasingly stressed. The focus moved from certain people who had problems to questions about why and how these institutions allowed specific groups to be excluded from full participation in society. Along with continuing recognition that certain people suffered the effects of problems, was increased recognition that these effects reflected basic flaws in society as well as in its institutions and their structures and processes.

A related development was the conspicuous movement away from individual treatment and therapy. The professional focus increasingly was on groups and communities, and the power and resources different groups might, and should, have within society.[7]

Not surprisingly, perhaps, the questioning attitude extended to human service professionals themselves. For example, it was not uncommon for funders and community activists to assume that human service professionals were either irrelevant or, worse, part of the welfare structure that needed reforming.[8]

As the 1960s ended, a new perspective emerged, one that questioned all institutions, including welfare. A greater awareness of social and political considerations developed. The notions of social structure and of opportunities were seen by some social workers and others as central to intervention in the social world. The phenomena of race and class and, to a lesser degree, gender, were seen as important considerations for society and for possible intervention. In a political and romantic movement in American history, human service professionals were often seen as technocrats and managers by proponents of social change. In short, politics and social movements dominated over alleged reason and science.

By the mid-1970s, political conservatism and a backlash to the disruption of the 1960s had occurred. With the Nixon presidency, the social questioning of the 1960s was replaced by the administrative concerns and questions of the 1970s. In this emerging context, a new social nexus—one that profoundly affected the human service professions—was introduced by conservatives into American society. That nexus had three components: the need for accountability, a strong focus on restricting the expansion of fiscal resources for welfare, and the assumption that welfare was inherently a negative structure.[9]

Mott's work details how these three factors came together during the Nixon period and its preoccupation with "goal impact" assessments of human service efforts.[10] It was within this particular period that the importance of scientific inquiry was introduced into American human and social services by fiscal and political conservatives and by some policy makers and administrators. At a very practical level, scientific methodology was seen as a tool to monitor social services and as an ideal way to evaluate the efforts and import of federally funded programs. Concern with the value of efficiency (fiscal) clearly took precedence over promotion of equality in opportunity structures (political and economic).

Perhaps the term, even the value, that came to be featured strongly in the Nixon period was *accountability*.[11] Accountability, which is basically a condition of a relationship between two (or more) parties, is always a consequence of power inasmuch as one or more parties must be answerable to some other party. In some instances, this answering or accounting to others may be voluntary or consensual. For example, one spouse chooses to be accountable to the other and to legitimate spousal claims. In other instances, an element of coercion or constraint may be present in the relationship—for example, a student to a teacher or an employee to an employer.

Relative to the helping professions, the concept of accountability reflects more of a coercive quality, simply because of the reality of funding. That is to say, the deliverer of services has to show funders that what was and is being done is appropriate to the expectations, values, and norms of the funding body and to the constituencies to whom that body relates.

Although the Nixon period continued the questioning tone of the 1960s, that tone was now tied to a series of related, albeit negative, values and assumptions concerning welfare and government's role in welfare. Within this value and assumptive context, an alleged scientific perspective became very relevant; scientific to some degree in the sense of how Madge, in part, has described science: " . . . systematic methods of data collection, suitable analytical tools . . ."[12]

To be accountable to the funding sources, funded service agencies now were required to demonstrate that they were offering the services for which they were funded, that as the providers of services they were using public resources efficiently. In some instances, they were also expected to show that the services they offered were necessary and effective.

As a systematic monitoring and evaluation strategy, science became a valued tool, a possible technology embedded in a larger set of values and assumptions that were political and even ideological in nature. Put another way, the introduction of selected formal scientific processes of monitoring in the human and social services occurred in the context of a politically conservative climate, a climate that had clear preferences concerning desirable and not-so-desirable populations, problems, and program strategies. What followed, then, was the political reality that human services that could not show that they were efficient and/or effective welfare responses often were cut or eliminated from funding.

So strong was the institutionalization of monitoring and evaluation within this conservative context—a context that led directly to contraction of resources for welfare—that certain phrases and descriptions became (and remain) constants. In critiquing the political climate in 1983, Segal and Specht used a variety of terms that captured the institutionalizing of the conservative research nexus.[13] For example, in referring to public aid, both in terms of amount and kind, they stated that the discussion tends to focus excessively on "budgetary limitations" and stresses "cost-effective utilization of all available resources." Similarly, in reporting the mood of the country in 1980, Palmer and Sawhill, in what apparently is a more "centrist" analysis, identified three major Reagan-period assumptions that had implications for welfare and the use of scientific inquiry: a demand for expansion of the military budget; a requirement for compression of the size and function of the federal government, including the area of human services; and a mandate for "new" program directions in human services.[14]

These interrelated assumptions were reported and basically accepted as fact in American society. Obviously, such value-related givens were not unrelated to what Nixon had set in motion some 10 years earlier. Equally obvious is that such assumptions could and did affect the interplay between science and welfare policy and programming. Budgetary constraints, limited resources, strong monitoring, and an ideology of less federal welfare and more local and private responsibility became inextricably related.

Yet the political use and abuse of an aspect of scientific inquiry and the promotion of accountability were not fully institutionalized within all sectors of the society. Meyer's comments in the mid-1980s captured a core of deep frustration in the profession of social work when she asked " . . have we unknowingly responded to a general political attitude of accountability—a prove it or move it demand that seems to permeate our lives?"[15] Very critical of the society's increasing specific use of monitoring, especially within the context of valuing the short term and the immediate, she stated: " . . . preoccupation with outcome measures and evidence of cost effectiveness may have as much to do with mechanistic, short-sighted, anti-humanist thinking as it does with budgetary concerns."[16] Meyer's pessimistic conclusion was that in these so-called practical times, agencies and human service professionals really cannot afford, in a variety of ways, to take the long view. To use Meyer's words: " . . . the cynical concern with the immediate fools the public."[17] Frequently, the instrumentality of concern with the immediate was, of course, the use of the "systematic methods of data collection," namely science.[18]

INQUIRY AND PROFESSIONAL DEVELOPMENT

It would be a grave mistake to conclude that the social work profession in the 1980s was fully aware of Meyer's points. In fact, a case could be made that the profession itself engaged in a series of internal developments over a 20-year period that inadvertently contributed to the particular nexus between conservatism and science that Meyer critiques.

In the 1960s, the social work field developed a strong political orientation that focused on community and organizational function.[19] This focus reflected and contributed to a perspective that social work was more than just individual work with clients. In this evolving perspective, not only was the amount of intervention with individuals questioned, but often the very profession and professionals associated with the case intervention strategy were as well.[20] In short, the late 1960s and early 1970s raised credibility and relevance issues within the profession of social work.

Accompanying these issues were specific battles within and outside the profession concerning not just units of intervention—individual, community, and social structure—but also disagreement over relevant concepts, for example, personality and development as contrasted with opportunity and power. Forces and interest groups that supported the changes and general cultural attitudes of the 1960s pushed for more structural analysis and political changes. Forces that resisted significant structural changes continued to prefer to focus on individuals and benefits and services to individuals.

However, the larger society grew weary of social disturbances and seemed to prefer the stability suggested by Nixon. Society at large thus issued messages to social workers, as well as to activists, that it preferred to have services focus on individuals rather than on communities and organizations in order to lessen social instability. Consequently, in the 1970s the boundaries for social change that affected social work and the helping professions were dramatically reasserted within the larger society by political forces and the government. Within the social work profession this period of turbulence led to a new emphasis upon individuals within an ecological perspective. The latter perspective became associated with a fertile period in the development of social work practice theory.

On one level, the 1960s and 1970s can be described as a period of explosion of contending practice theories within the social work arena. Theorists included Hearn, Gordon, Hollis, Reid, Pincus and Minahan, Bartlett, Meyer, and Germain—to name but a few.[21] Because of the number of and differences among practice theories, an imperative was set up within the profession to test and evaluate them. Apart from changes and developments within the larger society, that is, using scientific methods at least to monitor human services, the profession was developing a maturity that required that theories be sorted and conditions specified under which different practice perspectives seemed to work. In the sense of validating theory and practice, professional growth was now connected to science.

In the 1970s, the above development suggested that the profession had to become defensible, accountable to others outside the profession as well as to its own members. In short, issues of integrity and credibility could be achieved only if the profession could show that, whatever theory base was used, its interventions worked. True professionalism required the ability to show to others, as well as to fellow practitioners, that the practice intervention was effective; and if not, that it would be modified. Again, science and research became fused to a professional norm.

One of the most significant influences on the process of connecting practice and research was Briar, who, in a landmark work stated:

> I do not think clinical casework is nearly as effective as it ought to be . . . what the research indicates is simply that our batting average is too low . . . . Caseworkers should embark on a period of more effective models and methods.[22]

Stated in the late 1960s, this point of view, once set in motion, amassed many proponents over the ensuing years. One of the most significant has been Fischer, whose perspective reflects several key points.[23] He has argued that truly professional practice demands responsible use of available knowledge about effective strategies and techniques of intervention. A corollary in this analysis, of course, is that professionally it is irresponsible to use practice styles and interventions that have been demonstrated to be ineffective. Finally, Fischer has argued strongly against a single theory or school of practice, suggesting instead that an eclectic approach is probably desirable; science can assist in searching out what is useful and what can and should be used in the future.

The perspective suggested by Fischer and others in the late 1970s and 1980s led not only to an emphasis on research about practice and practice theory but also to a very positive tone of eclecticism and pragmatism. As Mullin has stated, given multiple approaches to helping people—the analytic, behavioristic, humanistic—and all variants within each, the profession became " . . . hopelessly deadlocked in the absence of ideological consensus and theoretical homogeneity."[24] Empiricism, specifically evaluation, came to be viewed as a way to identify pragmatic and effective interventions.

Accompanying this state of affairs, the larger social and political climate was also exhibiting (as stated previously) concern for effectiveness, efficiency, and accountability. This complex set of developments within the profession and within society, and their interaction, led many to conclude that social work should reflect and encourage pragmatism. Such pragmatism, it was argued, should not be justified by theory or even ideology, only by empirically demonstrated effective and efficient work with clients.

This process of fusing profession and science from the mid-1970s throughout the 1980s was not without its critics within the helping professions. Major criticism focused on the apparent anti-intellectual and atheoretical quality of pragmatism. Other criticisms attacked the particular relationship between science and practice as being mechanistic, extremely oversimplified, and, because of its stress on objectivity, biased in the direction of a scientific ideology.[25]

Apart from the merits of the fusion between practice and research, the result of the fusion was that increasing emphasis was placed by social workers on the more micro aspects of practice. That is, specific skills and practical application often became the central focus of practice, where practitioner empathy and other relational qualities promoted research and accountability to forces within and outside the profession. In the process, however, the broader concepts of society, opportunity, and power were overlooked. Correspondingly, units of attention and intervention moved away from the group and toward the client and/or the practitioner.

In 1983, after observing the political processes within the larger society and developments within the profession, Iatridis stated: " . . . the profession's continued avoidance of social theory and ideological issues is likely to make practical outcomes worse for its clients and to undermine its objectives."[26] Like other critics, he was suggesting that the movement from ideology was itself an ideology, a reinforcer as well as an effect of research.

Despite Iatridis's observation, it is fair to state that by the mid-to late 1980s the field of social work had arrived at a point where research and accountability were institutionalized. The title of Bloom and Fischer's 1982 book *Evaluating Practice: Guidelines for the Accountable Professional* captures well the flavor of institutionalization.[27] Similarly, Mantell's observation fairly accurately captures the practitioner's perspective when she states: " . . . to meet the cost containment challenges of the future and to better serve its clientele social work needs to expand its knowledge base . . . ," and it should do this by focusing on " . . . research on which interventions under which conditions achieve which specific practice goals."[28]

Note in the preceding remarks the recognition of responsibility and accountability to clientele and to funding bodies that in all probability will not expand resources. Also note the internalizing of the norm for self-monitoring to and for the profession itself. These observations are important because the very positive development of accountability to self (profession) and to client is born within the same period as accountability to funding bodies and contracting resources. In all instances, research was seen as a key medium for achieving accountability as well as for warranting the profession's sanction and the larger society's acceptance.

On a policy level these developments, which promoted systematic monitoring, were further reinforced by reliance on contracts, third-party payments, and bloc grants. Although it was a major breakthrough in the federal governments' assumption of responsibility for social services, Title XX, passed in 1970, relied on a strategy of state and local public agencies entering into contracts with other local agencies, often private agencies that would provide designated services for defined populations.[29] As positive as this was, the contracted or purchased services were given to individuals and families; larger social units, such as communities, were not directly dealt with. Specific groups subject to disproportionate levels of stress in society were not addressed, save through individual and family units that might be served through the auspices of a specific agency.

Correspondingly, because public funding became available mostly to those bodies that contracted to provide personal services, helping professions in the contract agencies became further niched with personal individual and family service strategies. As Kramer reported, this policy pattern of public funding to private agencies brought with it more demands for cost accounting and case management, while at the same time providing agencies with necessary financial resources to keep operating.[30] In this way, fiscal and service monitoring and reporting requirements, along with policy restrictions on programming as it relates to clientele and staffing, were simultaneously institutionalized. Perhaps what was lost, certainly overlooked, was suggested by Kahn and Kamerman: " . . . when income, housing, and medical care are inadequate, an inappropriate burden is placed on the personal social services. In such cases they will always be inadequate."[31]

Looking back at the purchase-of-service approach, one can detect concerns other than reliance on a personal services approach. For example, given the cutting of public resources for human services in the late 1970s throughout the 1980s, concern for the contracting and purchasing of services focused attention on contract compliance and resource allocation. Attention shifted from basic questions of whether the amount of resources should be increased and how, if at all, criteria (such as equality, compensation, equity, adequacy, productivity, redistribution, prevention) should be stressed.

In addition to the development of political conservatism and funding patterns and heavy emphasis on theory and research within the profession, social work was moving toward licensure in the late 1970s and 1980s.[32] Advocates continue to argue persuasively that licensing protects the community and clients. Licensing also serves the interests of the professional in terms of status, control of market, and reimbursement levels and rates from government contractors and from insurance companies. None of these benefits to the professional are inherently negative. However, it is somewhat problematical that in many instances the movement for state licensure became identifiable with the functions of counseling and treatment. Licensed human service workers were encouraged by licensing bodies to avoid dealing with the larger issues of income distribution, racism, and sexism. In the context of the previously cited developments in practice theory and research, licensure led to still another emphasis on the immediate world of the client, not the larger social units.

SEARCHING FOR RESEARCH AND ACCOUNTABILITY IN A DIFFERENT POLITICAL PERSPECTIVE

The preceding section attempted to trace the development of monitoring and science as they affected the social service area. As political conservatism, contraction of resources, professional development and interests, and uses of scientific inquiry became linked, individual client need came to dominate the perspectives and responses of practitioners and funders. Similarly, a particular ideology of science and objectivity emerged. In line with Gouldner's analysis, what was not apparent was that the new "objectivity" in the human service fields was occurring within, and was tied to, assumptions that promoted a specific range of purposes and interests for selected uses of scientific methodology.[33]

If, as Bannon has observed, justice is "a matter of better outcomes, not better intentions," then the critical questions center on defining those better outcomes and where we are now relative to them.[34] In a sense, the significant meta-scientific and meta-human-service consideration has to be the precise valuing and selecting of goals and the defining of current situations. Yet, in the past 20-odd years the so-called better outcomes largely have become individual outcomes; and the practice interventions largely have focused on the individual, and sometimes the family. The goals and outcomes might instead have focused on reducing the disparity between rich and poor; increasing supports for women and racial and ethnic minorities so they have full and fair access to the major social institutions; and reducing the need and risk associated with gender, race and ethnic origin.

In recent years, scientific inquiry and scientific methodology have not been wrong, only incomplete. As Abramovitz has stated: " . . . our techniques and our conceptual diagnostic frameworks have been too narrow. We have compartmentalized social welfare as we have compartmentalized the poor."[35] Selective use of scientific methods has been in many ways an unwitting instrument to this narrow compartmentalization. A number of suggestions might facilitate more positive use of science and scientific methodology within the human service area. They include:

- Identifying values and value options to be pursued. In recent years, the value of fiscal efficiency clearly has dominated at expense of the other values—social efficiency, redistribution, maximization of human potential, promotion of families and family functioning, prevention of problems.

- Defining problems/conditions. Notions of chances and risk could be stressed as they relate to different groups in society. Recognition that different chances and risks are associated with different social statuses—gender, race, age, social class, family structure—could be emphasized.

- Selecting goals that focus on groups and risk as well as those that focus on individuals and need.

- Designing and evaluating interventions that are preventive as well as restorative to groups and recognizing that such interventions are tied to bigger issues and structures in society. Offering easily accessible and usable health care facilities for poor young women so as to prevent birth defects and high rates of infant mortality is one example.

Using science relative to these suggestions would not make science any less political and any less value-laden in consequence. Rather, doing so recognizes that scientific methodology in the social world is always "contaminated" by context, that is, the questions articulated and the goals sought. If we understand this, then scientific inquiry can be used to answer Bannon's critical question: " . . . how do we change our arrangements for social organization so as to increase human welfare?"[36]

CONCLUSION

This chapter discussed the possible relationship between human service professions and scientific inquiry. Recognizing that professions are value-oriented, one can make a case that professions are "superior to" science. Yet, professions are influenced by the political context in which they operate and develop. Forces in the larger society, such as political and fiscal conservatism, pushed for monitoring of human service professions. Forces within the profession pushed for testing of interventions and theory. Both sets of forces resulted in scientific inquiry and professionalism converging and becoming tied to individuals and families. With such a convergence of forces, critical questions and goals often were lost. The chapter closed with suggestions that call for inquiry to be associated with different questions and goals.

Part two will focus on inquiry and policy within the context of political and rational forces.

NOTES

1. G.T. Powers, T.M. Meenaghan, and B.G. Toomey, *Practice Focused Research: Integrating Human Service Practice and Research* (Englewood Cliffs, NJ: Prentice-Hall, 1985), 1–5.
2. R.K. Merton, *Social Theory and Social Structure* (New York: Free Press, 1957), 552.
3. W. Gingerich, "Expert Systems and Their Potential Uses in Social Work," *Families in Society* 7 (April 1990): 220–228.
4. A. Hartman, "Still Between Client and Community," *Social Work* 345 (September 1989): 387.
5. G. Nelson, "Social Class, and Public Policy for the Elderly," *Social Service Review*, 56 (October 1982): 85–107.
6. An example of literature reflecting this development is R. Kramer and H. Specht, *Readings in Community Organization Practice* (Englewood Cliffs, NJ: Prentice-Hall, 1969).
7. *Ibid.*
8. I. Epstein, "Professional Role Orientations and Conflict Strategies," *Social Work* 15 (October 1970): 87–92.
9. P.E. Mott, *Meeting Human Needs: The Social and Political History of Title XX* (Columbus, OH: National Council of Social Workers, 1976).
10. *Ibid.*
11. T.M. Meenaghan and R.O. Washington, *Social Policy and Social Welfare: Structure and Application* (New York: Free Press, 1980), 121–23.
12. J. Madge, *The Origins of Scientific Inquiry* (New York: Free Press, 1962), 1.

13. S.P. Segal and H. Specht, "A Poorhouse in California, 1983: An Oddity or Prelude," *Social Work* 28 (July 1983): 319–323.

14. J. Palmer and I. Sawhill, eds. *The Reagan Experiment* (Washington, D.C. Urban Institute Press, 1982).

15. C.H. Meyer, "Planning vs. Bottom Lines," *Social Work* 28 (July–August 1983): 259.

16. *Ibid.*

17. *Ibid.*

18. Madge, 1.

19. *See* J. Rothman, "Three Models of Community Organization Practice," *Social Work Practice* (New York: Columbia University Press, 1968), 16–47; J.B. Turner, ed., *Neighborhood Organization for Community Action* (Washington, D.C.: National Association of Social Workers, 1968).

20. J.J. Hess, "Social Work's Identity Crisis," *Social Thought* 6 (Winter 1980): 59–61.

21. G. Hearn, *Theory Building in Social Work*. C. Toronto: University of Toronto Press, 1958; "Notes on the Nature of Knowledge" in H. Bartlett, A. Kaduskin, E. Thomas, H. Maas, W. Gordon, M. Murphy, eds., *Building Social Work Knowledge* (New York: National Association of Social Workers, 1964), 60–75; F. Hollis, *Casework: A Psychosocial Therapy* (New York: Random House, 1964); W.J. Reid and I. Epstein, *Task Centered Casework* (New York: Columbia University Press, 1972); A. Pincus and A. Minahan, *Social Work Practice: Model and Method* (Itasca, IL: Peacodk: 1973); H. Bartlet, *Analyzing Social Work Practice by Fields* (New York: National Association of Social Workers, 1961; C.H. Meyer, *Social Work Practice: A Response to the Urban Crisis* (New York: Free Press, 1970); and C.B. Germain, *Social Work Practice: People and Environments* (New York: Columbia University Press, 1979).

22. S. Briar, "The Current Crisis in Social Work Practice," In selected papers from the National Conference on Social Welfare (Berkeley: University of California Press 1967), 31.

23. J. Fischer, *Effective Casework Practice: An Eclectic Approach* (New York: McGraw-Hill, 1978); J. Fischer, "The Social Work Revolution," *Social Work* 26 (May 1981): 199–207; and J. Fischer, "Is Casework Effective? A Review," *Social Work* 18 (January 1973): 5–20.

24. E.J. Mullin, review of *Effective Psychotherapy: A Handbook of Research* in *Social Service Review* 53 (March 1979): 123.

25. Meyer, 259.

26. D. Iatridis, "Neoconservatism Renewal," *Social Work* 28 (March–April 1983): 123.

27. M. Bloom and J. Fischer, *Evaluating Practice: Guidlines for the Accountable Professional* (Englewood Cliffs, NJ: Prentice-Hall, 1982).

28. Comments of J. Mantell in support of empiricism as reported in Letters, *Social Work* 28 (July–August 1983): 335.

29. N. Gilbert, "The Transformation of the Social Services," *Social Service Review* 51 (December 1977): 624–641.

30. R.M. Kramer, "Public Policy and Voluntary Agencies in Welfare States," *Social Service Review* 53 (March 1979): 1–15.

31. A.J. Kahn and S.B. Kamerman, *Social Services in the United States* (Philadelphia: Temple University Press, 1976).

32. H. Land, "The Impact of Licensing on Social Work Practice," *Journal of Independent Social Work* 4 (April, 1987): 87–96.

33. A. Gouldner, *The Dialectic of Ideology and Technology* (New York: Oxford University Press, 1976).
34. G. Bannon, "Economic Justice: Which Way from Here?" *Social Thought* 6 (Winter 1980): 4–5.
35. M. Abramovitz, "Everyone Is on Welfare: The Role of Redistribution in Social Policy Revisited," *Social Work* 28 (November–December 1983): 440.
36. Bannon, 4.

PART TWO

Inquiry, Policy, and Politics

Collectively, the chapters in Part Two relate scientific inquiry to policy and interventions into the social world. Three major themes are stressed: scientific inquiry, its relation to knowledge, and the tensions that exist between rationality and politics in the area of policy.

Chapter 2 focuses on science, knowledge, and inquiry. Chapter 3 then explicates the complex issue of attempting to use scientific inquiry in multitiered social situations.

Against the backdrop of the issues of inquiry and knowledge in the social world, Chapters 4 and 5 focus on the nature of policy and how it is implemented, especially in human service organizations. In general, scientific inquiry is seen as a functional, though constrained, perspective that can be used in analyzing and assessing policy and programs.

In specific terms, Chapter 4 focuses on the substantive nature of policy, especially in terms of the interplay of politics and rationality, and suggests that description and analysis can assist in determining or inferring purposes of policy. Chapter 5 suggests that inquiry can assist organizations in determining who is actually served as well as how service is rendered. Obviously, inquiry can also identify what remains unaddressed, and what aspects of the environment—community and organizations—might need to be modified.

All the chapters in Part Two stress that choices have to be made relative to what is studied, to the purpose of policies, and to the strategies of intervention. Just as the process of inquiry is contaminated by interests operating in the social world, so too is the way in which policy is formulated and programs are evaluated.

CHAPTER 2

Science, Knowledge, and Inquiry

INTRODUCTION

There are a number ways by which we can try to understand the world around us. The process of inquiry need not be highly formalized and structured. Inquiry is a part of our everyday lives, and we all engage in it regularly by using informal systems of relating to the natural and social worlds. Although less systematic than other approaches, these everyday conceptions of reality are the means by which people organize their experiences and give meaning and understanding to their lives, including their behavior, patterns of interaction, and thoughts and feelings.[1] No matter how "sophisticated" or "advanced" modern techniques of formal inquiry may be, they have their roots in these mundane and informal ways of understanding.

Probably the most common formalized modes of inquiry are religion, literature, the visual arts, and science. Each of these mechanisms provides a set of guidelines or techniques for acquiring information about reality and for organizing that knowledge into a coherent whole. Whereas often there is some degree of compatibility among these methods, they can produce conflicting knowledge bases. Science and religion, for example, are often considered to be inherently at odds, with science undermining what religion may have to say about the world. As further evidence of this conflict, many religious leaders have considered the natural science theory of evolution to be a threat to their beliefs; others have raised concerns about genetic research and its potential for modifying existing life forms.

Although different means exist for comprehending the nature of social life and the physical environment, not all of them are equally valued. In modern society, the *scientific method* has gained preeminence among accepted modes of inquiry. It stresses certain values and sentiments that are seen as essential in modern life, such as rationality, logic, objectivity, and mastery and control of the environment. There is also a firm belief within our culture that science "works," that is, science is commonly perceived to be a successful and powerful means for acquiring knowledge and understanding. This perception has led to the feeling that science is a progressive force in human affairs. Furthermore, we as a society tend to idealize scientific motives. Restivo describes this as "the myth of purity"—"The notion of pure science has two basic referents. One is the production of ideas or knowledge through purely 'mental' acts, that is, pure contemplation. The second is the pursuit of 'knowledge for its own sake'."[2]

During the past century, science has certainly lived up to its expectations. Scientific theories and advancements have brought about a level of technological development that has transformed daily life. Despite some yearnings for more pastoral times, life's amenities in the late twentieth century are far superior in many ways to those of earlier times. For example, most of us can warm our homes when the weather turns frigid and cool them when it grows hot. We can travel across the world in a matter of hours; electricity and the machines it powers have made our lives quite comfortable. Especially in industrialized societies, people can anticipate enjoying these benefits longer than ever before, with life expectancy now two decades longer than it was at the beginning of this century.

Yet, science is not without its boundaries or dangers. With an understanding of atomic structure has come a technology for producing the most fearful weapons in human history—weapons that could destroy all of human life on this planet. More frightening may be what science does *not* know. Scientific enterprises have produced increasing quantities of information, but the understanding of that information is limited: nuclear power plants melt down, space shuttles explode, tornadoes wreak havoc, and leukemia kills people. In essence, science has acquired many facts, but not all of those facts are well understood. There is nothing inherently "right" or "wrong" with science and technology. Depending on how they are used, they can enhance or damage the quality of life. However, we need to recognize that science has become a "secular religion" that many accept without question.[3] There is a limited grasp of its strengths and weaknesses as a social force; in fact, science may not even be seen as a social force.

Because of the role of science in modern life, it is important to have a clear understanding of what science and scientific inquiry are. As a means for creating knowledge, science obviously affects how we preceive the world around us. More than that, however, it interacts with the social, political, and ethical contexts in which it exists. Scientific questions do not simply materialize from the purity of scientists' motives. Scientists are products of a culture and labor in organizations that are part of a political economy. Thus, some questions become relevant as points of scientific inquiry, but others do not. For example, at the turn of this century, medical scientists sought to understand how disease was transmitted, but their analyses were affected by the social structure in which they worked. That is, the theories of some doctors were more socially acceptable than those of others. According to Ehrenreich:

> Many physicians understood that low wages, unsafe working conditions, crowded and unsanitary housing, and so on, were at least as potent "explanations" of disease as was germ theory. State legislatures, however, heavily influenced by industrialists, landlords, and the like, could hardly be expected to grant medical authority to these doctors rather than to those who spoke with scientific expertise about the transmission of germs from individual to individual.[4]

To understand science, then, we need to examine more than just its guiding principles. We can understand its strengths only by also trying to identify its limitations as a means for creating knowledge. After looking at science in principle, we will turn our attention to the social and political context in which science is done and how these forces affect each other.

THE ACQUISITION OF KNOWLEDGE, EVERYDAY INQUIRY, AND SCIENCE

The Need to Understand

We need to understand the world around us, especially the social world in which we live and act. Without bringing a degree of predictability to our daily activities, we might not fully enjoy social life. This does not mean that perfect predictability is mandated, only that without a reasonable degree of it, chaos would prevail. For example, when we go to work we have some idea of what we will find; when we interact with a client, we have expectations about how that interaction will proceed; when we drive, we can anticipate how other drivers will behave. In fact, we may follow a "script," such as a set of procedures described in an operating manual. In sum, acquiring information and testing out predictions are a part of everyday life, a process that Babbie refers to as "native human inquiry."[5]

As members of society, we need not obtain most of our knowledge of the social and physical environments through first-hand experience. Through socialization, we learn most of the knowledge—including scientific knowledge—needed to function effectively as social beings. That is, through active participation in our culture we first acquire the wisdom of past generations; this experience guides our thoughts, feelings, and actions. Later because of the unique experiences of the generation into which we were born, we will likely modify what we learned. Levine describes this process:

> The individuals in a human population do not adapt directly and simply to their physical and biological environment but to the cultural (or sociocultural) environment that includes means for their individual survival and guides their adaptation along established channels. I use the term *culture* to mean an organized body of rules concerning the ways in which individuals in a population should communicate with one another, think about themselves and their environments, and behave toward one another and toward objects in their environments. The rules are not universally or constantly obeyed, but they are recognized by all and they ordinarily operate to limit the range of variation in patterns of communication, belief, value, and social behavior in that population.[6]

Sources of Knowledge

Knowledge comes from a variety of sources. Knowledge often takes the form of cultural traditions, where there is a sense of "rightness" because other people have acted in a certain way or expressed beliefs in the past. Some of our knowledge comes from religious authorities, government reports, celebrities and the like. Other knowledge comes from common sense, which often is derived from past experience and belief. Still other knowledge comes from intuition, insight, or hunches about what is right or wrong, correct or incorrect. Another common source of knowledge is mysticism, where we place our understanding of events in the hands of metaphysical or supernatural powers.[7]

Then there is science as a source of knowledge. As Chadwick, Bahr, and Albrecht point out, ''Many of us have succumbed to the mystique of science to the extent that we believe that most knowledge is a result of science. In fact, much knowledge is a result of experience and not the consequence of the rigorous application of the scientific method.''[8] This reliance on science as the primary way of creating knowledge developed largely because of legitimate concerns about the validity or accuracy of knowledge acquired in other ways. Authority figures frequently disagree with one another—one person's common sense flies in the face of another's—and although mysticism may help in understanding moral dilemmas, it exhibits serious limitations in dealing with pragmatic matters. There is a problem, then, with the notion of what knowledge is. Identifying something as knowledge does not mean what is accurate or credible. Knowledge can be challenged; in fact, it will change from one period of history to another. If that is the case, how can we trust what we presume to ''know''? Answering that question was the impetus behind development of the scientific method.

THE NATURE OF SCIENCE AND SCIENTIFIC INQUIRY

The Scientific Method

The scientific method, as summarized in Figure 2–1, is a notion that is familiar to most people in this society. After all, we have grown up in an environment that values scientific activities over all others. In fact, one of the principal means of achieving credibility in the modern world is to have our work labeled scientific, whether that work takes the form of understanding the nature of physical particles, economic systems, disease processes, social services, or even creation. For example, vast amounts of energy have been expended to establish certain fields as ''legitimate'' scientific enterprises. Psychiatry has followed other medical fields by conceptualizing problems as diseases, identifying diagnostic categories, and developing physical treatments in the form of drug therapies and surgical interventions. Psychology, in contrast, was modeled after the physical sciences and characterized as elaborating an overriding paradigm (or theoretical framework) in the form of behaviorism and emphasizing the use of experimental design as the primary means for examining phenomena. More recently, the social services have assumed a ''scientific'' stance as a means of enhancing their social respectability.[9]

What Is Science?   In our society, debate is commonplace as to what constitutes science. Indeed, one of the most deadly criticisms of a point of view or a

FIGURE 2-1   The Conventional View of the Scientific Method: Goals, Principles, and Means

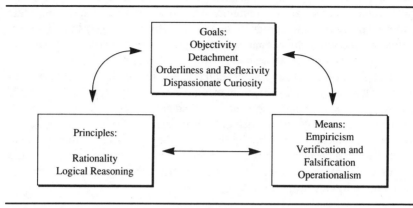

body of knowledge is to label it unscientific. An important example of this kind of criticism is the rejection of creationism by many members of the scientific community. In recent years, attempts have been made to establish creationism as a legitimate scientific alternative to evolutionary theory. Advocates assert that creationism's findings and theory should be included in high-school general science courses, along with the findings and theory of evolutionism. Contemporary evolutionists find themselves confronted by a battle radically different from past challenges, including the 1925 *Scopes* trial. According to Lessl:

> The new creationism, like the earlier version, has the full backing of a vocal, if not radically conservative, religious community; but unlike the earlier creationism, the modern movement began within the scientific community—not outside it. In the 1960s a minority of scientists with deep religious convictions began to form their own professional organizations and to publish their own scientific journals. These were not the backwoods preachers lampooned by H. L. Mencken during the *Scopes* trial; rather, they were the products of the same scientific establishment that triumphed in the face of William Jennings Bryan's Pyrrhic victory at Dayton. The new creationists are spearheaded by a corps of scientifically trained but religiously fundamentalist researchers who proclaim a creationist program of inquiry they believe will depose the established evolutionary paradigm.[10]

Many other instances can be identified where different groups of scientists are caught up in serious disagreements about perspectives, findings, and what qualifies as scientific. In the physical sciences, recent controversy has erupted over the existence of cold fusion as a means of producing energy.[11] In applying science to human affairs, dispute has been the order of the day. The human reproductive sciences, for example, always have been surrounded by controversy.[12] Matters such as when human life begins have been cast within the framework of verification by scientific principles. Even the end of human life has been debated among scientists, who by no means are uninterested in the nature and meaning of euthanasia or the use of heroic efforts to sustain life.[13] Some 50 years ago, portions of the scientific community espoused the eugenics movement, which advocated restricting the reproductive rights of individuals who were considered "inferior" according to certain scientific principles.[14] Indeed, the scientific method has been used to argue racial and gender inferiority.[15]

Still, no one—not even members of the scientific community—has agreed on a definition of science or the scientific method. In fact, debates over what "legitimate science" is often push opponents to brand each other not simply wrong but heretical. That is, protagonists seek to identify what is false and unacceptable or what violates scientific method. By doing so, they characterize that particular perspective as deviant and thus outside the realm of "proper" science. Lessl describes this process as similar to what occurs when there are serious controversies within religious institutions.[16]

Science and Its Practitioners.   To come to some understanding of science and its method, we should focus briefly on the practitioners of science. What we have seen up to this point is that fundamentally, scientists are no different than nonscientists. Scientists are human beings who live at a particular point in history and within a particular political, economic, and social structure. They share with other members of society a culture that includes certain values, attitudes, and beliefs about human nature and human behavior. They also share a concern about what Babbie calls the "common errors in personal human inquiry," by which he means those matters that call into question the accuracy and credibility of what we believe to be knowledge.[17] They identify themselves as scientists, then, because presumably science provides them with a way of avoiding the errors of everyday means for acquiring knowledge. That means, then, that scientists have a sense that what they do is distinctive, that some things are science and some things are not. Yet scientists and nonscientists alike still disagree over what is "proper science."

Method and Methodology.   In coming to grips with the problem of identifying the scientific method, we might heed the wisdom of Suchman who, more than four decades ago, pointed out the futility of arguing over whether a particular research design is scientific. As he noted so cogently: "The design is *the plan of the study* and, as such, is present in all studies, uncontrolled as well as controlled and subjective as well as objective. It is not a case of scientific or not scientific, but rather one of good or less good design."[18] Perhaps what we are dealing with in defining science and its method is essentially a particular way of examing or looking at phenomena, of collecting information or evidence, of making particular kinds of inquiries.

Method does not necessarily mean methodology. The actual means used for studying phenomena vary widely among different sciences. In fact, different methods may be used within the same field, as in the use of visual observation versus radiotelescopes in astronomy. As Siegel points out, we need to distinguish between scientific method and scientific technique. That is, different techniques may be used in making actual inquiries, but the scientific method focuses on the means for acquiring evidence. In science, observation is the method of study: "Indeed, it seems clear that this is the case: in all of the sciences mentioned, observation plays the role of generating data, or facts, which are used to test hypotheses, perhaps to generate them, to contribute to the formulation of generalizations, and so on."[19] However, there is more to science than just making observations. We want to make observations that are as accurate, valid, and credible as possible. That points us toward certain other matters that are also essential components of the scientific method.

Rationality and Logic

Rationality and logic are two of the most distinctive characteristics of science. In fact, most scientists take a good deal of pride in describing themselves as rational and logical, traits that have transcended the world of science and entered our daily lives. We complain, for example, about people we find to be irrational in their judgments or illogical in their decision making. In effect, we make value judgments based on our perceptions of people as logical and rational creatures.

Rationality as a Guide to Action. In the social services, rationality has gained increasing prominence in policy decisions. Finsterbusch and Motz describe what they refer to as the *rational model* for policy decision making, consisting of five components: specifying goals, identifying various options for achieving the goals, constructing criteria by which to evaluate action options, analyzing the advantages and disadvantages of each option relative to the criteria established, and selecting the option with the most advantages and the least disadvantages. If such a model could be realized, they claim, it would have several strengths: "This is the logical way to proceed in order to make the best decision possible in terms of the goals. It represents pure efficiency. It excludes traditional, emotional, and political considerations because they interfere with the maximization of goals."[20] They go on to say that this is an idealized model, based on the tenets of the scientific method. Unfortunately, it is unrealizable in practice, because it does not consider that knowledge about a particular problem is limited as well as potentially costly to obtain. It also ignores the fact that there will be competing groups involved in decision making about public policy, groups whose values are likely to be in conflict.

At the same time, an idealized model can provide helpful guidance in that it can help in organizing and evaluating options, even if political factors will affect the decision-making process. Clearly, such a model stresses the need for information and the need to assess the quality of the information at hand. As

Faludi notes, one can accept as a given that political and moral factors will be part of the policy and planning process, but that does not rule out using rationality as a decision-making rule, in effect as a methodology or technique.[21] That brings us to the substance of the concept of rationality: it is based on reasons. That is, we have to provide a set of reasons or standards that guide us in making decisions.[22] Thus, to call an activity rational, we must have sound reasons for carrying it out in a particular way, whether the activity is deemed scientific or not.[23]

Rationality is not solely the domain of science. It has utility in other enterprises as well, especially when decisions are needed. A number of biases may affect one's options in making decisions, especially in the human services where decisions are likely to affect lives. For example, human service professionals make decisions about who should get certain medical services, who deserves certain types of education, or who is entitled to housing. Rationality appears to be a pragmatic way to avoid some common problems to which people—whether they call themselves scientists or social service providers and decision makers—are prone.

Rationality as Reasoned Judgment.   A good way to approach the concept of rationality is to consider it in terms of what Hoover calls reasoned judgment:

> *Reasoned judgment* is a staple of human understanding. A reasoned judgment bears a respectable relationship to evidence. Because people inevitably have to act in the absence of complete evidence for decision making, the term "judgment" is important. Judgment connotes decision making in which all the powers of the mind are activated to make the best use of available knowledge.[24]

In effect, the rationality of science revolves around its *commitment to evidence*. According to Siegel:

> If SM [scientific method] is properly characterized as a commitment to evidence, then science's rationality is a direct consequence of that commitment. SM is to be seen as an embodiment of rationality—SM is the way that rationality manifests itself in science. For SM is structured so as to emphasize *reasons:* testability, objectivity, impartiality, and other features and ideals of science are functions of science's regard for evidence.[25]

Rationality as a scientific principle, then, focuses our attention on the use of evidence as a means for making decisions. In this sense, rationality is instrumental, that is, a means to an end; it involves the use of a methodology that we need to apply if we are to reach our goals. With science, the goal is a commitment to evidence as a means for making sound judgments, and we are rational to the extent that the methodology actually aids us in arriving at such judgments.

Logic as a Guide to Reasoning.   Sound reasoning requires the use of logic, a system of principles we can use in arriving at conclusions. Logic, then, as the application of rationality to a particular problem or inquiry, is the process of sound reasoning. Oftentimes, logic is illustrated by comparing it to mathematical inquiries, where the process of reasoning is axiomatic or based on self-evident propositions or truths. For example, hardly anyone would challenge the arithmetical statement that two plus two equals four. In effect, we are dealing with a method of reasoning that is based on certain principles or underlying assumptions. We need to keep in mind, however, that there is no guarantee that those underlying principles are correct. A method of logic is acceptable so long as it is applied consistently and a group of experts arrive at a consensus in their conclusions. Although the principles may be incorrect or the method may lead to an incorrect conclusion when applied to the natural world, a method can still be internally consistent and acceptable.[26]

Elements of Logic.   In general, several elements are common to logical reasoning as it is applied in the social sciences. These principles must be applied systematically and consistently. First of all, a given factor or concept cannot cause another one that occurred prior to it. For example, the explosion of gasoline in an auto engine cannot cause the ignition switch to fire a spark. In other words, if *A* causes *B*, then *A* must precede *B* in time. In the social sciences, such relationships can be problematic. For example, do certain personality characteristics lead to alcoholism, or does chronic excessive drinking bring about certain traits? Which comes first, the drinking problem or the traits?

Second, a given object cannot fall into two mutually exclusive categories. For example, a person cannot be politically liberal *and* conservative at the same time; nor can one simultaneously be male and female. Classifying objects in the social sciences often can lead to confusion, though, because categories can be vague and overlapping—as in some diagnostic assessments, where boundaries may be obscured.

Finally, one phenomenon cannot produce mutually exclusive results. Winning the lottery, for example, cannot make one wealthier *and* poorer at the same time. Once again, this principle may create problems. In the human services, for instance, such mutually exclusive outcomes could occur as a consequence of welfare reform programs if recipients receive job training only to work at low income levels and without health-insurance coverage. Their incomes may increase in absolute terms but not in line with increases in expenses. In such cases, is the quality of life better or worse? Or both at the same time?

Clearly, these principles may not always work in actual practice. Even in the physical (or so-called hard sciences), difficulties arise in applying them adequately, for example, in the concept of light as both a wave and a particle (a phenomenon that falls simultaneously into two mutually exclusive categories). The goal in logical reasoning, however, is to follow the principles as closely as possible. Ultimately, further research and the development of theory will presumably eliminate anomalies.

Types of Logic.   There are two general categories of logic: deductive logic and inductive logic. *Deductive* logic derives conclusions from general principles by first establishing an explanation for particular phenomena based on assumptions about certain concepts, including relationships among them. We then deduce specific conclusions or outcomes from that set of assumptions. Deductive reasoning, the more familiar category, is akin to mathematical reasoning, including symbolic logic. Deductive reasoning often is illustrated by the use of syllogisms, which present a general statement, identify a particular case, and then allow us to draw a conclusion. The conclusion is simply an exercise in logic with no need at this point to check the conclusion against actual experience. The following statement is an example of deductive reasoning: "All individuals with incomes below $5,153 fall below the poverty line. Paul's income is $5,434. Therefore, Paul does not fall below the poverty line."

Inductive logic starts by making observations and then develops generalizations about those particular facts, working from the specific to the general. The inductive approach stresses the use of evidence, emphasizing the overriding need for verification in scientific enterprises. In looking at recipients of particular social service programs, we might find a preponderance of those with certain characteristics. That information would allow us to make a general statement about who is most likely to be a client. It might also direct our attention to further research on why some people become recipients and some do not. If we looked at alcoholism programs, for example, we would find that employed men are most likely to receive treatment services. We could then generalize that most alcoholics in treatment are employed men. We would then know that there is a relationship between gender and treatment for alcohol problems.[27] Inductive logic often leads to further questions. In our alcohol treatment example, we might do further research to explain why that observation-based generalization was found.

Whereas deductive logic stresses the value of generalized explanations—typically referred to as theory—inductive logic stresses the value of evidence. Both categories are seen as important elements in the scientific method. In fact, many writers argue that the two approaches will be used in a cyclical fashion.[28] For example, we may start by deriving specific expectations from a particular theoretical perspective. If such expectations are unconfirmed or only partially confirmed by evidence, then we may try to modify our previous generalizations by applying an inductive approach. However, those new generalizations may require verification, leading to a new series of deductive statements. New evidence in turn may contradict revised generalizations, leading to a search for more new principles, and so on, thus creating a cycle of activity.

The Conventional Image of Science What has been presented so far is the traditional explanation of elements of the scientific method—the conventional wisdom about what science is. Critics of this approach complain that rationality and logic cannot guarantee correct conclusions. Even mathematics cannot escape the influence of social forces. According to Harding: "Mathematicians in this century . . . have found it impossible to justify the axioms of mathematics with any logical principles that are not more dubious, more counter-intuitive, than the mathematics they are supposed to justify. So it is doubtful that the duty of providing a firm grounding for the truths of mathematics can be assigned to logic."[29]

Logic and rationality, then, have their limits. We need to keep in mind that we are dealing with a way of reasoning, which implies that "truth" will be self-evident. Yet, in that sense, any method is arbitrary in that no one methodology can guarantee validy.

Rationality if often presumed to be a single entity, but that is probably not the case. There are many alternative forms of rationality, some of which may have precedence or acceptance at a particular time or within a particular scientific community.[30] As noted earlier, the goal of rationality is to make judgments about phenomena based on sound reasons. Yet this "sweet reason" is a matter of legitimation and construction, that is, a product of social, political, and economic forces. As Lincoln and Guba have pointed out, to challenge rationalism does not mean rejecting it out of hand:

> Rejecting rationalism (on the part of others) does not mean automatic acceptance of irrationalism. Rather, it may mean acceptance of multiple rationales, or conflicting value systems, or even separate realities. The parallel is drawn to a statistical argument, that of accepting or rejecting the null hypothesis. If one rejects the null hypothesis, it does not mean that only one other alternative may be accepted. There are a variety of alternatives that may account for the rejection of the null hypothesis. Rejection of the null only means that the null hypothesis is rejected. By the same token, rejecting rationalism is not tantamount to accepting irrationalism. Between rationalism and irrationalism, there exist an infinity of rationales and realities.[31]

The limits of rationality and logic can be seen in the research process itself. As Phillips has pointed out, we need to make a distinction between what he calls *logic-in-use* and *reconstructed logic*.[32] Logic-in-use refers to what the scientist did in carrying out research, whereas reconstructed logic refers to what was done in a written or verbal report. The question is not so much the veracity of the scientist because individual scientists have only a limited awareness of their own behavior. In addition, norms for scientific reports limit what is actually reported. In fact, scientific reports probably reflect a much higher level of organization than is actually the case, leading to an idealized image of science. Rationality and logical reasoning clearly are affected by such norms and perceptions.

Objectivity

Hardly any social scientist would still argue that science can be truly objective. Most acknowledge that values and ethics affect the scientific process. All the same, that disclaimer does not negate the value placed on objectivity in conventional orientations toward science. To a large extent, the intent of being rational and logical is to become objective—to become independent of (or separate from) what is studied. Put another way, the purpose of the scientific method is to provide a means by which scientists can limit as much as possible, the influence of sources of distortion, such as personal values and sentiments, on their understanding of the objects of study. In this way, scientists can become relatively dispassionate and neutral inquisitors, presumably without being encumbered by a vested interest in what facts emerge or whether hypotheses and theoretical propositions are supported or refuted.[33] According to Knorr-Cetina:

> To the objectivist, the world is composed of facts and the goal of knowledge is to provide a literal account of what the world is like. The empirical laws and theoretical propositions of science are designed to provide those literal descriptions. If the knowledge of scientific accounts is reality represented by science, an inquiry into the nature of the real becomes an investigation of how the logic of scientific accounts preserves the lawlike structure of the real.[34]

Current debates in the philosophy of science regarding scientific realism demonstrate a continuing concern with objectivity and with the nature of scientific facts and theories.[35] Whereas social scientists may be more equivocal about objectivity than many other scientists, objectivity still is a concern. Babbie acknowledges that objectivity has its limits and that subjectivity enters the making of scientific judgments, just as it does in other human endeavors. He then introduces the notion of intersubjectivity, which suggests that we can treat a phenomenon as having a degree of objective existence, so long as there is agreement that it does indeed exist.[36] In effect, the principle of intersubjectivity uses agreement or consensus as a criterion for establishing the existence of objectivity.[37] For example, if a number of social scientists believe that a particular instrument produces a measure of intelligence, then we have a means for identifying the existence of that phenomenon.

In the human services arena, concerns about objectivity have led to the application of tools such as the American Psychiatric Association's *Diagnostic and Statistical Manual,* third revised edition, known as the DSM-IIIR. Yet the DSM-IIIR is a matter of consensus, also a social construction and the product of professional politics whereby certain terms come to have meaning.[38] This suggests that social scientists participate in the social construction of scientific reality in the same way that we all participate in the social constrution of everyday life.[39] Scientific knowledge—which includes facts, assumptions, propositions, theories and such—is a matter of agreement (consensus), existing at a particular point in time within a specific social and political context. By stressing the appropriate use of accepted methods and consensus, we may have produced what Denzin would call the *fallacy of objectivity,* whereby we use only our own perspective to try to understand phenomena and either ignore or fail to recognize the existence of other perspectives.[40]

Objectivity can be conceptualized in other ways. It does not necessarily have to mean objectifying concepts or detachment between the observer and the observed. As Kirk and Miller note, the concept of objectivity can be used to refer to an underlying value of the scientific perspective.[41] They suggest that we use objectivity to refer to taking "intellectual risks." That is, when scientists propose ideas or describe their observations, they open themselves to critical assessment by their peers. Other scientists may present conflicting empirical evidence or judgments of the underlying logic. What makes science different from other methods of inquiry, then, is its commitment to evidence and to having the work of one scientist open to examination by others.

Orderliness

Even though few descriptions of scientific activities make note of this characteristic, the previous discussion makes it clear that science is concerned with orderliness. Scientific activities are organized around certain principles and rules of procedure; that is, there are certain ways to think and behave. Furthermore, the goal of scientific enterprises is generally to bring structure to the phenomena that interest scientists, whether their interests lie in understanding the social or the physical environment. Because science is founded on process, structure will be brought to the result. Because scientists are reflexive and systematic in their thoughts and activities, they seek to bring order to apparent chaos. They keep detailed records of what they see and think, and much of what they do concerns organizing facts and ideas to examine theories or hypotheses.

This orderliness flows from the reflexive process, which is a means for limiting the influence of personal biases. As Phillips describes it:

> The reflexive process refers to a process of self-examination, where factors normally hidden are brought into plain view. For example, the scientist learns to probe his own fundamental assumptions, or paradigms, so that these can be opened up to testing, as opposed to setting dogmatic boundaries for investigations. All human behavior is reflexive to the degree that it is based on some understanding of the individual's relation to his environment. For example, within the socialization process we learn to define ourselves as distinct entities via observing the reactions others have to us. Scientific procedures carry the reflexive approach a good deal further.[42]

In order to be reflexive, it helps to be systematic (or organized) and objective, both in thought and in action. To be scientific, then, we need to be dispassionate and contemplative; to pursue knowledge for its own sake; to examine and define concepts rigorously; to state hypotheses following certain principles; to document carefully our methods of observation; to develop theory logically and rationally and to be willing to expose our theoretical and empirical work to possible refutation.

The scientist is stereotyped as a careful individual who wears a white lab coat and carries a clipboard to record what he or she does. Data are carefully recorded and stored, whether they concern cell structures or opinions about presidential candidates. The scientist, then, painstakingly seeks to be accurate. Data must be valid and reliable, and theory must be constructed in a coherent and logical form from which deductions can be drawn. Deductions can then be transformed into hypotheses, which can be tested by comparison with observations made of appropriate phenomena in the real world. Being reflexive and systematic are fundamental to the scientific process. The conventional perception of science, then, is that it is orderly and linear.[43]

Images, of course, do not necessarily reflect actual events. Phillips makes note of this in his distinction between logic-in-use and reconstructed logic, where he contrasts the actual research process with the process of communicating research. The point is that scientific endeavors may be idealized by established conventions for the presentation of results. The reality of doing science often leaves a lot to be desired, and there is likely to be a good deal of disorder in most research projects. In a typical survey project, for example, disorder can occur if:

- Questions are taken in different ways by various respondents;
- Some interviewers work more conscientiously than others;
- Errors arise in coding questions;
- Data are omitted or entered incorrectly when electronically processed;
- Analysts misunderstand what variables should be analyzed;
- More than one option exists for organizing and presenting data; and
- Statistical outcomes are open to alternative interpretations.

Thus, calling something scientific does not make it infallible. The goal of a research project is a product that is acceptable to a variety of audiences, including funding sources, decision makers, other scientists, and the general public. Oftentimes, the research process will be presented so as to give it the appearance of being more orderly and systematic than may actually be the case. The rate of deliberate falsification of results is probably very low,[44] but research often involves a "fudge factor" or some inadvertent preening to make the project and the investigators look as good as possible.

The same process occurs in the human services, where agency credibility is enhanced by the appearance of an orderly office environment that mimics scientific style. For example, bureaucratic manuals provide guidelines for making decisions, computers give a look of accuracy and precision to client information, word processing and desktop publishing produce impressive-looking reports. Yet, all such activities are subject to the same collection, processing, and analysis problems noted in the research process.

Knowing and Knowledge

Knowledge has been a recurring theme throughout this chapter, largely because scientific enterprises have been characterized as intending to improve on existing knowledge or to create new knowledge. It might be helpful at this point, then, to examine the nature of knowledge—what it is and what it means to "know" something.

Understanding knowledge is no simple task; philosophers and scientists have grappled with this problem for centuries. Understanding how and why we know what we know is the purpose of epistemology. In most discussions of social science and research methods, efforts to explain knowledge generally revolve around identifying different types or sources of knowledge.[45] In relating social research to social service practice, Powers, Meenaghan, and Toomey went a little further by trying to identify how different types of knowledge can inform practice methods.[46]

Describing where knowledge comes from or classifying knowledge into a set of categories begs the issue of identifying specifically what it is. A further complication arises from our implicit, matter-of-fact understanding of knowledge—we simply know things. We learned facts, ideas, concepts, and explanations through formal and informal means; sometimes we acquired knowledge through personal experience. Yet, as the earlier discussion of objectivity suggests, understanding what we mean by knowledge—what it means to know—is no simple feat.

Knowledge is not founded on objectivity, for it is constructed by individuals and groups. Thus, to have knowledge relies on having agreement among different people. Perhaps Namer has summarized knowledge simply by calling it ''everything that passes for knowledge, i.e., that is legitimated as such by a particular authority in a particular society.''[47] In other words, knowledge is a product—one produced by a group having the power to create and legitimate that product. In the sciences, knowledge is produced by following the appropriate and socially accepted methods, such as laboratory experiments and field surveys in the social sciences. That knowledge is then legitimated scientifically through verbal and written communications, including presentations at professional conferences and publication in professional journals. Legitmacy is enhanced if an investigator's findings are cited in other work, included in review articles and theoretical statements, and described in textbooks. Namer further suggests that the legitimation process may require acceptance by the mass media and by the public.

What defines knowledge is subject to historical and societal forces. For something to become knowledge, it has to have the support of institutional authorities who apply particular means for generating knowledge. Those means will change over time, as demonstrated by the conflict over methods of inquiry between religious and scientific authorities. We may like to think of knowledge as truth, as something that can withstand the test of time, but as noted earlier in this chapter, all knowledge is subject to variation and change when looked at from one society to another or from one era to another. Denzin puts it quite simply: ''Knowledge and truth are political constructions.''[48] For him, there is no equivocation regarding the social construction of knowledge or reality.

Whether we are dealing with knowledge in the context of science or that of the human services makes no difference—what we ''know'' is created within a political, economic, and social context. Therefore, we ''know'' that some people are caught in a cycle of poverty because they cannot hold a steady job; or that AIDS afflicts some populations more than others; or that an alcoholic in a state of denial must reach ''rock bottom'' before becoming motivated to break the addiction.

Empiricism and Positivism

Earlier in the chapter, we discussed Siegel's assertion that ''commitment to evidence'' is at the heart of contemporary science.[49] He characterizes the scientific method as stressing the need for explanatory adequacy, for empirical testing, and for inductive support. This is the conventional approach to science, revolving around empiricism and following largely in the positivist tradition. From this perspective, verification and falsification are important matters, as is operationalism in creating the means for observation.

Having a commitment to evidence means that a major goal is to find documentation or facts that support ideas. Getting such evidence in an accurate manner is what makes science a special type of human activity. As Harding describes it:

> The common view . . . is that science's uniqueness is to be found in its method for acquiring reliable descriptions and explanations of nature's regularities and their underlying causes. Authors of science texts write about the importance of value-free observation as the test of beliefs, and especially about collecting observations through the "experimental method." We are told that it is the refined observation characteristic of experimental method that permitted Galileo's and Newton's views to win out over Ptolemy's and Aristotle's.[50]

To obtain evidence that will be scientifically acceptable, we need to rely on the doctrine of empiricism, which asserts that observation is the means for acquiring scientific knowledge. As Sanders and Pinhey explain: "The core of scientific knowledge is empirical observations—seeing, hearing, feeling, smelling, tasting—that is, obtaining information through the senses. We can see things to the extent that we can describe their features and/or measure them."[51] Only what we can observe, directly or indirectly, can be trusted. To establish the existence of a phenomenon, we must have concrete sensory documentation, an approach so well established that nearly all social science textbooks advocate empirical observation—even to the point of labeling it a doctrine.[52] Clearly, empiricism emphasizes a reliance on facts.

Empiricism draws heavily on the tradition of positivism in science. Positivism developed during the nineteenth century, when philosophers of science struggled with the nature of science itself, as well as with distinctions between the natural and the social sciences.[53] Could both strains of science, they asked, follow a common method and, if so, what would it be? As positivism developed, it came to center on a group of European philosophers known as the Vienna Circle. They drew on the work of Ernest Mach, who was convinced that science would develop only through the application of operationalism (see below). As an approach to science, positivism focused on facts, essentially assuming the existence of an objective reality that could be observed directly. Unobservable phenomena, especially those that were unobservable in principle (e.g., emotions, thoughts, motivations) were distrusted. Collecting facts and understanding the world could be separated in principle from any inherent personal biases in scientists as human beings. In effect, this philosophy took an extremely positive attitude toward science as a mode of understanding—thus the label "positivism."

Although most social scientists would no longer advocate the extreme position taken earlier in this century by "logical positivists," this tradition has had a profound impact on current conceptions of social science. Most contemporary social scientists would probably find the principles of scientific realism more acceptable than classical positivism, because scientific realism readily accepts the use of theory, the need to interpret scientific theory in realistic or pragmatic terms, and the assumption that scientific progress occurs in a progressive and developmental process. Scientific realism, though, also argues that science can be largely value-free because of the principles embedded in the so-called scientific method.[54] A separation between positivism and scientific realism may apply more to epistemological debates in the natural sciences than to the social sciences. Where social scientists have taken issue with empiricism has been in the discussion between quantitative methods and qualitative methods, where there has been a call for a different orientation toward observation as well as the meaning of observation itself.

Verification and Falsification.   The positivist tradition emphasized the need for empirical verification. Making a deduction or phrasing a hypothesis was well and good, but generalizations were acceptable only if one could produce evidence of their accuracy, based on sensory observations. Scientists are not directly concerned with truth but rather with whether their ideas have utility. That is, do they work? This is the essence of scientific realism. As Hoover notes:

> The term ''truth'' is red meat for philosophers, and they are welcome to it. Science prefers to operate in the less lofty region of falsifiable statements that can be checked by someone else. Every good scientific proposition or generalization is stated in such a way that subsequent observations may provide either supporting evidence or evidence that raises questions about the accuracy of the proposition. By making the degree of verification a permanent consideration in science, a good many rash conclusions can be avoided.[55]

The good scientist, then, is a skeptic, who needs to *see* what was done. For instance, in developing a principle that will explain a phenomenon or a relationship between certain variables, a scientist is responsible for stating the hypothesis in such a way that it can be found false. That is, what are the conditions under which *contrary* evidence could be obtained.

Operationalism.   Another concept that developed out of the positivist tradition and has come to have great importance in the contemporary social sciences is operationalism. Originally, the purpose of operationalism was to provide a means for dealing with the ambiguity that characterized most theoretical or abstract concepts. Concepts would be defined only in terms of how they could be observed or measured. Later, the means of observation came to be largely synonymous with the process of measurement as quantitative methods achieved more prominence in the social sciences. An example is the definition of the concept of intelligence as an individual's score on an IQ test. The main goal of operationalism then is to delimit or restrict the meaning of concepts. If intelligence is a score on a test or if fear is the level of galvanic skin response, then those concepts can be observed and facts about them communicated without ambiguouity.

Critics have pointed out a number of problems with operationalism as a technique for empirical observation.[56] For example, operational definitions are very shallow, ignoring the fact that concepts generally have a broader degree of meaning. Perhaps operational definitions work well with physical phenomena such as temperature, which can be understood as scores on a thermometer, or weight which can be measured as scores on a scale. However, social phenomena cannot be so easily restricted without sacrificing meaning. Can love be understood by quantifying hugs or kisses? Can racism be understood solely as avoidance of one group by another? Operationalism, in fact, forces one to make choices about what will be observed and measured, and it often draws implicitly on theoretical orientations. In designing an IQ test, exactly what content should be included and how should it relate to formal education as well as to informal modes of learning? Operationalism as a means for reducing ambiguity is clearly a proposition that is open to challenge.

Scientific Inquiry as a "Stylized" Inquiry

The conventional image of science is as a method of arriving at conclusions that are accurate and based on facts. Because of the success that the physical sciences have had in manipulating the environment, science has achieved a dominant position in our society as a mode of inquiry. Scientists are seen as dispassionate, selfless individuals driven by their curiosity to understand the natural world or by their commitment to better the human condition. When something becomes accepted by the scientific community as fact or as knowledge, then we have great confidence in it. Yet, as we have seen, that characterization of science and its knowledge base is questionable.

What do scientists do to make their ideas acceptable? There is no doubt that scientists follow rules of procedure intended to produce knowledge in such a way that the common problems of human inquiry can be neutralized. To what extent that neutralization occurs has become a matter of serious debate among scientists and epistemologists. The conventional argument is that what makes scientific knowledge different from other kinds of knowledge is the very perspective of science.[57] Its method—that is, its reliance on rationality and logic, on the goal of objectivity, on verification of principles and hypotheses—leads scientists to question and to challenge. Because of the scientist's commitment to evidence, scientific explanations—unlike other types of explanation—are open to challenge based on experience or observation. Yet, as Harding points out, many so-called scientific endeavors have been driven by unquestioned assumptions scientists make about the social, political, economic, and moral order.[58] How, then, can we say that science is any more exempt from the influence of such assumptions than is any other way of creating knowledge? Scientific knowledge does not emerge out of a social vacuum.

Part of the problem in understanding science as a social process is the legacy left by earlier practitioners. Until the twentieth century, science—especially social science—was not a mass phenomenon. That is, large laboratories were not necessary in the physical sciences; nor were computers and statistical packages necessary (or available) in the social sciences. Many scientists essentially were amateurs: they could walk along the beach collecting shells to classify; they could create new devices, such as telephones, light bulbs, or airplanes without the benefit of labs; they could examine their clients or colleagues so as to understand psychological processes. In other words, they did not need much in the way of resources or training to consider themselves scientists.

Being a scientist today is a different story, and to be accepted as one requires participation in a process of legitimation.[59] This process involves extensive education and the completion of appropriate degrees. To have some autonomy as a scientist generally requires a doctorate, especially if the goal is to be a university-based scientist. Educational credentials, though, are only the beginning, and the legitimation process is a long-term affair.

The Practice of Science: Research and Publication

Despite a number of large research institutes, corporate settings and government bureaucracies in which research takes place, most social scientists and social service researchers still practice their craft in university settings. In large research-oriented universities, professional survival (in terms of tenure and promotion through the various professorial ranks) is tied to publication of research. Even in corporations, institutes, or government bureaucracies, publication is expected. Success as a social scientist, then, can be operationalized and measured by frequency of publication, which also serves to legitimize one's ideas.

As mentioned earlier, doing research is not enough. A successful scientist must communicate what has been done in such a way that the information will be accepted for publication. At the present time, that generally means engaging in quantitative empirical research, which often requires extensive individual commitment. If one needs funding to carry out the research, one must develop a proposal to submit to various public and private organizations. Government agencies and private foundations have priorities, and research topics that do not fit within those priorities have limited possibilities for funding. In addition, proposals undergo peer review, whereby a panel of social scientists judges the adequacy of the proposed research. Proposals that are accepted typically require at least one revision and resubmission. The entire process can take several years.

After research has been completed, the social scientist writes a report. In most cases, preliminary results will be submitted for presentation at a professional conference, allowing the researcher to get some initial reaction to the ideas in the paper. Then the report will be revised and submitted to a professional journal. In most fields, there is a hierarchy of journals in terms of reputation. The more reputable journals take pride in their high rejection rates—often as great as 80% to 85%—of submissions. Even if peer review is favorable, few articles are accepted without revision. Completing an article and having it accepted for publication can consume another two or three years, particularly if its content is at all controversial.

Some research can receive broader legitimation if it appears in textbooks; textbooks are careful to avoid controversy. Sometimes ideas can reach even wider audiences by dissemination through the popular media; those social scientific "findings" or "explanations" that support the social and political order (such as research on welfare reform and workfare) are most likely to achieve this type of legitimation.

What does this tell us about the scientific enterprise? Perhaps the simplest way to conceptualize it is as a stylized mode of inquiry, which allows social science (or any other science) to be characterized as a ritualistic activity. This means that certain conventions must be followed in completing the research, such as the use of experimental design or survey methods. Preferably, a large amount of data will be generated and processed by computer. Analysis of the data should include the use of multivariate statistics. The article must adhere to a set format: statement of problem; presentation of a conceptual framework and a review of relevant and recent literature; description of methodology, including the type of research design, the means by which the variables were operationalized, and the nature of the sampling; presentation of results, including tables of numbers; and statement of conclusions, including an interpretation and assessment of the results. If the ritual is completed adequately, then the article may be judged acceptable for print, which publicly legitimates it as part of the scientific world of knowledge. Publication is, in some respects, the most important part of the process and is taken quite seriously.

CONCLUSIONS

Creating scientific knowledge is a social process, subject to the same vagaries as other human endeavors. Scientific ideas, then, need to be evaluated in terms of the social context in which they achieve legitimation. For example, the so-called scientific racism of the nineteenth and early twentieth centuries is no longer acceptable—no one would contend today that either craniometry or biological recapitulation is a sound scientific idea.[60] Yet, biological determinism is still a scientifically acceptable principle that even receives significant media attention as the new science of sociobiology or is applied in terms of genetic influences on certain types of behaviors or problems, such as alcoholism.[61,62] Clearly, science should not be conceived as a value-free enterprise, for no social process is free of value assumptions.

All the same, the scientific method is generally treated as the most reasonable way to understand the world around us. Its stress on objectivity and rationality fits the ethos of our time. We live in a mass society characterized by large-scale bureaucracies where explicit rules and regulations are seen as necessary for decision making. This is especially true in the human services, where the goal is to treat clients in consistent and orderly ways. As Mack and Pease note: "The effort to create an organization that provides an efficient coordination of diverse human behavior toward a common goal leads to the formalization of social structure."[63]

Many principles of science have come to be seen as ways to rationalize and objectify human service programs. Concepts such as operationalism and verification can do more than merely guide our activities; they also can legitimate them. As noted in Chapter 1, the scientific method provided a means for systematically monitoring practice activities and for evaluating the impact of interventions. According to Briar and Fischer, the true professional must be able to demonstrate that what he or she does works.[64,65] In other words, we need to *operationalize* our interventions (*independent variables*) and expected outcomes (*dependent variables*) so as to *empirically verify* our *hypotheses* (or treatment goals).

The language and style of science implies an objectivity and separation of observer from observed, which we now realize does not exist. Adopting that language to the needs of the human services does not mean we are acting without being influenced by the political and social context in which those services are provided any more than is the case in scientific enterprises. Because the social sciences have had a profound influence on contemporary social service organizations and practitioners, it is important to understand how the social sciences have been used and abused in trying to understand the social world. That is the focus of the next chapter.

NOTES

1. N. K. Denzin, *The Research Act,* 3rd ed. (Englewood Cliffs, NJ: Prentice-Hall, 1989), 70–71; R. Amundson, "Science, Ethnoscience, and Ethnocentrism, *Philosophy of Science* 49 (1982): 236–250.
2. S. Restivo, "Modern Science as a Social Problem," *Social Problems* 35 (1989): 215.
3. H. J. Sherman, *Foundations of Radical Political Economy* (Armonk, N.Y.: M. E. Sharpe, 1987): P. Smith, *Killing the Spirit: Higher Education in America* (New York: Viking, 1990).
4. J. H. Ehrenreich, *The Altruistic Imagination: a History of Social Work and Social Policy in the United States* (Ithaca, N.Y.: Cornell University Press, 1985), 56.
5. E. Babbie, *The Practice of Social Research,* 5th ed. (Belmont, CA: Wadsworth, 1989), 7.
6. R. A. Levine, *Culture, Behavior and Personality,* 2nd ed. (New York: Aldine, 1982), 3–4.
7. Babbie.
8. B. A. Chadwick, H. M. Bahr, and S. L. Albrecht, *Social Science Research Methods* (Englewood Cliffs, NJ: Prentice-Hall, 1984), 4.
9. Ehrenreich.

10. T. M. Lessl, "Heresy, Orthodoxy, and the Politics of Science," *Quarterly Journal of Speech* 74 (1988): 18–19.

11. See, e.g., several editorial summaries in the *Economist*. "Cold fusion: some heat, not much light," *Economist* 311 (April 15, 1989): 94; "Fusion frenzy [research into cold fusion at the University of Utah]," *Economist* 311 (April 22, 1989): 27–28; "Cold fusion: not what it used to be," *Economist* 311 (June 3, 1989): 84.

12. A. E. Clarke, "Controversy and the Development of Reproductive Sciences," *Social Problems* 37 (1990): 18–37.

13. M. Henderson, "Beyond the Living Will," *Gerontologist* 30 (1990): 480–85; T. Miller and A. M. Cugliari, "Withdrawing and Withholding Treatment: Policies in Long-Term Care Facilities," *Gerontologist* 30 (1990): 462–68; T. M. Smeeding, *Should Medical Care Be Rationed by Age?* (Totowa, NJ. Rowman & Littlefield, 1987).

14. R. J. Lifton and E. Markhusen, *The Genocidal Mentality* (New York: Basic Books, 1990).

15. R. Bleier, *Science and Gender: a Critique of Biology and Its Theories on Women* (New York: Pergamon, 1984): A. Fausto-Sterling, *Myths of Gender: Biological Theories about Women and Men* (New York: Basic Books, 1985); S. J. Gould, *The Mismeasure of Man* (New York: W. W. Norton, 1981).

16. Lessl.

17. Babbie, 8–17.

18. E. A. Suchman, "General Considerations of Research Design," in *Handbook of Research Design and Social Measurement,* ed. D. C. Miller (New York: Longman, 1983), 50.

19. H. Siegel, "What Is the Question Concerning the Rationality of Science?" *Philosophy of Science* 52 (1985): 256.

20. K. Finsterbusch and A.B. Motz, *Social Research for Policy Decisions*, (Belmont, CA: Wadsworth, 1980), 24.

21. A. Faludi, *Critical Rationalism and Planning Methodology* (London: Pion Ltd., 1986), 10.

22. Siegel.

23. L. Laudan, *Progress and Its Problems* (Berkeley: University of California Press, 1977).

24. K. R. Hoover, *The Elements of Social Scientific Thinking,* 3rd ed. (New York: St. Martin's, 1984) 8–9.

25. Siegel, 532.

26. B. S. Phillips, *Social Research: Strategy and Tactics,* 3rd ed. (New York: Macmillian, 1976).

27. W. B. Sanders and T. K. Pinhey, *The Conduct of Social Research* (New York: Holt, Rinehart, & Winston, 1983), 10.

28. Babbie, Denzin, 100 (note his concepts "abduction" and "retroduction"); H. W. Smith, *Strategies of Social Research,* 2nd ed. (Englewood Cliffs, NJ: Prentice-Hall, 1981).

29. S. Harding, *The Science Question in Feminism* (Ithaca, NY: Cornell University Press, 1986).

30. R. G. A. Dolby, "Reflections on Deviant Science," in *On the Margins of Science: the Social Construction of Rejected Knowledge* (Sociological Review Monograph 27), ed. R. Wallis (Keele, Staffordshire: University of Keele, 1979), 9–47.

31. Y. S. Lincoln and E. G. Guba, *Naturalistic Inquiry* (Beverly Hills, CA: Sage, 1985), 91.
32. Phillips.
33. R. C. Bogdan and S. K. Biklen, *Qualitative Research for Education* (Boston: Allyn and Bacon, 1982), 217; S. Fuller, *Social Epistemology* (Bloomington: Indiana University Press, 1988), 149.
34. K. Knorr-Cetina, "The Fabrication of Facts: Toward a Microsociology of Scientific Knowledge," in *Society and Knowledge: Contemporary Perspectives in the Sociology of Knowledge,* ed. N. Stehr and V. Meja (New Brunswick, NJ: Transaction Books, 1984), 223-24.
35. R. N. Boyd, "The Current Status of Scientific Realism," in *Scientific Realism,* ed. J. Leplin (Berkely: University of California Press, 1984), 41-82; E. McMullin, "A Case for Scientific Realism," in Leplin, 8-40.
36. Babbie, 45.
37. Lincoln and Guba, 292.
38. W. J. Scott, "PTSD in DSM-III: a Case in the Politics of Diagnosis and Disease," *Social Problems* 37 (1990): 294-310.
39. P. L. Berger and T. Luckman, *The Social Construction of Reality* (New York: Doubleday, 1963); Stehr and Meja.
40. Denzin, 8.
41. J. Kirk and M. L. Miller, *Reliability and Validity in Qualitative Research* (Beverly Hills, CA: Sage, 1986), 10
42. Phillips, 9.
43. Harding.
44. Gould.
45. E.g., Babbie; Chadwick et al.; Sanders and Pinhey.
46. G. T. Powers, T. M. Meenaghan, and B. G. Toomey, *Practiced Focused Research: Integrating Human Service Practice and Research* (Englewood Cliffs, NJ: Prentice-Hall, 1985).
47. G. Namer, "The Triple Legitimation: a Model for the Sociology of Knowledge," in Stehr and Meja, 209.
48. Denzin, 38.
49. Siegel, 528.
50. Harding, 41.
51. Sanders and Pinhey, 9.
52. Chadwick et al., 422.
53. E.g., Lincoln and Guba; Denzin; McMullin; D. Nachmias and C. Nachmias, *Research Methods in the Social Sciences,* 2nd ed. (New York: St. Martin's, 1981).
54. Boyd; Harding.
55. Hoover, 50-51.
56. Lincoln and Guba; Denzin.
57. K. R. Popper, *The Logic of Scientific Discovery* (London: Hutchinson, 1959).
58. Harding, 42.
59. Namer; M. E. Spencer, "The Imperfect Empiricism of the Social Sciences," *Sociological Forum* 2 (1987): 331-72.
60. Gould.
61. Bleier; Fausto-Sterling; see G. Cowley, "How the Mind Was Designed," *Newsweek* (March 13, 1989); 56-58, for an example of coverage in the mass media.

62. K. M. Fillmore, "The 1980s Dominant Theory of Alcohol Problems—Genetic Predisposition to Alcoholism: Where Is It Leading Us?" *Drugs & Society* 2 (1988): 69–88.

63. R. J. Mack and J. Pease, *Sociology and Social Life,* 5th ed. (New York: D. Van Nostrand, 1973), 186.

64. S. Briar, "The Casework Predicament," *Social Work* 13 (1968): 5–11.

65. J. Fischer, "Is Casework Effective? A Review," *Social Work* 18 (1973): 5–20; *Effective Casework Practice: An Eclectic Approach* (New York: McGraw-Hill, 1978).

CHAPTER 3

Applying Scientific Inquiry in the Social and Political World

INTRODUCTION

During the twentieth century, all of the sciences have been transformed in dramatic ways. The number of scientists alive now probably outnumbers those who lived in the past. Scientific knowledge has been produced at a phenomenal rate, and the ramifications of this knowledge have pervaded our physical and social environment through its impact on our technology. Our lives have been changed forever—for better or worse. To a large extent, this development can be traced to the natural and medical sciences, which have demonstrated proficiency in their subject matters to the nonscientific community through the products of their technologies.[1]

Because many scientific advances have had a direct impact on our lives, science has come to have great value in modern society. Much of our economy revolves around continued advances in the level of knowledge, and science and technology have become major employers in recent decades. Similar developments have occurred in the social sciences, although not as extensively. The social sciences have come of age lately, in that they have attained substantial social and economic worth.

THE DEVELOPMENT OF MODERN SOCIAL SCIENCE

Beginnings

The social sciences can trace their histories over two centuries, emerging a century or so after the natural sciences caught the imagination of philosophers with the publication in 1687 of Newton's work on the laws of motion.[2] By the end of the nineteenth century, empirical social science had emerged, particularly in the work of Durkheim. Yet, until the middle of this century, there was little interest in social science research outside the academic community, and there was little or no support for research from private philanthropic organizations, industry, or government.[3] Only gradually did the social sciences demonstrate their worth.

Social scientists first obtained research funds in the early part of this century, and the results of these projects became prototypes for later large-scale enterprises. Collins and Makowsky credit sociologist William I. Thomas as the first recipient of major funding in the social sciences.[4] In 1908, he received $50,000 from a wealthy Chicago heiress to finance his research on ethnic relations. That windfall ultimately led to the publication in 1919 of one of the first major studies on minorities in the United States, Thomas and Znaniecki's classic *The Polish Peasant in Europe and America*.[5] At that time, $50,000 was an extremely large grant, especially in light of the fact that until 1990 the AARP Andrus Foundation, a major private foundation that funds gerontology research, had a maximum grant size of $50,000.

Thomas may have been the first academic-based social scientist to receive a significant amount of money, but other research activities were also being funded at the same time. By the turn of the century, industrialism had profoundly affected the lives of the working class in American cities, and some social reformers and philanthropists became concerned about living conditions. The Russell Sage Foundation provided the funding for what would be called "the Pittsburgh Survey."[6] The foundation added an additional $17,000 to their initial $7,000 to carry out the biggest study ever undertaken of an American city and the lives and welfare of its working people. This piece of research was far ahead of its time in many ways, because it was intended to be *applied*—that is, to provide information that could be used in guiding interventions that could affect social conditions.

John M. Glenn, director of the Russell Sage Foundation in 1909, described the Pittsburgh Survey:

> The plan of the survey proposed a careful and fairly comprehensive study of the conditions under which working people live and labor in a great industrial city, and a fair public statement of facts discovered. It was hoped that these facts would lead to the prompt application of some practical measures, whose value to the community would be readily recognized, and that with respect to such conditions as are firmly rooted in custom and convention, they would afford a basis for efforts to secure legislative or other remedies. It was hoped, too, that they would constitute a body of evidence, such as had never had bearing on our national civilization, and that they would supply a foundation for further study in a deeper and more comprehensive way of conditions whose consequences are little understood, although they affect vitally our whole community life.[7]

This effort produced six volumes, published between 1909 and 1914, including analyses of the conditions of women and men workers, work-related accidents and injuries, and an overview of household conditions. Survey and observational methods were used, as well as secondary sources of data, to yield a sophisticated body of work even by today's standards. This may well represent the beginning of human services research in the United States.

Intelligence Testing as a Technological Tool

Understanding social conditions did not seem to appeal to the public imagination quite as strongly as studying individual abilities or performance, so that psychology became the first social science to attract the attention of nonscientists. In the second decade of this century, American government became interested in psychology as a result of the convergence of two powerful social forces: war and the promotion of professional interests by practitioners of a particular academic discipline. To prove their worth, physical scientists had successfully applied practical solutions, based on their theories, to problems in the natural environment. A similar strategy was applied by psychologists, who during the outbreak of World War I in Europe and under the leadership of Robert M. Yerkes, were trying to promote acceptance of their discipline as a science through the use of intelligence testing. As described by Gould:

> Wars always generate their retinue of camp followers with ulterior motives. Many are simply scroundrels and profiteers, but a few are spurred by higher ideals. As mobilization for World War I approached, Yerkes got one of those "big ideas" that propel the history of science: could psychologists possibly persuade the army to test all of its recruits? If so, the philosopher's stone of psychology might be constructed: the copious, useful, and uniform body of numbers that would fuel a transition from dubious art to respected science.[8]

During this period, research and theory on intelligence and its relationship to education lent a degree of academic respectability to psychology. The intent of this work, in the United States and in Europe, was to develop a technology that could be applied to societal problems, similar to applications of engineering to the physical environment based on the theory and research of the physical sciences. The goal in psychology was to develop instruments that could be used to identify which students should be placed in what types of educational programs, a theoretical and applied perspective that continued to be in vogue until at least the 1960s.

Demonstrating Worth in the 1930s and 1940s

Later developments during the first half of this century furthered interest in the potential applications of social science theory and research in a number of ways. First, many social scientists in the 1930s were not dispassionate or detached observers of the human condition; they were reformers with goals similar to those of participants in the Pittsburgh Survey. As a result, social scientists looked upon their field as a means for acquiring the information needed to deal with the social problems of their times. This was especially the case with sociologists who were part of the Chicago school, whose interests ranged from criminology and juvenile gangs to race relations and to the urban environment and its ecology.[9]

Second, industry began to develop an interest in the potential of "social engineering." Western Electric Co., under the direction of the Bell Telephone laboratories, supported a series of industrial studies on work environment and productivity.[10] The notion of "scientific management" also came into prominence through the theories of Frederick Taylor when office automation started to grow at a rapid pace after World War I.[11] Changes in industrial and office settings brought about competing concerns with efficiency, productivity, and human relations (or humane work environments). Industrial psychology and industrial sociology emerged from this.

Third, government took a further look at the utility of social science in dealing with social problems, this time because of the crisis in American society brought on by the Great Depression. Finding the expertise of economists especially useful, the federal government, for the first time, hired economists as bureaucrats and researchers. From that time economists have been at home in government and policymaking circles, as well as in private industry. According to Finsterbusch and Motz: "Recognition of the value and relevance of economists and their work has given impetus to the acceptance of the other social sciences."[12]

Fourth, the 1930s saw the development of research on consumer behavior and the emergence of sample survey organizations. In addition to consumer-oriented research, there were early polling organizations (including the Gallup organization), which published their polls of popular opinion as syndicated newspaper columns, a tradition that continues today. In addition, there were developments in sampling methods. For example, face-to-face surveys, which used carefully drawn quota samples intended to provide "representative" samples, were successful in predicting the 1936 election. Such successes, based on the adaptation of social science research and theory to practical application, helped survey research achieve respectability.[13] (In this case, the goal of the technology was to forecast elections.) Whereas it was nearly 1940 before academic social scientists developed a corresponding interest in survey methodology, the social survey has emerged as the primary form of research in the social sciences and probably the most common image of social research in the public eye as well.

Finally, war once again came into play; in fact, World War II was probably the pivotal point in the status of the social sciences. Large numbers of scientists joined the military, where they engaged in extensive long-term projects. Not only were psychologists prominently involved, sociologists and anthropologists also were quite active. These military studies led to the publication of Stouffer's *The American Soldier* volumes and probably were instrumental in leading to research on *The Authoritarian Personality*.[14] There also was a clandestine connection between social science and the military during World War II. As historian Robin Winks has documented, academic social scientists were heavily involved in intelligence operations prior to and throughout the war.[15] In fact, one of the most famous developments in the social sciences, the Human Relations Area Files, were originally called the Cross-Cultural Survey and served as a prime source of information for the Office of Strategic Services and later for the Central Intelligence Agency.

Coming of Age

The social sciences did not lose the momentum gained during World War II. After the war, most social scientists who had served in the military returned to their academic settings. Because of relationships formed with bureaucrats in the War

Department (later the Department of Defense), these social scientists received substantial funding for their research throughout the 1950s and 1960s, particularly from the Office of Naval Research and the Advanced Research Projects Agency. Connections subsequently were made to other funding sources, including additional government agencies (such as the National Science Foundation and the National Institute of Mental Health) as well as private foundations (such as the Ford Foundation and the Rockefeller Foundation).

In the mid-1960s, new research opportunities grew out of the Great Society and the War on Poverty programs, which required that an explicit proportion of appropriations be spent on research and evaluation. In addition, much support was provided by the major foundations, many of which have strong ties to corporate interests.[16] However, with these resources came a shift in the thrust of research: in the early–World War II years, the emphasis was on "basic" or theoretically oriented research, whereas in the mid-1960s the emphasis shifted to "applied" research, especially in the form of program evaluation. Furthermore, university-based researchers could not keep up with the volume of activity, and the 1970s saw an explosion of policy organizations, research institutes, and the like, many of which took their lead from the Rand Corporation, one of the first social science and policy-making "think tanks."[17]

Even though there were cutbacks during the 1980s in support for social science research, these cutbacks were selective, affecting mainly basic (or theoretically oriented) research. Some areas, such as welfare reform (i.e., mainly workfare) research, have actually seen increases in the level of support. Federal expenditures for poverty research grew from about $1 million in 1965 to about $75 million in 1980. Haveman identifies 10 "major" social welfare experiments, noting that they cost a total of $1.1 billion (in 1983 dollars), "of which about $450 million can be attributed to research and administrative costs."[18] Social science has apparently come of age and proven its worth; there is no question that, when it is responsive to government and corporate interests, it profits well.

METHODS AND WORTH

Spencer argues that, unlike the natural sciences, the social sciences have not established that they "work," "since they cannot manipulate the social world in the same way that the natural sciences are able to manipulate the natural world."[19] Some critics may feel that social science has "fallen from grace" in policy-making circles, but that is certainly arguable.[20] Social science seems to have established and maintained a degree of credibility, because large-scale survey research and program evaluation projects are daily and ongoing activities. At least two major factors were instrumental in these developments, both of them products of emulating positivism in the natural sciences.

First, the social sciences (as noted in Chapter 2) adopted the principle of operationalism, ultimately coming to stress quantitative methods. With the access to mainframe computers and statistical packages that marked the 1960s, the social sciences could model themselves after the classical physical sciences. Prior to that time, large-scale projects were difficult to complete because of the massiveness of data processing and analysis. Using McBee cards and compiling data by hand were inefficient and untidy methods, compared to punch cards and computers as tools for storage and analysis. As quantitative data became easier to manage, the products of social science research (i.e., reports that included impressive numeric tables and charts) became more credible and persuasive because of appearance alone. Furthermore, social scientists could mimic the language of other scientists, in that they now collected their data using "instruments"—questionnaires and forms, not thermometers and scales but "scientific" instruments no less.

Second, the social sciences adopted experimentation as the ideal or prototype for research design. Although this methodology would never become the most commonly applied procedure, it could still serve as the model for how research should be done. The importance of experimental design lies in its ability to determine causal relationships among variables, and positivism identified "scientific explanation" with "causal explanation."[21] Because it is extremely difficult to use "true" experimental design in actual practice in the social sciences, alternatives were identified in the form of quasi-experimental and nonexperimental designs; terms such as *internal validity* and *external validity* were used to define the relative strengths and weaknesses of these alternatives. As a result, it was possible to carry out large-scale applied research projects that at least modeled themselves after so-called true experimental design. These developments can be readily seen in the program evaluation literature, which drew heavily on the notion of quasi-experimental design (see Chapter 10). During the past 20 years, program evaluation has achieved legitimation as a methodology through the convention of publication, manifested in three stages: publications about program evaluation in standard methodological and substantive journals; development of peer-reviewed journals devoted to this methodological field; and adoption of program evaluation as a topic to be included in social science research methods textbooks.

As noted earlier, quantification and experimental design have received substantial criticism in recent years. Nonetheless, these factors have helped the social sciences demonstrate their social worth. For better or worse, the conventional image of social science is what is "bought" beyond academic circles. This is not to suggest that the traditional social science method should be accepted without qualification; serious problems are incurred in the way social science is generally conceived and practiced, problems that may be exacerbated because social science research has become a commodity that is indeed "bought."

SCIENCE AND TECHNOLOGY AS COMMODITIES

One purpose of science is to generate information. Thus, if our research interests lie in developing or improving theoretical insights about certain phenomena, then we would describe our activities as *basic* research. If our interests lie in making policy decisions regarding human services—transportation, parks and recreation, or income maintenance needs—generally we will need to acquire information that helps us find solutions to specific problems; then we would describe our activities as *applied* research. Applied research typically yields a product, and in the natural sciences these products are often concrete objects or devices (airplanes, autos, stereos, and the like). The medical sciences also produce objects, such as prosthetic devices and medicines; furthermore, they produce tangible technologies, such as organ transplantation. In these examples, the outcomes of applied research may well be "commodities." We need to recognize, though, that basic research also yields an outcome that can be a commodity. For example, information or knowledge can be a product or a device; ideas can be owned as commodities, an ownership that can be protected legally by copyright, just as a device or technique can be legally protected by patent. As commodities, ideas can be bought and sold and made profitable.

Science, Disinterestedness, and Personal Gain

The quantity of valuable goods produced by scientists has accelerated since World War II, particularly in the natural and medical sciences. Yet the traditional image of the scientist has remained constant—someone motivated by intellectual curiosity rather than monetary gain. The traditional normative expectations in science call for the scientist to avoid proprietary motives; that is, a scientist should disdain personal gain as a motive.[22] Direct participation in converting an idea or research outcome into a commodity with commercial value generally has been deemed improper behavior for a scientist. The scientific community, then, is no different from any other human community: the behavior of its members is guided by norms that specify appropriate and inappropriate behavior. Presumably, these norms have helped science achieve its goal of advancing the state of knowledge over the course of time.

However, acceptance of some of these normative expectations declined during the post–World War II years, and the behavior of scientists relative to what they do with their discoveries has changed. Etzkowitz identifies two norms, communism (or communalism) and disinterestedness, both of which he believes have undergone important transformations:

> Communism requires that research results be shared with peers. The only "property rights" allowable for scientific discoveries are the honor and rewards that derive from recognition as their originator. Full and open communication represents the enactment of this norm; secrecy is its antithesis. Disinterestedness denotes the form that the relationship of scientists to society should take: the outcomes of scientific research are freely given to all who would use them in exchange for freedom from outside influence on the direction of scientific inquiry.[23]

As discussed in Chapter 2, verification is an important ingredient in the scientific method. Yet, without open communication of results, verification of findings is difficult if not impossible. That means that scientists must be willing to share ideas, not only through publication but also by sharing directly. The underlying question, then, concerns the extent to which scientists are willing to allow peers access to their data. Put another way, does the norm correspond to actual practice? Whether there is correspondence is a critical issue, because, as Ceci points out: "Some philosophers and social scientists who study normative practices in science fear that the eagerness to establish proprietary rights is leading to a closed system in which the refusal to allow colleagues to examine and replicate findings ultimately will impede scientific progress."[24] Unfortunately, results of his surveys on this question are not encouraging. Although most of his respondents indicated willingness to share their data bases, many reported they were aware of colleagues who had refused to do so, even if the research was funded by public money.

In a study of contemporary academic and industry connections at a private, research-oriented university, Etzkowitz found that entrepreneurial norms were emerging among many scientists.[25] Often, they rationalized their guardedness by stressing uncertainty of continued federal research funding. The implication seemed to be that although they preferred the existing norms, it was difficult to accommodate the traditional image when research monies issued from industry, where proprietary matters cannot be ignored. As a result, many researchers were forging links with industry or creating their own companies, thus establishing property rights to their discoveries. The university itself encouraged these endeavors, for it too would benefit by establishing proprietary rights to scientific discoveries.

Knowledge and Property Rights in the Social Sciences

It is not only in the natural and medical sciences that research products have become commodities; similar events have occurred as well in the social sciences. For the social planner, information can be invaluable, especially when it is current and the individual or organization that can provide it has a product that may have significant monetary worth. Such information can be marketed in two ways: Organizations can sell their ability to produce scientifically reliable and valid information when it is needed, or, they can sell access to needed information that they already have.

Controlling Access to Information: Restricting Who Can Produce.   As already discussed, scientists believe they support unrestricted access to each other's data or information. Yet, that is not always what they practice, especially now that social science has become "big business." Research on welfare reform illustrates the point. During the past 15 years, a small number of private research institutes, including the Manpower Demonstration Research Corporation (MDRC), Abt Associates, the Urban Institute, and Mathematica Policy Research, have come to dominate this research area. Many state governments contracted with these or other organizations for evaluation research on their programs. For example, in 1988, the state of Ohio awarded a multimillion-dollar contract to Abt Associates, which submitted an impressive proposal in response to an invitation from the Ohio Department of Human Services. To understand how corporate interests can lead to limited access to information, it is instructive to examine the literature review included in that proposal. A total of 46 items were included in the list of references, of which 24 (52.2 percent) were attributed to corporations. Only 11 items were disseminated through conventional social science sources, 6 as journal articles, and 5 as books. As Kilty and Jackson noted:

> The fact that over half of the documentation for previous research on welfare pro-grams came from corporate sources and over 60% from nonpublished sources indi-cates that much of this literature is likely to be inaccessible to many social scientists. Without ties to the appropriate organizations or individuals, it would be difficult to identify these materials and to make use of them.[26]

Controlling dissemination of information and access to data is a form of power; the more control an organization or group of organizations has, the more dominant it becomes in identifying what issues will be addressed by social re-search. An organization that can set the agenda will have a clear advantage in the supposedly competitive process of acquiring research resources.

Controlling Access to Information: Restricting What Is Produced.   An-other means for marketing ideas is to create a product and then sell it to interested parties, a strategy that is becoming more and more common in the social services and in the social sciences. An example is a publishing company that markets a resource book of agencies providing services for alcoholism or for the aged, comprised of lists taken from government publications. In some cases, books that purportedly provide exhaustive national lists are priced at $45 or more, whereas similar materials are provided at no charge or nominal charge by such agencies as the National Institute on Alcohol Abuse and Alcoholism. Not all practitioners or agencies have ready access to federal or state directories or to libraries that receive these materials on a regular basis. Furthermore, some consulting firms and research organizations try to market survey results under questionable circum-stances. Several years ago, for example, an organization in Columbus, Ohio, wanted to market the results of a community "needs assessment" survey to interested social service agencies. Yet, the project had been carried out using public monies, with the understanding that the materials would be made available to any local agency or group without charge. As social science research continues to produce information that is perceived as valuable, the impact of proprietary concerns is likely to become even more serious.

SOCIAL RESEARCH AND THE HUMAN SERVICES

The Development of Large-Scale Social Services

Prior to the Great Depression, human services were limited in the United States. Some public services were provided by state and local governments, but most social services were carried out by private, often religious-affiliated, philanthropic organizations that at the time exemplified the American spirit of voluntarism. Unfortunately, as the depression of the 1930s worsened, our social structures proved incapable of humane or timely response to the human misery produced by the depression. New institutional responses became necessary, one of which was the first major federal social welfare program in history—the Social Security Act.[27]

Although Social Security generally is identified with old-age pensions, it was designed to provide more, including national public welfare comprised of five major programs: (1) state assistance to the aged (Title I); (2) the Social Security system (Title II); (3) unemployment compensation (Title III); (4) assistance to families with dependent children (Title IV); and (5) assistance for the blind and disabled (Title V). In effect, Social Security established public welfare in the United States.[28] As noted earlier, these developments led to government interest in social science research and the entry of economists into federal agencies.

The next major era of expansion in public social services occurred in the 1960s. Michael Harrington's *The Other America* shocked a complacent and self-satisfied America into acknowledging that there was poverty in the midst of plenty. Upon reading the book, President John F. Kennedy was moved to commission a study of the problem. After Kennedy's death, President Lyndon B. Johnson declared an "unconditional war on poverty" in his 1964 State of the Union address.[29] Social scientists were involved from the beginning of these federal efforts, first as investigators and later as planners and strategists.

Linking Social Services and Social Science

As the War on Poverty programs unfolded, research became integrally involved in them, in the form of demonstration and evaluation projects and later including what came to be called needs assessments. Although research had previously had some limited impact on human services, the two were now formally linked. Indeed, social services practitioners adopted social science theory and research, not only as a means for acquiring information but also as a mechanism for establishing their professional credibility.[30] Many of the leaders of the social service community now enthusiastically adopted the scientific method as a basis for demonstrating the legitimacy of their interventions.

Social Service Research Methods

Practice and Accountability.   Demonstrating the validity of their activities became a major goal of human services professionals by the 1970s. To what extent practitioners were successfully intervening in the lives of their clientele became a matter of increasing concern, with the language of empiricism and operationalism now identified as a means for documenting the impact of professional interventions.[31] On the practice level, research steadily centered on what has come to be called "single-case design" or "single-subject research."[32] The goal of this approach is to provide the practitioner with information that will inform his or her practice, by documenting through tangible means that treatment goals were met.

Unless this evaluative process is formalized, assessments of individual practice are considered to be essentially subjective. Single-case designs calls for establishing clear intervention goals on the part of the practitioner and the client. These goals then can be assessed by objective measurement of relevant behaviors, attitudes, beliefs, or levels of knowledge, which should change if the intervention is having an impact. In essence, practitioners now have a means for holding themselves accountable, an endeavor that all "good" professionals should undertake. This technology has achieved significant acceptance among advocates of research in the social services and is now commonly taught in social service educational programs.

Planning, Program Evaluation, and Needs Assessment.   On the policy, planning, and decision-making levels, concerns with research led to development of two somewhat interrelated technologies: program evaluation and needs assessment. Beginning in the late 1960s, many federal human service programs mandated evaluation of program impact. How this assessment should be done generally was not specified. Often, the research projects were in the form of demonstrations, where the sole intent was to establish that the program had an effect. However, control group comparison was not generally included in these programs, which meant that program impact could not be documented unequivocally.

As program evaluation sought to establish itself as an acceptable methodology in the social science community, it adopted the principles of experimental design, with an emphasis on control and causation. In effect, the intent of this type of research came to be, first, to document experimenter control over the research situation and, second, to establish causal relationships between program interventions and client behaviors. Experimental programs became commonplace in a variety of social problem areas, including public welfare, criminal behavior, alcohol and substance abuse, and mental health problems.[33]

As services were expanded, another type of research emerged. Federal regulations soon required that, prior to development of new services or expansion of existing services, need levels be established by planners, which led to development of needs assessment studies to document the extent of need, particularly among identifiable target groups. Often, needs assessment is treated as an essential element in program planning, providing the baseline information needed for program evaluation.[34]

Like single-case design, program evaluation and needs assessment bring objectivity to the analysis of social service program effectiveness. Because concern over undue social, economic, and political influences on social services and social research has waned, descriptions of these research technologies focus on their ability to generate objective facts that can be used to guide the development of social services.

THE CONTEXT OF SOCIAL RESEARCH AND WHAT IS BEING ASKED

Social research does not take place within a vacuum. Whether we are concerned with basic research to extend knowledge and enhance our understanding of social processes, or with applied research to develop information that can be used to solve existing social problems, social research takes place within a social, political, and economic order. As Estes and Binney have pointed out, we need to understand "that scientific knowledge is socially produced and reproduced—knowledge is not inherently unbiased, objective, or politically neutral, as it is often represented." Furthermore, they note, "as the knowledge base is constructed and accepted, becoming part of the collective stock of knowledge, it becomes a force of its own with social, political, and economic consequences."[35]

The critical issue in understanding how context affects the social research process is to focus on how that context frames which questions will be asked. The next sections provide examples of how social science research is affected by the social environment.

Desegregation

In the mid-1970s, the U. S. Commission on Civil Rights funded a major study on desegregation in public schools. The commission contracted with the RAND Corporation for a preliminary study design, and RAND produced a traditional research design emphasizing objective measurement of conditions. The design led to serious conflicts among those involved in deciding whether the study should be carried out. As Mornell describes it:

> At the center of debate during this period were assumptions underlying the proposal in the RAND design to compare segregated and desegregated schools on a variety of measures, a plan which we perceived to ask, in effect, whether segregation was preferable to desegregation. As noted at a commission meeting where the issue was discussed, we felt that this was comparable to asking whether slavery was preferable to emancipation, as measured by a comparison of economic productivity under both conditions. The appropriate stance for the commission, we felt, was to restate its support for desegregation as a constitutional and moral imperative and then ask how desegregation could most effectively be implemented.[36]

Two competing assumptions were at work. First was the idea that desegregation should be approached as a social science problem, where the goal would be to design a careful research study contrasting desegregation with segregation. This would be an objective assessment, where scientists would not allow their personal values regarding segregation or desegregation to have an influence. Second was the idea that desegregation was the law of the land and an ideal to be achieved, a perspective that would render a comparison between segregation and desegregation meaningless. Thus, attention would focus on other types of research questions, such as how to implement desegregation programs effectively. The political and social context, then, affects the research process on a fundamental level: by directing attention to certain research questions over others.

Welfare and Work

Similar context problems plague the study of poverty and public welfare programs in that assumptions are made about the desire for work and the skill level of Aid to Families with Dependent Children (AFDC) recipients. Further assumptions are made about the ability of the job market to absorb increasing numbers of labor force participants. Yet, the research is designed following traditional principles of experimentation, where the impact of social, political, and economic factors— including the level of unemployment, the adequacy of pay levels and fringe benefits, the extent of child care and the like—cannot be taken into account.[37] It has not been established that most welfare recipients do not want to work; in fact, it has been shown that most welfare clients receive benefits for short durations and enter the labor force when jobs are available. For many, the problems in staying off welfare center on social structural factors such as the availability of child care, access to medical care for their children, and transportation. Nonetheless, the research presumes that the problems are individualized, particularly the lack of proper work habits, skills, and educational levels.

Aging as Pathology

Estes and Binney, in describing what they refer to as the "biomedicalization of aging,"[38] are concerned that gerontology is becoming embedded in the field of medicine. This trend, they fear, leads to a concept of the aging process as a medical problem and an approach to practice that focuses on medical conditions. In general, medicine is concerned with individual organic pathologies, and intervention strategies focus on the individual, where there is an inevitable chain of biological decline and disability. Research questions, then, focus on individual pathology, even though many people now live longer, healthier, and more active lives than ever before. Furthermore, biomedical factors influence how we perceive the basic social and behavioral dynamics of aging. Again, we can see that only certain questions become raised, largely relating to disease and disability. Yet social factors affect the well-being of older people. Limited income, housing problems, and transportation difficulties may affect the lives of older people even more than disease processes. Unfortunately, social and economic forces become obscured or ignored when problems are viewed from a biomedical perspective.

Alcohol and Abstinence

One last example of how social context affects research will be drawn from the treatment of alcoholism. During the 1970s, controversy erupted over nonabstinent drinking goals as an objective of treatment. In 1976, the RAND Corporation published a report that suggested that many so-called problem drinkers and alcoholics return to normal drinking after treatment, whether or not they are encouraged to do so. Actually, similar research findings had first been published in 1962, and a number of researchers had developed programs to teach people with drinking problems to become social drinkers again.

This research led to a furor among the alcohol establishment, particularly the policy makers, program administrators, and practitioners. Mark and Carol Sobell, two social scientists who advocated social drinking for alcoholics and published a series of papers documenting their claims, received the most attention. Complaints about their research ranged from methodological challenges (such as research design problems and inadequate follow-up of cases) to allegations of scientific misconduct (such as omitting contrary data and even altering data). They were first attacked in a paper appearing in *Science,* the prestigious journal of the American Association for the Advancement of Science, and later became the target of an exposé by the TV show "60 Minutes." The result was a congressional investigation of the veracity of their research.

This controversy has had a profound impact on research on the etiology and treatment of alcoholism and drinking problems. Even though more than 25 years of research have documented consistently that some people with drinking problems recover on their own and return to social drinking, that finding is unacceptable to the treatment community, which largely subscribes to a biomedical model of alcoholism. Certain research questions cannot be asked, at least not if one hopes to acquire research funds. If individual scientists persist in raising unacceptable questions, then massive efforts may be directed at discrediting them professionally and personally. The Sobells left the United States for the Addiction Research Foundation in Canada, where they could continue their research program. Sadly enough, they were ultimately exonerated of the charges placed against their research—although "60 Minutes" never saw fit to make note of that.

CONCLUSION

From the framework of the sociology of knowledge, we see that scientific reality is socially constructed, as everyday reality is a matter of social construction. What this principle means, then, is that a "fact" has no "meaning" until it is interpreted; and that interpretation takes place within a social context of political, economic, and moral assumptions and preferences. Is a mother with two children who is on AFDC lazy and promiscuous or the victim of social forces? Was the alcoholic who went back to social drinking someone who fell off the wagon and who eventually will have trouble again or someone who was never really an alcoholic in the first place? Is the elderly woman who sits in her house every day the victim of degenerative biological factors or someone who has no access to transportation? What should we make of the "fact" that the number of prison inmates in the United States doubled between 1981 and 1987? What does the "fact" that the number of working women rose from 38 percent in 1960 to 52 percent in 1981 mean? Is it necessary for both spouses to work, or do their extra earnings simply provide luxuries?

As we can see, social context guides us in asking particular questions. Is it fair to ask the question "Do most married women need to work?" Obviously, certain assumptions underlie that question—assumptions about the nature of family structure, assignment of responsibility for child care, and the nature of work (e.g., paid work versus unpaid work, level of commitment to work outside the home).

Social scientists are products of their culture, as are nonscientists. Yet, they also face other forces, among them conventional scientific wisdom. A successful social scientist must carry out research and publish it in peer-reviewed journals. Most scientists learn quickly which research questions are "acceptable" to raise, that is, which ones are publishable. Furthermore, doing research takes resources, and most scientists learn quickly which research questions are "acceptable" to potential funders. Creating scientific facts, then, is a process of demonstrating that one's evidence is credible.[40] In the social services and applied research, that includes the social science community, the planning and decision-making community, and the larger political and cultural community.

We turn our attention next to the way in which science is used by policy-makers in formulating policy and translating those policies into services. Adopting a scientific stance provides the appearance of objectivity and rationality in the policy process, but social services still exist within a political and social context—even when that context is ignored.

NOTES

1. M. E. Spenser, "The Imperfect Empiricism of the Social Sciences," *Sociological Forum* 2 (1987): 362.
2. R. Collins and M. Makowsky, *The Discovery of Society,* 3rd ed. (New York: Random House, 1984), 21.
3. Much of this section draws on material from a paper by K. M. Kilty and A. Jackson, "Social Science as Big Business: the Case of Welfare Reform," presented at the Annual Meeting of the Society for the Study of Social Problems, San Francisco, August 1989.
4. Collins and Makowsky, 189.
5. W. I. Thomas and F. Znaniecki, *The Polish Peasant in Europe and America* (Chicago: University of Chicago Press).
6. P. U. Kellogg, ed., *The Pittsburgh Survey: Findings in Six Volumes,* Volumes 1–4 (New York: Charities Publication Committee) and Volumes 5 and 6 (New York: Survey Associates). Volume 1: *Women and the Trades* (1909); Volume 2: *Work-Accidents and the Law* (1910); Volume 3: *The Steel Workers* (1910); Volume 4: *Homestead: the Households of a Mill Town* (1910); Volume 5: *The Pittsburgh District Civic Frontage* (1914); Volume 6: *Wage-Earning Pittsburgh* (1914).
7. J. M. Glenn, in Kellogg, vol. 1, 1.
8. J. Gould, *The Mismeasure of Man* (New York: W. W. Norton, 1981), 193–194.
9. A. Oberschall, *The Establishment of Empirical Sociology* (New York: Harper & Row, 1973).
10. Collins and Makowsky, 196.
11. I. Robertson, *Sociology,* 3rd ed. (New York: Worth, 1987), 460.
12. K. Finsterbusch and A. B. Motz, *Social Research for Policy Decisions* (Belmont, CA: Wadsworth, 1980), 4.
13. P. H. Rossi, J. D. Wright, and A. B. Anderson, eds., *Handbook of Survey Research* (Orlando, FL: Academic Press, 1983).
14. S. A. Stouffer et al., *The American Soldier: Studies in Social Psychology in World War II* (Princeton, NJ: Princeton University Press, 1949); T. W. Adorno, E. Frenkel-

Brunswik, D. Levinson, and N. Sanford, *The Authoritarian Personality* (New York: W. W. Norton, 1950).

15. R. W. Winks, *Cloak and Gown: Scholars in the Secret War, 1939–1961* (New York: William Morrow, 1987).

16. G. W. Domhoff, *Who Rules America Now?* (Englewood Cliffs, NJ: Prentice-Hall, 1983).

17. H. J. Aaron, *Politics and the Professors: the Great Society in Perspective* (Washington, DC: Brookings Institution, 1978).

18. R. H. Haveman, *Poverty Policy and Poverty Research: the Great Society and the Social Sciences* (Madison: University of Wisconsin Press, 1987), table 9.1, 184–185.

19. Spencer, 362.

20. R. P. Nathan, *Social Science in Government* (New York: Basic Books, 1988).

21. F. Collin, *Theory and Understanding: a Critique of Interpretive Social Science* (New York: Basil Blackwell), 75.

22. H. Etzkowitz, "Enterpreneurial Science in the Academy: a Case of the Transformation of Norms," *Social Problems* 36 (1989): 15.

23. Ibid, 14–15.

24. S. J. Ceci, "Scientists' Attitudes toward Data Sharing," *Science, Technology, and Human Values* 13 (1988): 45.

25. Etzkowitz.

26. Kilty and Jackson, 17.

27. M. A. McSteen, "Fifty Years of Social Security," *Social Security Bulletin* 48 (August 1988): 36–44.

28. H. R. Rodgers, Jr., *Poor Women, Poor Families* (Armonk, NY: Sharpe, 1986).

29. Kilty and Jackson.

30. J. H. Ehrenreich, *The Altruistic Imagination: a History of Social Work and Social Policy in the United States.* (Ithaca, NY: Cornell University Press, 1985).

31. S. Briar, "The Casework Predicament," *Social Work* 13 (1968): 5–11; J. Fischer, "Is Casework Effective? A Review," *Social Work* 18 (1973): 5–20; J. Fischer, *Effective Casework Practice: an Eclectic Approach* (New York: McGraw-Hill, 1978).

32. J. C. Nelsen, "Single-Subject Design," in *Social Work Research and Evaluation*, 3rd ed., ed. R. M. Grinnell, Jr. (Itasca, IL: Peacock, 1988); D. H. Barlow, S. C. Hayes, and R. O. Nelson, *The Scientific Practitioner: Research and Accountability in Clinical and Educational Settings* (New York: Pergamon, 1984); D. H. Barlow and M. Hersen, *Single Case Experimental Designs: Strategies for Studying Behavior Change* (New York: Pergamon, 1984).

33. C. C. Attkisson, W. A. Hargreaves, M. J. Horowitz, and J. E. Sorensen, eds., *Evaluation of Human Service Programs* (New York: Academic Press, 1978); F. G. Caro, ed., *Readings in Evaluation Research* (New York: Russell Sage Foundation, 1971); R. H. Haveman, ed., *A Decade of Federal Antipoverty Programs: Achievements, Failures, and Lessons* (New York: Academic Press, 1977); K. M. Kilty and A. Feld, "Professional Education in Understanding and Treating Alcoholism," *Journal of Studies on Alcohol* 40 (1979): 929–42; K. M. Kilty, "Longitudinal Analysis of a Demonstration Rural Outreach Alcoholism Program," *Journal of Studies on Alcohol* 45 (1984); 124–30; E. J. Posavac and R. G. Carey, *Program Evaluation: Methods and Case Studies*, 3rd ed. (Englewood Cliffs, NJ: Prentice-Hall, 1989).

34. Rossi et al.

35. C. L. Estes and E. A. Binney, "The Biomedicalization of Aging: Dangers and Dilemmas," *Journal of Gerontology* 29 (1989): 588.

36. E. S. Mornell, "Social Science and Social Policy: Epistemology and Values in Contemporary Research," *School Review* 87 (1979): 298.

37. Kilty and Jackson.

38. Estes and Binney.

39. D. J. Armor, J. M. Polich, and H. B. Stambul, *Alcoholism and Treatment* (New York; Wiley, 1978); E. M. Pattison, M. B. Sobell, and L. C. Sobell, *Emerging Concepts of Alcohol Dependence* (New York: Springer, 1977); M. L. Pendery, I. M. Maltzman, and L. J. West, "Controlled Drinking by Alcoholics? New Findings and a Reevaluation of a Major Affirmative Study," *Science* 217 (1982): 169–75; M. B. Sobell and L. C. Sobell, eds., *Moderation as a Goal or Outcome of Treatment for Alcohol Problems* (New York: Haworth Press, 1987).

40. Spencer.

CHAPTER 4

Policy, Politics, Reason, and Inquiry

INTRODUCTION

Chapter 1 discussed the general context in which a relationship among large-scale political forces, the development of social work, and the selective uses of science was forged. Chapters 2 and 3 focused in detail on the peculiar difficulties of engaging in scientific inquiry in the social and political worlds.

Chapters 4 and 5 continue the discussion, focusing on the nature of policy and the operationalizing of policy at the agency level. Chapter 4 asserts that the political nature of policy and the choices afforded those who make policy strongly affect the manner in which science and scientific inquiry is used by professionals.

Six major topics will be covered in this chapter:

- policy in terms of its rationality and other characteristics;
- policy as pervasive social phemomena;
- policy as an inherently political process and product that affects the boundaries of rationality;
- the purposes, including political, in developing and focusing policy responses;
- the professional and political choices in programming strategies;
- the functional use of inquiry within all of the preceding political and volitional aspects of policy.

POLICY AS RATIONALITY AND OTHER CHARACTERISTICS

Generally speaking, there are two key approaches, even traditions, to a discussion of policy. One heavily relies on a rational problem-solving process and emphasizes the features of selected phenomena and conditions that may be present in society. The other approach, which will be discussed below, stresses political forces, power, and political processes. To the degree that there is clear articulation and description of the phenomena, eventual shared agreement on the phenomena's dysfunctional components, and a state or goal to be pursued, then rational intervention can occur.[1] Some products of this rational and logical process are called policy.

Reason, Systematic Gathering of Data, and Variable Perspectives

In one sense, policy is a public statement to the effect that something "ought to" occur, and if it does, that it can be rational and instrumental in addressing some condition(s) in a society. Whatever policy or policy proposal is ultimately offered is largely shaped by the process of systematic gathering of data concerning the current situation.

For example, increased social awareness of conditions facing parents and children is an element in building a case for possible policy in the area of child care.[2] Large numbers of households can be identified as single-parent households, and an even larger number can be tabulated wherein both parents work. Within both types of households are children who must be cared for. Employers need workers from both types of households. Briefly, then, general features of the problem can be identified.

This assessment of the current situation, through systematic inquiry and statistical reporting of numbers by household category, suggests several rational possibilities. One of these is for the government to become involved more directly in addressing the set of conditions that affect families and employers. Other rational possibilities might include answers that do not lead to public statements of what ought to be—for example promoting the cultural notion that "appropriate" parenting means a parent staying at home, or fostering individual and collective decisions that reflect a cultural preference for fewer children, no children, scaled-down life-style, and such. A still different approach might be for employers to become very active in handling the child-care problem; for example, providing day care, permitting job sharing, or improving child-care benefits. In pure form, the employer approach could be private and voluntary in nature or involve a partnership with the government. In modified form, this approach could allow or require tax credits or other incentives.[3]

In examining this rational approach, two points are worth noting. First, many of the solutions suggested above are indeed rational for different audiences and to different degrees. That is, in all probability, a selected alternative will make sense for those who select it. Second, however, a preferred rational approach will be riddled with some significant values. For example, if person *A* stresses the value of availability of child care and the rights of women to pursue personal and career goals, then the option of government involvement may be perceived more favorably. If, on the other hand, person *B* argues that the value of parenting is *a priori* defined primarily in terms of a parent being in touch with the child physically during the day, then not only might government involvement not be required, it could be perceived as another problem. In short, the values and perspectives one brings to the rational approach not only affect the proposals, they also can affect the discussion and description of the problem. Thus, the process of viewing and approaching policy as a rational enterprise quickly runs into the variable and political dimensions of policy, which will be discussed in detail later in the chapter.

Policy Instrumentation: Normative Guide and Collective Wisdom

Despite the preceding observations, policy initially can be seen as rational. Policy, in its basic form, is an instrument designed to promote or achieve some "ought to be." That "ought to be" could be more gainful employment, reduction of infant mortality, and so on. As an instrument, policy can reflect different social forces over periods of time; the "ought to be" can focus heavily on something that should occur in the future—full employment or available housing for all. In so doing, the state or goal to be pursued can be viewed as a solution to a problem or dysfunction about which society has some level of awareness.[4]

Policy can also be viewed as rational in terms of being a normative guide. As such it can guide people—including professionals and clients—in their present actions.[5] Viewed from this perspective, policy instructs people in the "right" ways to apply, or react to applications for, benefits or help. In this respect, policy can be viewed as systematically defined procedures and guidelines.

Still another way in which policy can be seen as rational, especially if one looks behind current guidelines, is as the collected wisdom of people through time.[6] That wisdom can have emerged from cumulative shared experiences, or it can be the wisdom of officeholders. Through repetitive experiences and through examination of "better" answers, the guidelines as well as the solutions and goals become clearer.

Policy and the Allocation of Resources

Policy might even be seen as rational in relation to the use and distribution of resources. In this instance, policy can be developed so that resources are allocated systematically, relative to selected criteria (need, seniority, even equality). In this example, policy is rational in recognizing the need for criteria and in applying criteria to potential recipients. As will be discussed later, this example certainly is not necessarily rational in the selection of one set of criteria over another.

POLICY AS A PERVASIVE SOCIAL PHENOMENON

Whether or not one accepts policy as basically rational, it is nonetheless endemic in our society, occurring in the public and private aspects of life.[7] For example, the government produces policy concerning many aspects of our lives—citizens "ought to" pay taxes, send their children to school, be free to worship in the manner they choose, and so on. In addition, some employees work in organizational environments in which they "ought to" appear for work on time, get X number of vacation days, and so on. Similarly, some private organizations (such as social agencies) "ought to" provide after-school services to neighborhood residents, offer professional services to runaway adolescents, and so on. In short, "ought to" statements—whether they stress solution, guide, or wisdom—are commonplace in our public and private lives.

Each area of our lives, the public and the private, encompasses several institutional sectors or components. Though each sector is distinct, it is increasingly necessary to see and understand that these sectors often *interrelate* with each other, even across the public and private boundaries. For example, although private banks and businesses function within the larger economy, each has its own policies. Even so, in most instances they are affected significantly by *public* policy decisions made by the Federal Reserve Board and numerous government regulatory bodies. In short, the public and private areas are not totally distinct and insulated from one another; in many cases, the interpenetration is achieved through the reality of policy.

In related fashion, policy may be generated within our religious congregations, private schools, clubs, and other organizations. In all instances, the policy produced will reflect some mixture of the promotion of solution and goals, the "right" way to proceed, or a "better" way that has been discerned or learned over time.

In looking at the public and private aspects of life and the different sectors within each, two points are worth noting. First, interpenetration of the public and private has become more pronounced. Increasingly we witness situations wherein policy in the private area is not purely private. For example, private schools receiving public funds may not discriminate on the basis of race. The "ought to be" stance of the public sector can take precedence over, or constrain, the "ought to be" statements, (even unwritten ones) of the private sector. Further, the "ought to be" of serving a particular group may be tied to public funding patterns, which can affect the nature and extent of services eventually offered to certain groups.

Second, within the aspects of public and private life, there is always the issue of relative dominance of institutional sectors. For example, does the economic sector have more influence over the educational sector? If yes, is that dominance in turn reflected in the type and amount of policy written in each sector? Across aspects of life, the same issue of relative significance and possible dominance often can be detected—policy developed for public schools often impinges on policy in private schools, e.g., curriculum requirements or deployment of special services in school districts. In short, policy routinely produced in all aspects of our lives—public and private—neither is produced nor operates in a vacuum. Policies initially indigenous to one aspect of our lives invariably interact with others, and across different institutional sectors. Collectively such policies will constrain and influence the public/private structure of our lives.[8]

Policy and Levels of Policy Interpretation

Besides being shaped in the public and private aspects of our lives, policies can be made on a variety of levels and in a variety of ways.[9] In the public arena, policy can be made on the national level (young men 18 years of age "ought to" register with the Selective Service System). It can also be detected at the state level (anyone driving under the influence of drugs and/or alcohol "ought to" have his or her driver's license revoked). Policy is evident at the local level as well (employees of city government "ought to" live within the city's corporate boundary).

In examining levels of policy one should not assume they apply to only the public or the private aspect of life. For example, the National Rifle Association (NRA), Catholic Charities, and General Motors all make national or corporate headquarters' policies, and their federated or constituitive units often make additional policies. In both instances, however, the interpenetration between and among levels is likely to occur, and it often will be disproportionate in effect, in terms of constraints upon the local organization and it policies. Further, to make it even more complex, the interpenetration is likely to include not only different levels of interpretation, but also different aspects of life (private and public) and different institutional sectors previously raised.

Sources of Policy

Policy, whether formed in the public or private arena, can be formulated in a variety of ways. Public policy can be generated by any and all units of government—*legislative, executive, judicial.*[10] Looking at different phenomena, we can see one or more of these units, at some level, getting involved. States historically have passed laws about whether abortion "ought to be" considered legal or illegal. Over time, the Supreme Court has said women "ought to" have some level of personal privacy, which could extend to decisions, within guidelines, concerning the fetus. In this example, different levels of government, as well as different potential sources of policy, can be easily identified. In the same policy area, Congress and the president agreed, as did the Supreme Court eventually, that *Roe vs. Wade* did not necessarily mean that women had a right to public funding for abortion. Thus, the second policy on abortion—funding—interacted with the "right" to privacy, the net effect being that the policy restricted some women but not others.

All three units of government make policy. Whereas legislation is the most obvious attempt to make public policy, and whereas court decisions are often dramatic and significant, much policy is administrative in origin. Executive orders and other administrative and agency directives are extremely important in today's society. Rourke has identified this area as potentially the most undemocratic and uncontrollable aspect of policy, because appointed administrative officials are not easily or routinely subject to the purview of either legislators or citizens.[11]

POLICY, POLITICAL PROCESS, AND PRODUCT

Perhaps the most significant characteristic of policy, one that dominates the second major approach to policy, is politics.[12] Although policy may be considered to be rational in a variety of ways, it is also dramatically political in several ways, including the initiation, the ongoing processes and development, and the consequences of policy. Several specific political aspects of policy are discussed below.

Before discussing the political nature of policy, however, the term *politics* should be clarified. In this discussion, it refers to the recognition of, and subsequent action by, groups and individuals of their interests that are directly tied to their positions in social relationships.[13] This concept suggests that what people and groups perceive and ultimately want is directly tied to the social structures in which they are located and from which they operate.

Political Interests and the Shaping of Problem Perceptions

Nelson, Ross, and Staines have discussed the role interests play in the initiation of policy when they suggest that policy does not automatically occur as a rational solution to a problem.[14] Initially, there has to be recognition that some interests are not being met, that one or more groups are experiencing dysfunction. Central to this unfolding is the fact that perceptions and definitions of social problems are not automatic.[15] In discussing battered women, Davis notes that the interests of certain women clearly were not met for many years. Yet society, including many women, failed to see or note the problem of abused women. What was required was shared recognition that a problem befell certain people (women) and that the interests of women were not served.

Given this connection between problem and group, and problem and interests, women's groups came forward to help shape awareness of the problem in the larger society. In doing so, they developed a logic/rationale to initiate the process of seeking solutions—ultimately, policy and program responses intended to serve and protect women.

Interest Groups and Decision-Making Processes

Besides observably shaping social perceptions within society and therefore serving as a precursor to policy, politics is also apparent in the process of formulating policy. In this regard, many groups, despite recognizing their own interests and wishing to have them met through policy responses, are unable to persuade others to acknowledge the need for rational solutions or changes. More realistically, there is recognition that certain interests may be better served if special-interest groups are formed, e.g., veterans groups, the American Medical Association or the National Rifle Association; and if those special-interest groups direct most of their efforts toward key policy decisionmakers (such as legislators).[17]

Now in the formation of a special-interest group perspective and the eventual instrumental activities that may be undertaken by such a group, other political features can be discerned. At the top of the list is the fact that key decisionmakers have interests that are directly tied to the fact that they *are* decisionmakers. For example, a legislative official might need to cultivate a constituency in order to be reelected, which requires a simple majority of voters. In some regards, then, the pluralistic democratic process can be viewed as an exchange game: On one side an interest group presents demands to people who, alone or in concert with other groups, can produce policy responses that promote the interest group. On the other side the decision-makers may be looking for a way to build a constituency that ultimately can produce a simple majority of electoral support. In negative terms, the decision-maker is trying to prevent special-interest groups from withdrawing support.[18]

However, the policy process is rarely, if ever, this simple. The special-interest groups cited are only a few of many; therefore, a potential interest group may be overlooked. If this happens, the decision-maker often cannot respond as desired, or the interest group may not, by itself, be strong enough to activate the desired response from the decision-maker. The interests and agendas of other interest groups may compete to influence the decision-maker. If so, inactivity is likely be the result, because decision-makers are not best served by offending any one (or more) interest group.

When one interest group is counterbalanced by a contending interest group, there is the politically compelling reason to enter into coalitions with still other interest groups, so that the leverage of combined political forces swings the balance for the decision-maker toward seeing that his or her interests are best served by moving in the direction of the stronger coalition.[19]

The strong coalition, however, rarely is limited to one policy proposal. Rather, each special-interest group is likely to use the coalition strategy to promote its discrete interests and issues. Consequently, coalitions can be temporary structures.

Thus, these are the specific political features of the policy-making process:

- Articulation of interests;
- Attempts to influence decisionmakers in light of those interests;
- Coalition building to maximize leverage;
- Likelihood of shared issues, sometimes referred to as an agenda, by related interest groups; and
- Responses by decision-makers to ensure future support or prevent erosion of critical support from a coalition of interest groups.

In looking at the process of policy making, it is critical to understand and appreciate the difference between actual and potential political resources.[20] If potential resources are not brought to the political process, then they cannot produce policy responses that could help a situation or group. The corollary is also true. For example, many fine proposals can be offered to help families, children, and welfare recipients in this country, but such proposals—as "rational" and as "good" as they may be—often do not get serious attention because the potential beneficiaries lack political "clout." On the other hand, policy proposals affecting the elderly routinely get serious attention. Why? The elderly's resources, the numbers of elderly voters and their group awareness and degree of organization are extremely high. One consequence of this imbalance of power is that the elderly receive a lot of attention in the area of policy whereas children and welfare recipients do not. Years ago, Dahl referred to the latter situation as slack resources, which are not strong enough to activate the decisionmakers.[21]

Another feature in the process of policy making is that the process itself tends to work against any overall grand design or singular comprehensive plan.[22] Rather, the ongoing emergence of special-interest groups and fluid and changing coalitions make for a process that is disjointed and somewhat incremental in nature, a feature discussed in the following section.

Allocation of Resources

If we now move from the *process* of policy making to its *consequences,* particularly the allocation of resources, we again see the political side of policy. Rarely, if ever, does a social unit have enough resources to meet all the interests and desires of all its groups and actors. The same can be said of the larger society (and has been in the past 15 years). That being the case, the basic political issues concerning policy often involve *who* will get *what* and *how* it will be distributed. The back side of this political issue is, obviously, who will *not* get what for which problems or conditions? Inherent in these very thorny issues is the question raised earlier: which institutional sectors (e.g., military, education) should receive more or less consideration?

In attempting to examine these key policy questions, the only broad consensus is likely to be that these critical issues and questions do exist. Reasonable people, especially those operating within an interest-group perspective, no doubt will differ substantially on answers or sometimes even on framing the questions. Given this, then, the importance of process and the power of interest groups are germane. Allocation of resources for specific questions raised is likely to be a function of the perceived power of different interest groups that comprise the critical constituencies.

This discussion of process and allocation is not to suggest that attitudes and values are not important—they are, especially in the context of explaining or justifying allocation of scarce resources. Discussion of why and how the policy will work, including the key area of resource distribution, typically will involve phrases like "for the good of the community," or "to promote the well-being of our senior citizens.'' Explanations such as "we need the support of the elderly" or "we are concerned about reprecussions if we don't satisfy the banking establishment" are not typical justifications.

Nonsystemic Policies

The final area to be addressed here has to do with politics and incrementalism, referred to in the above discussion. In relating the discussion of process to the topic of resource allocation and consequences, one is likely to find that different policies do not relate well to each other. In fact, because of the reality of different goals and problems being pursued by different interest groups and coalitions over extended periods of time, one is likely to find a disjointed and nonsystemic mixture of policies to placate different constituencies. For example, congressional policymakers consistently have voted for subsidies to tobacco farmers, while, concurrently and alternately, funding research and prevention efforts to eliminate smoking or to study cancer. Similarly, state and local legislators have developed policies to discourage or limit drinking and smoking, while at the same time developing taxing policies that, in a sense, require the continued existence of certain behaviors as well as the very companies and sources of revenues that facilitate the allegedly questionable behavior.

Relative to incrementalism, policy can evolve or be made over an extended period of time, in response to different problems and political forces. The result of this is that, at any time, pieces of policy can be constructed, perhaps in piecemeal fashion. The policy that gets created thus may be "small" relative to the true scope of a problem, and policy may be seen as less than adequate to meet the desired change of some political groups. Examples of incrementalism abound in American society, and they include incremental responses in such areas as day care and health insurance.

PURPOSES IN POLICY RESPONSES

Inherent in the question of *who* will receive *what* and *how* is a more basic question: Are distinct political purposes to be served by certain policies? Purposes of policy are rarely self-evident. In fact, even if a policy has a stated purpose, it is wise, given the reality of interests and power, to probe for the "real" reasons behind it.

Several social policy analysts have discussed the range of possible purposes and functions of social policy. Perhaps the most suggestive discussions allow for distinctions among different interest groups and among recipient groups.

Policy as Reward

One possible purpose of policy is to reward a group. Gilbert and Specht point to veterans groups who, because they have contributed to society, are recipients of policy benefits.[23] Further, veterans are well organized and well versed in playing the politics of welfare. The elderly are also often approached as a group that ought to receive policy consideration—in fact, special consideration. In terms of their demographic patterns, voting patterns, strategy of not making distinctions within the group (i.e. wealthy/not wealthy, male/female), and political sophistication in the policy arena, the elderly have fairly recently been approached as a group that is special.[24]

The elderly and veterans rely on policy and derived benefits as compensation for prior contributions. In fact, behind most policy that rewards valued interest groups is a "payback" quality, so much so that the term *entitlement* is correctly applied to the benefits directed to all members of the rewarded group. Recognizing the potential and actual political power and resources of these two groups, policymakers of all political persuasions have found it in their own self-interests to institutionalize entitlements for these groups.

Policy as Necessary Response

A second possible purpose in the creation of policy is to handle unavoidable necessity, such as a conflict in society. Typically, the conflict involves values on one level and interests on another. Aid to Families with Dependent Children (AFDC) is such an example. This policy states that public financial assistance should be given to households with children that do not have adequate family financial resources.[25] Such a lack of resources, the policy recognizes, adversely affects the growth and development, perhaps even the survival, of the children. Yet as clear as this recognition is, there is also another recognition that, it is argued, such public assistance can produce depencency, including intergenerational dependency, on public assistance. On a value level, then, the value of caring for children is counterbalanced somewhat by the value of self-sufficiency, especially as the latter may apply to adults in the household.

The interest of the child(ren), then, are counterbalanced by the negative impact on taxpayers. Further, the financial interests of others in the economy can be affected adversely by the diversion of economic resources from the market to taxes that pay for these benefits. It is argued that the interests of the larger private economy are affected adversely by this type of policy, because money that could be used for consumer items that have more of a multiplier effect throughout the economy goes instead to groups who will use the resources for survival items, or other items that tend to have less of a multiplier effect on the economy. Given this strain between values and interests of the different groups, policy has been created that reflects the multiple pressures: funds are made available to families for child care, but payment is (and, it is argued, should be) limited, so as not to devalue the notion of self-sufficiency or to divert excessive or substantial sums of money from the private economy. This way, policy allows individuals to make choices about consumer items, a type of freedom is promoted, and self-sufficiency as a norm remains.

Policy as Investment

A third possible purpose behind policy has to do with investment, financial and otherwise.[26] This policy perspective recognizes that purposeful use of benefits serves the interests of several groups; that is, there can be multiple recipients. Our society is riddled with policies that reflect this recognition: tax abatements so that certain industries or corporations will locate in certain portions of the country and provide jobs; subsidies for certain groups for in-kind benefits such as housing, so that the availability of those benefits will stimulate builders to make housing available and to create jobs; and provision of other in-kind benefits, such as food stamps, to ensure an active buyers market to assist food processors and store owners.

In these and other instances, policy is made with an ostensibly designated benefit and population, e.g., food stamps and the poor. However, the "real" recipients may be—in the case of food stamps—store owners, food distributors, food processors, and farmers. In other areas—tax abatements and housing—policy positively contributes to the interests of entrepreneurs, stockholders, unions, school districts, stores, and local taxing bodies.

Policy that reflects this perspective is always marked by multiple recipients, and often the key recipients, though not seen, have power and interests that are well served by the policy. So strong is the reality of this policy orientation that often it is virtually impossible to "sell" a proposed social policy to assist one group unless it can also be shown to serve multiple recipients and bestow multiple economic rewards.

Policy as Stabilizer

A fourth possible purpose for policy is stability, or order within the social arrangement.[27] In a very real sense, this is related to investment purposes, but the payoff benefits the social *and* economic sectors. The principle of multiple recipients and multiple interests still applies.

Policy examples from the 1960s and 1970s typify this purpose. For example, legislation at all government levels provided for summer employment for youth, higher welfare payments, and so on, and reflected a belief that a dollar spent in certain ways could forestall rioting, unsafe streets, or delinquency. In all of these instances, the policy that provided costly benefits ultimately would, it was argued, serve other citizens and maintain a stable social life and environment.

As we settle into the 1990s we see that some of the early policies promoting stability and order have been institutionalized. Operation Headstart, admittedly functioning at a reduced level, is an example. Pragmatically, the surviving social investment policies have developed constituencies and interest groups that help maintain them. In some cases—again Operation Headstart is an example—it has subsequently been found that children directly involved in the policy are less prone to crime and delinquency. Stated another way, some fiscal involvements are accepted by the larger society, and some are seen to contribute to ongoing conformity in the social world, i.e., they are good social and fiscal investments.

However, in the Reagan and Bush administrations the more routine occurrence was the cutting back of public investments and the resorting to a private and volunteer approach.[28] The norms of contraction of welfare and reliance on charity will likely continue so long as social disruptions are few and have little negative impact on key groups in the larger society.

Policy and Human Development

A fifth possible purpose behind policy may be identified as developmental. Here public policy is viewed as assisting and promoting a broad range of people across a broad range of areas—health, recreation, personal growth, aesthetic and survival concerns, and so on. In recent years this purpose rarely has been found in policy, because of "limited resources;" more pressing demands in other sectors (building up military and defense, bailing out the savings and loans); and the advancing acceptance and reliance on a user-fee strategy (those who use the service or benefit should pay for it).

Policy in the areas of schools, libraries, and recreation has typically contributed to and reflected a developmental purpose, but even these socially accepted areas evince contraction of resources, the encouragement of voluntarism, and the charging of fees. It is not uncommon, for example, for public schools to require sports players and their families to pay for a sports program—uniforms, equipment and such. Similarly, summer school and extension courses now require large fee payments.

As the developmental policy recedes, certain effects become evident: first, affected populations and groups receive less service or no service; second, those who can will resort to private alternatives for continued services; third, stratification of benefit recipients likely will occur; finally, that portion of the population able to pay for its own services is apt to be progressively cut off socially and politically from populations that cannot pay. In this last instance, the fiscal cutback leads to a social consequence that is detrimental to certain recipients and groups.[30] Recent developments of two-tiered responses in health care, education, and day care are examples of marked qualitative differences in benefits that reflect and contribute to group differences and separations, e.g., between racial groups and social classes.

PROFESSIONAL AND POLITICAL CHOICES IN PROGRAMMING STRATEGIES

Behind each policy purpose discussed are identifiable choices and values. Initially, these values relate to *whom* is chosen to be a recipient and *what* benefits are to be provided. These choices can be examined in terms of possible program strategies, i.e., the *how*. Wolins's work describes programmatic options and strategies and is elaborated on below.[31]

Programs as Substitutes

One strategy is to develop programs that are substitutes for "normal" institutional arrangements. For example, a child who needs parental care and nurturing may not have a steady parent figure or may have one who cannot act in the child's best interests. In this instance, the program response is for a substitute to perform the appropriate nurturing and caring functions, either foster care, child-care institutions, or adoption programs.[32]

Behind this substitute strategy lies a common theme of institutional malfunctioning, either temporary or long term. Further, substitute strategy tends to occur only *after* need is demonstrated, which suggests that the values of prevention and broad development are minimal or absent. Frequently, programmatic response is in the context of a perception that ideally the "other" institution should perform the service; that "others" should be responsible but because "they" can't (or won't), "we" (society) ought to do what we can without violating the rights and responsibilities of other individuals and stuctures. In simpler language, substitute programs can reflect a classic push–pull effect on the larger society, in that the program response is never simply to assist a client but often is riddled with symbolic statements to other actors and constituencies.[33] These statements can reinforce values and valued groups. They can also devalue other values and/or other groups.[33]

Programs That Prepare

A second program strategy prepares participants to use other institutions more appropriately. A fundamental program might give information about resources, so that a program recipient can then use the information constructively. For example, a parent wishing to enrich a child's artistic development might need to know what music enrichment programs are available to preschoolers; once this is known, the parent can then act. This example reaffirms the inherent value of individual choice and individual responsibility. A program to provide information, although simple, ultimately is significant in that it serves as a link between would-be users and providers.

More complex programs give more than information; they might provide opportunity for personal insight, resolution of psychological conflicts, or ventilation of feelings. Whether the services are called counseling, therapy, or treatment, these programs are useful because they allow recipients to grow, to interrelate more effectively with others and in other institutional contexts.

Depending on how inclusive the definition is as to who can use these programs and for what range of issues, these programs can be far more than substitutes. Programs that prepare can assist people in their personal development and might reflect a more preventive focus. However, sometimes they are narrow in focus and often presuppose that a need is present.[34]

Programs That Alter the Environment

A third program strategy recognizes that the recipient of a program response exists within an environment that might have to be modified or changed. This program strategy often presupposes a need that either is enmeshed in, or caused by, the environment.[35] For example, a single parent may need financial assistance to care for a young child; the parent also may need a job but cannot meet the parenting responsibility if he or she pursues a job. The parental function can occur only if the community makes available low-cost or free day care. Without the day care, only the financial need can be addressed (to some degree) through public assistance. Altering the environment by providing day care theoretically can allow both levels of need to be addressed. Obviously, the nature of the alteration and the number of people included will affect whether this program strategy is broadly developmental and preventive or, ultimately, need-driven and focused on social control.

Programs and Social Order

The last program type to be identified here focuses on social order or social control. A program anchored by social control reflects a strong commitment to having the social world predictable, where various actors can anticipate one another's actions. In this kind of program, intuition, perhaps even previous experiences of the larger society, suggest that certain interventions can have particular effects on the social arrangement. Gans, Galper, Cloward and Piven, and others have recognized that the nature of many welfare expenditures and programs is keyed to social control.[37]

Social order program strategies are plentiful: At one level, much of public assistance benefits could be considered actual investments in containing and managing populations and groups that could be disruptive to the larger community. Similarly, public housing and food stamps might be construed as programs focused on ensuring some level of recipient compliance. Perhaps less dramatic are programs that hire teenagers in the summer.

More subtle programs in community mental health centers and schools focus on "leveling" the behavior of recipients. These programs can teach such skills as how to present oneself in public, how to dress appropriately, how to apply and interview for jobs, parenting skills, and the like. Such leveling allows for normal activities to occur in the larger community and society with minimal dysfunctions and cost.

POLITICAL FACTORS AND THE NEED FOR CRITICAL ANALYSIS

In reviewing the range of possible purposes of policy and identifying the type of program strategy employed, several points are worth noting. First, the policy/program arena is complex. Recipients themselves rarely can account for or fully explain why a policy or a program has come into existence. In many of the examples discussed, others benefited from the policy and program response. Obviously, this specific consideration requires the analyst to consider the issue of interests and to ask whose interests are being served in addition to the so-called client or recipient. Inherent in analyzing issues is the complexity of multiple, varying, and contending interest and value positions. This being the case, both policy and program will reflect not only the key interests but also the way power is used by the different interests.

Second, this discussion implies that problems of would-be clients or groups probably will not be prime activators of policy and program responses. Rather, it is when problems become dysfunctional for significant or powerful others that the policy and program response is more likely to be set in motion; and it will be set in motion relative to the reality of interests.

These first two points, who is affected in what way and who has power, raise the consideration that, in a technical sense, the "best interests" served may be quite removed and distinct from the interests of the designated benefit recipients.

Finally, this discussion raises the possibility that many welfare and human service responses ultimately are geared to maintaining relationships among groups, rather than merely meeting the obvious needs of certain groups. This possibility suggests that when policy is directed at large numbers of minorities, the not-so-subtle function of the concern may be to ensure that the minority remains a minority, not just in statistical terms but also in terms of power and influence.

If this is so, then the mere numbers of needy people served and the examination of their key characteristics, in and of itself, cannot lead to the conclusion that the program is "valuable." Specification of the program type, accompanied by an empirical assessment of who receives directly the benefit, is but a beginning step in the inferential process of critiquing possible purposes and functions of policies and programs.

THE FUNCTIONAL USE OF INQUIRY

From the preceding sections it is clear that policy is heavily political in nature. All this means is that interests and power are significant in the process and the substance of policy, as well as in the programs that ultimately are utilized to carry out the policy. This political reality does not suggest that science plays no role; on the contrary, systematic inquiry can play a major role, a role that ultimately is constrained and shaped by larger political forces and processes.

The point of the discussion so far is to identify the logic and utility of scientific inquiry. For those who are in applied fields there are three major ways in which to apply scientific inquiry:

- Identifying the current situation, especially in terms of relationships between policy or policy proposals, and the "objective" state of affairs;
- Observing, the process of making policy; and
- Monitoring the consequences of policy that is implemented.

In all three areas, a working premise may be explicated: The more one can tabulate and identify what is going on and who and what is at stake, the more informed and appropriate may be the resulting policy and practical choices and behaviors.

Identifying the Current Situation

The first thing scientific methodology can do is to help specify and describe the situation facing a policy or policy proposal. Generally speaking, this will involve *describing the numbers of people who now face some situation, e.g., illness, truancy, and so forth.*[38] Once this is done, the tabulation of who has the problem or condition can be further specified in terms of major demographic variables— age, gender, race, family structure, education level, occupation, and income level. The point here is to examine the correlation between certain characteristics and the problem or condition. By doing both steps, one not only begins the process of specifying need, one also identifies the reality of differential risk or higher levels of chance among the different groups.[39] For example, it is possible to tabulate the unemployment rate at 7 percent; but looking at unemployment by age and race might show the rate of unemployment to be more than twice as high for teenagers and more than three times as high for black teenagers. With this tabulation and the use of cross-tabulation analysis the problem or condition can be distilled into more understandable and precise units. This process can be continued by looking at what has happened over time, especially as it involves selected demographic variables. In this way, it can be ascertained whether the condition or problem remains stable over time, or whether it is more pronounced relative to certain demographic characteristics. At this stage, scientific inquiry can assist only in identifying numerical patterns; the significance or weight of such patterns is more in the realm of social and political interpretation.[40]

After patterns over time have been identified, inquiry can also assist in *specifying the consequences or effects of the condition or problem.* Consequences can be categorized as benefits and costs.[41] These two terms, however, inherently are tied to the vantage point of the analyst, as well as to the interests emanating from, and associated with, the analyst's vantage point. For example, an analyst working with a school board may identify loss of revenue as a critical cost in reviewing the truancy rate in a school district. Other people and groups sitting elsewhere may not see this particular cost as "the" cost; they may not even see this consequence as a cost. Therefore, tabulation of costs and benefits is permeated with unstated assumptions and biases tied to unique positions and vantage points.

The review of costs and benefits, from a quasi-scientific perspective, should follow the dicta to report everything and to avoid suggestive terminology. Although these two exhortations may be wise, and although normatively they must be employed, they are very hard to carry out. In the first instance, "reporting everything" cannot be done; judgments have to be made as to relevance of consequences. In turn, judgments may well be affected heavily by political and cultural forces working on the person or groups conducting the inquiry. Further, despite our efforts to the contrary, we may be trapped by a limited vocabulary, or one that has negative connotations in common cultural and/or professional usage.[42]

In this mine field, the tabulation of consequences occurs. Moving through the process of reporting consequences, one may identify a range of factors or groups that either win or lose as a result of the problem or condition (e.g. certain landlords may "win" and certain tenants may "lose"). The review process should be careful in documenting the range of "winners" and "losers," for this documentation ultimately can allow for assessment of how significant "need" is or may be for different groups in shaping the policy process and product. Again, this assessment will probably tip "pure" science over into the realm of politics, subjective interpretation, and, possibly, political strategy.

An example: It is one thing to identify those who have AIDS, both in terms of absolute numbers and certain patterns, e.g., more males than females, more active homosexual males than heterosexual males. It is something else again to identify fully the consequences of AIDS and to whom. By extending the tabulation to include assessment of costs, one can begin to identify the possible group motivations and processes that may come into the area of current and future AIDS policy. In this exchange, the obvious potential recipient—the AIDS patient—may not be the compelling reason why policy is made; rather, it may be the people who fear becoming affected. As will be discussed below, those who think they might be affected by the problem/condition not being addressed are liable to influence policy. In the AIDS example, this has translated into policy that is not strongly related to caring for people with AIDS.[43]

Most problems or conditions have a history, so there is some likelihood that *prior attempts have been made to solve or address a given current situation.* Inquiry should attempt to identify whether such responses exist and what level of success they achieved. Unfortunately, in many areas where prior efforts have been attempted, feedback has been limited, inconclusive, or nonexistent.

A final thing systematic inquiry can do relative to specifying and understanding a problem/condition is to identify the *range of causal explanations* being employed. Again, the role of science and politics is blurred. In the social world, almost all social problems or situations conventionally defined as negatives have a limited range of possible causes. Causal explanations fall into four basic categories:

- Personal explanations which focus on individual (sometimes family) factors, including genetics, psychology, and religion to name just a few;
- Cultural explanations, which focus on the properties or characteristics of a group;
- Social explanations, which suggest that there are features of our social world, such as opportunity structures, discrimination, and so on, that are intimately tied to the problem/condition; and

- Major structural explanations, which suggest that such critical variables as lack of property ownership, gender, or racial status ultimately explain certain problems/conditions.[44]

In the social and political world, the fact that there are several often contending explanations should not come as a surprise. A major reason for such explanations is that the social order is extremely complex and interrelated. This, as well as the interests and self-serving imperatives of the differing academic fields, make some level of nonconsensus the norm for most social problems and conditions. Yet for most problems/conditions, a particular explanation (sometimes more than one) becomes prevalent. In this stage of systematic inquiry one should review the range and determine which explanations win acceptance among which interest groups and interest perspectives.

Inquiry and the Process and Substance of Policy

Distinct from the problem/condition being examined, there should be inquiry into the policy, or proposed policy. Such inquiry should focus on both the substance and the process of the policy. Initially this can involve identifying the source of the policy—law, administrative order, court decision. If the policy is a proposal, at what stage is the proposal—is it merely an idea, or is it formulated and officially under review?

Once this is done, the substance of the policy (or proposal) can be described and summarized. This will include identifying who is covered and with what benefits. Identification of who is covered allows for the eventual specification of who is *not* covered. In examing the possible *fit between the policy and the problem/ condition,* special attention can be given by policy reviewers to whether the policy has a *target(s)* that corresponds to those *groups most in need* and/or *with higher rates of risk.*

In an ideal world, policy or proposed policy would relate well to problems or conditions that are well understood. The policy would certainly cover those in need of particular benefits and would pay special attention to the groups who have greater amounts of risk. In short, there would be in the policy some emphasis on specifying target group(s) and even preventing certain problems/conditions from ever materializing—most especially among those groups at greater risk.

However, in the real world policy is often made without full assessment of what is. Therefore, some policy and policy proposals do not match up very well with the "real" facts of a problem/condition. This is largely related to the fact that some policy is made as a result of the political clout of certain interest groups and not the "facts" of the situation. An example occurred in 1988, when the Catastrophic Medical Care Act was passed. The act was a response to need and to the political power of the elderly and their interest groups, especially the American Association of Retired People (AARP). However, the assessment of *what* was needed was inadequate, and as a result the major concern of the elderly was completely uncovered in the policy, namely, long-term care benefits. Similarly, there was little analysis of *who* needed the catastrophic care and what the tax surcharge on all the elderly would produce in terms of the ratio of those taxed to those who might eventually receive the program benefit.

In addition to coverage of need and risk, policy can also be examined in terms of purposes and goals. Even though policy may have the "right" intention to cover the "needy" and/or address those more at risk, the policy may also remain relatively nonspecific. So at this point the inquiry should be into the thrust or direction of policy. Are there specific statements that address preventing certain conditions, e.g., reduction of infant mortality rates, and a special emphasis (target group) on reduction in higher-risk areas?

Inquiry and Implementation of Policy

Systematic inquiry can do more than help to examine policy for current problems/conditions. Systematic inquiry also can help examine how policy comes to be implemented in programs.[45] That topic is discussed in considerable detail in the following chapter, so it suffices to say here that inquiry can assist in the specification of activities and efforts in programs, the effects of programs, and the level of satisfaction among program recipients.

Inquiry also can help examine who *is* served as contrasted with who "should be" served according to policy and/or according to the actual profile of those in need or at risk. Thus, inquiry can assist analysts in critiquing the allocation of resources, including professional skills.

Just as comprehensive inquiry can help identify interests and interest groups in the initiation of policies and proposals, inquiry also can help specify the range of interests served by the policy and program. As discussed in Chapter 5, a key interest group often is the very agency that provides programs.

The preceding discussion can help identify a possible nexus between research and evaluation, coverage and allocation of resources, and identification of interests served by the policy in action. Thus, the products of such inquiry can be used in promoting purposeful rational change in any of the areas cited. In a sense, this becomes the ultimate function of inquiry—providing a rationale and framework for possible change activities.

However, the connection between inquiry and change rarely is this direct and clear. Volitional and political elements affect policy not only at the national and state levels, but also at the stage of implementation. Implementation often takes place in local agencies and organizations, and as such it is subject to the dynamics of organizations and to the interest perspectives of staff administrators and boards. In some instances, these dynamics and perspectives can constrain and influence how inquiry is defined and pursued in specific settings. Chapter 5 will look more closely at the actual implementation of policy at the agency level.

CONCLUSION

This chapter reviewed the nature of policy. Although the rational aspects of policy were cited, the political aspects also were stressed, especially in terms of interest and power considerations. A range of possible purposes of and for policy, as well as specific types of program strategies, were reviewed. Throughout the discussion, the focus was on specifying key political questions of *who* receives *what* and *how*. Pursuing answers to these questions can pave the way for inferring answers to the political question of *why* the policy exists.

Systematic inquiry was presented as a way to help achieve a more inclusive sense of what problem/condition a policy could attempt to address. Inquiry could help specify need and risk, key interests at stake in the policy area, results of existing intervention efforts, and identification of existing causal explanations of problems. Inquiry also can help examine the implementation of policy in terms of actual coverage, allocation of resources, and evaluation, a topic that will be covered in more detail in Chapter 5. The logic and results of scientific inquiry can be used to help promote purposeful change of policy and programs, but such change often is constrained by the political forces and processes described at the outset of this chapter.

NOTES

1. A. Kahn, *Social Policy and Social Services* (New York: Random House, 1973) is an example of a rational and analytic approach to policy, and discussion of H. Blumer, "Social Problems as Collective Behavior," *Social Problems* 18 (Winter, 1971): 63–77.
2. J. T.D. Bandler, "Family Protection and Women's Issues in Social Security," *Social Work* 34 (July, 1989): 308 and N. Gilbert, "An Initial Agenda for Family Policy," *Social Policy* 24 (April, 1979): 447–450.
3. R. Maroney, *The Family and the State: Considerations for Social Policy* (New York: McGraw Hill, 1990), 287–288.
4. S. Kammerman and A. Kahn, *Social Services in the United States* (Philadelphia: Temple University Press, 1976), 4.
5. J. P. Flynn, *Social Agency Policy: Analysis and Presentation for Community Practice* (Chicago: Nelson-Hall, 1985), 13.
6. T. Dye, *Understanding Public Policy* (Englewood Cliffs, N.J.: Prentice Hall, 1981), 19.
7. Flynn, *op cit.*, 2–7.
8. T. Meeneghan and R. Washington, *Social Policy and Social Welfare: Structure and Applications* (New York: Free Press, 1980), 131.
9. Flynn, *op.cit.*, 4–6.
10. *Ibid.*, 4–6.
11. R. Hamel, "The Fate of Democracy in a Technological World," *The Futurist* 13 (May 1979): 115.
12. Dye, *op.cit.*, 19–45, especially discussion on process model.

13. This perspective is suggested by the classic book on power, N. Polsby, *Community Power and Political Theory* (New Haven: Yale University Press, 1963).

14. G. Nelson, "Social Class and Public Policy for the Elderly," *Social Service Review* 56(1) (March 1982), 86–107; and R. Ross and G. L. Staines, "The Politics of Analyzing Social Problems." *Social Problems* 20 (Summer 1972): 18–40.

15. J. Seeley, "Social Science? Some Probative Problems," in M. Stein and A. Vidich (eds.), *Sociology on Trial* (Englewood Cliffs, NJ: Prentice-Hall, 1963), 61.

16. L. Davis, "Battered Women: The Transformation of a Social Problem," *Social Work* 37 (July–August 1987): 306–10.

17. Dye, 19–45.

18. *Ibid.*

19. *Ibid.*

20. T. M. Meenaghan, R. D. Washington, and R. Ryan, *Macro Practice* (New York: Free Press, 1983), 117–19.

21. R. Dahl, *Who Governs? Democracy and Power in an American City* (New Haven: Yale University Press, 1961).

22. C. E. Lindblom, *The Policy Making Process* (Englewood Cliffs, NJ: Prentice-Hall, 1968); C. E. Lindblom, "The Science of Muddling Through," *Public Administration Review* 19 (Spring 1959): 79–88; Dye, 36–38, 232–57.

23. N. Gilbert and H. Specht, *Dimensions of Social Welfare* (Englewood Cliffs, NJ: Prentice-Hall), 67.

24. D. M. DelVito, T. R. Dye, *Social Welfare: Politics and Public Policy* (Englewood Cliffs, NJ: Prentice-Hall, 1987), 75–77.

25. *Ibid,* 115–18.

26. M. Wolins, "The Societal Function of Social Welfare," in N. Gilbert and H. Specht (eds.), *The Emergence of Social Welfare and Social Work* (Itasca, IL: Peacock, 1976), 112.

27. J. H. Galper, *The Politics of Social Services* (Englewood Cliffs, NJ: Prentice-Hall, 1975); D. A. Rochefort, "Progressive and Social Control Perspectives on Social Welfare," *Social Service Review* 55 (December 1981): 568–91.

28. D. M. Dinitto and T. R. Dye, *Social Welfare: Politics and Public Policy* (Englewood Cliffs, NJ: Prentice-Hall, 1987), 161.

29. D. L. Bowden and J. L. Palmer, "Social Policy: Challenging the Welfare State," in J. L. Palmer and I. V. Sawhill (eds.), *Reagan Record* (Cambridge, MA: Ballinger, 1984), 117–215.

30. *Ibid.*

31. Wolins, 119.

32. *Ibid.*

33. Galper.

34. Meenaghan and Washington, 21–24.

35. Wolins, 117–119.

36. *Ibid.*

37. H. Gans, *The Urban Villagers* (New York: Free Press, 1962); R. Cloward and F. Piven, *Regulating the Poor: The Functions of Public Welfare* (New York: Vintage Books, 1971).

38. R. R. Mayer and E. Greenwood, *The Design of Social Policy Research* (Englewood Cliffs, NJ: Prentice-Hall, 1981), 19–41.

39. M. Bloom, *Primary Prevention: The Possible Science* (Englewood Cliffs, NJ: Prentice-Hall, 1981), 94–95.

40. Meenaghan, Washington, and Ryan, 23–24.
41. *Ibid.*
42. J. Horton, "Order and Conflict Theories of Social Problems as Competing Ideologies," *American Journal of Sociology* 71, (May 1966): 701–13.
43. R. Bayer, *Private Acts, Social Consequences: AIDS and the Politics of Public Health* (New York: Free Press, 1989).
44. Meenaghan and Washington, 38–39.

CHAPTER 5

Operationalizing Policy: Organizational Forces and Inquiry

INTRODUCTION

Previous chapters discussed how political forces in the larger society and in the helping professions helped shape how scientific methodology came to be utilized in the helping professions. The issue of how to allocate scarce resources became a precipitating factor for inquiry at the agency level.

The focus of this chapter is the more positive use of research in an organizational context. A premise of this discussion is that a more inclusive use of research can allow organizations and professionals to consider more comprehensive options within a larger value context, including those choices that allow for the consideration of scarce resources.

THE ORGANIZATIONAL LEVEL: MISSION, POLICY, PROGRAM

Professionals in the human services generally do not exist as discrete individuals who offer benefits to clients; typically, benefits are offered through an agency. *Agencies* are entities established by law or by voluntary agreement to address a specific situation, be it a range of problems or populations, through specific policies and organized programs. Whether public (by law) or private (by charter and incorporation), most agencies today reflect a complex organization model. That is, the human resources of the organization tend to be organized deliberately in a vertical and horizontal fashion.[1] Specific workers are assigned specific roles that require them to perform certain functions, and the defined roles and functions are always seen in relation to others—those above and below as well as those parallel to a given role and worker (see Figure 5–1).

How the agency is organized is never an accident; a variety of influences and constraints affect agency structure and operations. Some influences can emanate from the law that established the public agency. For example, the law could dictate that a public health department ''serve people with infectious diseases

FIGURE 5-1   Complex Organization Model

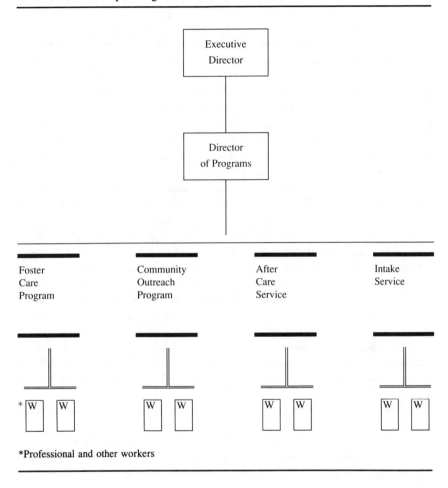

*Professional and other workers

and work to ensure that the public is protected from exposure to infectious and contagious conditions.'' The law may or may not specify that the public health agency be directed by a physician and have a staff to carry out the mandated functions. Whether the law specifies who will work under the physician (or other individual), some entity—the physician, a public health board, or an administrator—will define functions to be assigned to different roles and how the roles will interrelate.

A private agency is guided by the same process. A civic and/or sectarian group incorporates itself and spells out its purpose and goals. Once this is done, the human resources are assembled, with functions and roles evolving over time. Public and private agencies alike are apt to spend a long time defining roles and the ways in which workers will relate to one another in their given roles. Typically this leads to written job descriptions.

For the private agency, this evolutionary process is directed by the organization's mission statement.[2] An organization's *mission statement* is a rather broad philosophical statement that reflects the preferences, purposes, and values of the incorporated body. For example, a certain agency's mission statement might articulate that the agency "affirms the central role of the family and the needs for supportive and preventive services to maximize family functioning in a rapidly changing society." In the public sector, agencies established and funded by legislation often incorporate similar statements, which direct agency personnel in terms of what it should focus on and, perhaps, how to organize the workers.[3]

As significant as mission and legislative statements may be, they often are very general in nature. Two important agency products help bring the agency's mission into sharper focus: *agency policies* and *program designs*.[4]

Agency policies are statements about what should be done, and in some cases what cannot be done, relative to the ongoing operations of the agency. Specifically, the policies state how workers can and cannot go about carrying out the organization's mission. *Program designs* drive an agency's specific organized behaviors and activities in light of its policy and mission. Of the three formal elements that influence the organization and its staff—mission, policy, and program—program is the only one that has a direct behavioral reference point. The behaviors of people, helpers, and recipients can be observed in a program. On the other hand, one basically only reads and hears about mission and policy. Figure 5-2 depicts how these elements operate in an agency.

The process shown in Figure 5-2 can be characterized as moving from the general and rather abstract (mission) toward the specific and observable (programs). Do not assume from this figure, however, that the agency always operates in a predictable linear process—from mission to policy to program. Sometimes a written mission and specific programs are in place, but there may be no written policy about the programs. Other times, policy, although established prior to implementation, may not have been written down but nonetheless is fairly clear. In still other instances, the program can precede the policy, and the policy may not ever come to be written. In such a case, people and experiences at the program level may have led to decisions or choices that in a sense became policy. For example, initially there may have been no written policy on serving substance abusers in many family agencies, but staff at the program level may have evolved into a pattern of service without ever having produced a formal policy statement to that effect. Or administrators may have added programs focusing on certain populations or problems primarily because external funding was readily available. Sometimes these ongoing responses can lead agencies to make formal policy that justifies programs already under way.

FIGURE 5-2   Systemic Components of an Organization

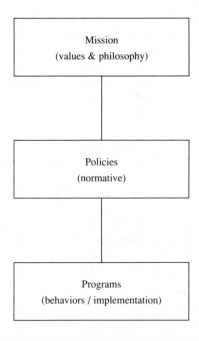

ORGANIZATIONS AND THEIR ENVIRONMENTS

Agencies are not just vertically stratified bodies with mission and policy statements to guide their programs. Although all agencies go through the same evolutionary process, they never do so in a vacuum. This means that what each agency does will influence what other agencies do in their mission-to-program processes. For example, two proximate but different agencies may serve families and provide counseling to couples. This could prompt a third family-oriented agency to focus more on parenting problems rather than relationship problems. Although all three agencies may have very similar mission statements, each agency's eventual program response might be somewhat different, simply because of the presence and number of other family agencies and their programs.[5]

Not only do agencies have to deal with the reality of other agencies having similar mission statements, they have to deal with other organizational pressures. Some of these pressures emanate from funders, which, whether dealing with tax dollars or voluntary contributions (for example, United Way) have certain expectations.[6] Funders' expectations can influence agencies' statements of policy, e.g., persons below a certain income level must be given priority. Such expectations can also influence an agency's operations in terms of location and how clientele will be addressed.

Another potential pressure can come from the community in which the agency operates. For example, over time, an agency may have evolved a set of policies and programs through which it feels it is doing something important and in keeping with its mission (philosophy and values.) However, the community in which the agency operates may have changed dramatically and now may have expectations and preferences that differ from those of the agency. If so, the community might seek to influence how the agency operates.[7] This does not mean necessarily that the agency could (or should) move in the direction of the community, away from its own tradition and mission. Yet, community pressure could produce tension, perhaps even spurring the agency to change its programs.

In short, the very process of change complicates the mission-to-program process. Increasingly the helping services have come to institutionalize systems theory, including open systems theory at the agency or organizational level.[8] This mode of thinking suggests that organizations have a responsibility to change internally in light of alterations in their environment. Such change could occur at the program or policy level and, in unusual circumstances, even at the mission level.

Figure 5–3 captures some of the elements in the open systems perspective, which could influence the mission-to-program patterns.

In Figure 5–3, "extra" organizational forces—community, funders, and other agency programs—ideally are processed by the agency in its ongoing operations and structure. More specifically (and as indicated earlier in this section), the agency scans and interprets its environment to adjust to what is occurring outside itself. In turn, other agencies adjust themselves to changes within the agency depicted. Central to this processing of an agency's ongoing operations are the professionals within that agency.

CHOICES IN TRANSLATING POLICY INTO PROGRAMS

It is at the program level that professionals have the most influence, for it is here that they translate policy into action and behaviors. Dolgoff and Feldstein, among others, have referred to this as workers being policy practitioners.[9]

To understand the translation process it is useful to introduce two related phenomena that affect the policy/program relationship: operationalization and implementation. *Operationalization* refers to how the policy will be made "real." In most cases, when applied to policy/program, the term means basically the same as it does in research, namely, that a thought, concept, or value has to be made explicit and observable. With respect to policy, the explication is related to the basic policy considerations of *who* gets *what* and *how*. *Implementation* refers to the organized behaviors and actions that are carried out, that make policy become

FIGURE 5–3   Open System Model of Organization

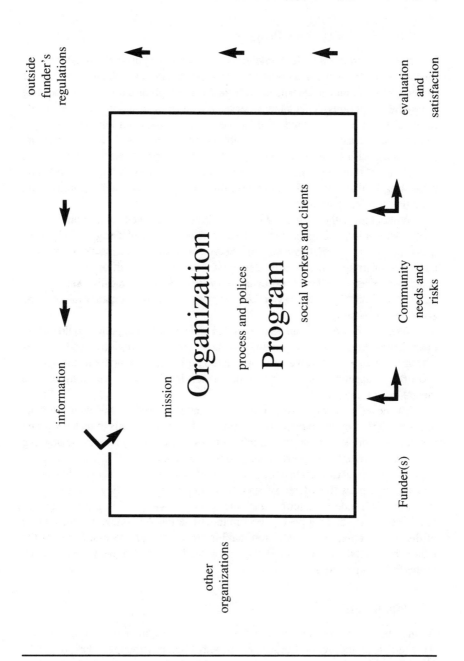

alive, real, and observable in light of specific thoughts, values, and choices concerning the possible *who, what,* and *how.*

Mission, Policy, and Program

By using a concrete example, namely, an agency whose purpose is to address the mental health problems in a community, we can begin to see the interrelation of mission, policy, and program, as well as the conceptual choices in translating policy into programs. This agency serves a suburb of a major city, and, as its mission states, it "was established" to serve individuals and families who may need supportive assistance . . . and to prevent mental illness . . . and to promote the mental health of the larger community." This type of mission statement is typical in that it anchors the agency in serving needs, preventing problems, and promoting health. Similarly, it focuses the agency to individual, family, and community reference points.

Without any other source of direction, this mission statement would not be overly helpful in guiding agency professionals in specific offerings of help, i.e., actual programs. Therefore, over time and through the collective experiences of staff, administrators and boards, the agency develops a point of view or norm concerning what "ought to" occur at the program level. Typically, this norm is influenced in part by those "extra" forces cited earlier—community funders and other agencies' programs.

When agency policy can be formulated and written, that policy could clarify the rather general mission statement's focus on serving "individuals and families who may need . . . ." Developed and stated policy could now focus the agency "to offer counseling and other therapeutic services to those who may require mental health programs"

The developed policy gives more focus and specificity to the agency and its program staff. Yet, there remain opportunities for professionals to make ongoing choices, to exert some creativity. Such choices are most likely seen in the ongoing program behaviors, which translate policy into action.

The degree of discretion or choice will vary from agency to agency depending on such factors as the degree of specificity in developed policy, the degree of specificity in funders' requirements, the level of awareness in a given agency relative to choice and degree of freedom in translating the policy, and the culture of the organization and its decision-making structure and process. Some of the major choices that might be faced at the program level by an agency are discussed in the following sections.

Population

At one extreme, an agency could serve almost every segment of the population.[10] An example is the public library. Even with libraries, though, there might be some emphasis on population residency within the library district. At the other extreme could be a family agency with a program focusing only on women, or women with children, or women returning to the job market, and so on.

Typically, the program offered reflects a commitment to some distinct group(s). This commitment can occur by design, it can reflect a conscious playing out of value or it can even reflect an organizational value or preference for a certain group (or groups). Such preferences may or may not involve some type of bias against a certain group(s) of which the agency and staff may not be aware.

At the program level in some agencies, choices are tied to considerations such as what other programs are available and what staff competencies and areas of expertise are available in a given program and agency. Such factors lead to a logic of "served" populations, in contrast to "referred" populations.

Geographic Area

Some agencies are required to serve everyone who resides within a designated service district. Some service districts, however, can cover very wide areas and offer programs that are centralized so as to extend the specialized program to everyone who may require it. In this instance, the geographical area is so big that the service district includes scores of smaller geographical communities. On the other hand, some agencies may relate only to specific and limited geographical areas.

In many cases, the problem and/or population to be served can lead to selecting a geographical area based on the service emphasized, e.g., a well-baby clinic for poor people. Because of the high correlation of population characteristics (such as income and family patterns) to spatial distribution patterns, program decisions on populations and geographical areas can become highly interrelated.

At the program level, especially if the program is operating at full capacity or has a waiting list, it is sometimes difficult for staff to readily ascertain which geographical areas and communites are well served and which are not. The imperatives of daily operations and the selective (possibly skewed and noncomprehensive) perceptions of staff may lead program personnel to miss significant patterns of served and unserved areas and groups.

Program Approach

A third aspect of program decision making has to do with how the program will approach a specific phenomenon.[11] For example, a community mental health agency serving gays and lesbians might use a personal problem/dysfunction approach, where the target addressed is basically individual in nature. Another program serving the same population might approach the matter wth a civil rights orientation. In this instance, the target addressed ultimately might be the sources of discrimination (such as employers and landlords). Still another approach might focus on the social stress suffered by gays and lesbians. Here the approach could involve individual work and supportive work but would do so within an interactive and ecological perspective, which would encourage the staff to deal with issues and targets beyond the individual client.

Nature of Benefits

Related to program approach is the nature of benefits. Obviously, when an individual problem perspective is used in a program, when the unit to be addressed is the individual, and when the perspectives to be employed by program staff depend on sickness concepts, it is logical to expect that the program benefit will be treatment or counseling. In this particular situation, the overall group perspective would be deemphasized, perhaps lost, at the intervention level. On the other hand, if, a shared condition/situation is stressed in a program, e.g., gay discrimination or elderly rights, then it is equally logical to find that program benefits change. Benefits could then become provision of information, provision of legal and organizational expertise, as well as possible support and assistance in dealing with certain organizations.

Program Modalities

In a less dramatic form, program choices concerning the nature of benefits might include variety in program modalities. Programs that are therapy and treatment-oriented can offer individual or group services; they can reflect humanistic psychology approaches, in-depth analysis, transanctional analysis, reality therapy, and so on. Modalities also can vary the length of time the program is offered to the populations served—short-term, long-term, or indefinite treatment periods.

Need and Risk

After benefits are defined and offered, a program must address how it will handle need and risk. Here again, there can be considerable variation at the program level. At one extreme, the program might choose to focus on individuals in need, as confirmed either by the client or a significant other (another professional or a family member). In this case, the logic at the program level is to individualize and assess the client's situation, and then to develop and implement a plan for, and with, the client.

At the other extreme a choice might be to recognize that a particular group is at high *risk* for a condition or problem.[12] For example, drug users who use dirty needles are at high risk of contracting AIDS precisely because of what they share— the needles. Teen mothers—precisely because they are younger—are at great risk of developing physical problems themselves and of bearing babies with physical problems. It would be logical for programs in these cases to deal with larger numbers of people who share the risk, and if possible, to deal with the factors that impinge upon their situations, e.g., use of needles or use of dirty needles, proper use of prophylactics or abstinence, providing more prenatal care, and so on. This approach is potentially logical on several levels. First, it may be more efficient. That is, the ratio of spent dollars to people dealt with is better. Second, it may be more effective in terms of actually preventing large numbers of people from getting some problem. And finally, it may even be more logical if one factors in fairness and justice, that is, doing what may be effective for risk populations simply because they are at disproportionate risk. In all of these instances, although clients may receive certain benefits as individuals, recognition of the element of shared risk can infuse the program design and strategy.

Levels of Intervention

Once risk and need are addressed, choices about intervention strategies at the program level can be considered.[13] Programs can reflect responses to those already in need—referred to as *tertiary intervention.* Save on a case level in terms of reoccurrence, this kind of tertiary intervention does not focus on prevention but with containing or treating an already present need. With this strategy, prevention occurs only to the degree of deterring relapse or worsening of the condition.

Secondary intervention and *primary intervention* have a somewhat different focus. There is tremendous confusion regarding these terms. They reflect an appreciation for the goal of prevention and tend to consider the concept of disproportionate risk as it relates to shared features of groups and their environments. Secondary interventions can focus on aspects of the physical/social environment of certain groups who live in shared spaced (drug users in a given area who share needles) Secondary intervention also could focus on how agencies and other organizations in the area relate to groups at higher risk and in more need. Primary intervention relates to behaviors and life-styles that seem directly related to certain conditions/problems (cigarette smoking and cancer, eating/drinking patterns and cardiovascular disease). In other instances, primary intervention could focus on social status and its relation to certain phenomena (lower social class and higher infant mortality rates, higher school dropout rates and higher frequency and severity of mental disorder). Primary intervention could focus on modification of behaviors and life-styles or diminished opportunities and benefits associated with lower social status.

In all of these primary and secondary intervention examples, the shared features of cohorts or groups are stressed and the goal of preventing need materializing from risk is also stressed.

Definition of Resources

In considering types of program intervention, the issue of defining a resource becomes central.[14] In needs-driven programs, especially those using a sickness perspective, it is logical to identify those trained in personality and behavior theory as experts and as resources to be utilized in the program. Besides being logical, this pattern of resource definition also can be pursued where dictated by client/staff ratios. This means there is a fairly good balance between the number of trained staff and the number of individuals seeking help at a given time.

At the other end of the spectrum, if group risk is considered, along with the large number of at-risk members within that group, the gross imbalance between those to be helped and the helpers can be appreciated. When resources are so strained, prevention approaches tyically require that professionals perform activities that go beyond treating individuals, such as teaching, advocacy, and the like. Correspondingly, professionals in prevention programs often attempt to expand local resources to maximize the number of people and efforts devoted to prevent risk from turning into need.[15]

Choices concerning the definition and expansion of resources are not limited to prevention programs, however. Some agency programs actively use volunteers, former clients, and even current clients as part of existing programs. For example, older parents of developmentally disabled children can be used in programs that work with younger parents of children recently diagnosed as developmentally disabled. Or recovering alcoholics can (and often do) work in programs that serve alcoholics and their families. For every program that uses volunteers, there is probably an equal number that exclusively use professionals.

Evaluation: Maintaining/Changing Programs

Finally, there is consideration of the basis for maintaining program activities, including considerations of whether there is a need for the current program and how pressing that need is relative to other needs and risks that could be addressed. Without going into the process of need/risk determination (which is discussed in Chapter 8), the point to consider is whether the agency can scan its environment and say yes, there is a range of needs and/or risks for which our current program responses are appropriate.[16]

Also involved in this consideration is the related, though separate, issue of program results.[17] This consideration determines whether the program can measure its results and effects. Although this topic will be discussed in detail in Chapter 10, the issue here, briefly, is whether the program outcome has helped in achieving goals. Obviously, if there is neither evaluation nor specification of goals, then the program is vulnerable to charges of ineffectiveness. Short of the total absence of outcome evaluation, a program can monitor staff and/or client activities and perhaps elicit some sense of client/former client satisfaction with the program. (This is the more likely scenario.)

All of the above evaluation possibilities can affect a program—for example, having or not having a need/risk determination process and the type and nature of evaluation. Often the evaluation choices can be seen in the way an agency operates: Does it do more than a funder requires? Is it interested in reviewing and modifying programs when no external demand or pressure demands it?

RESEARCH AND CRITICAL INQUIRY OF PROGRAMMING

If staff and administrators wish to use research methodology as well as a research perspective in a positive way at the program level, they should consider the population(s) served, the community, and the host agency and community resources.

Population

The first question—*Who is being served?*—involves systematic collection of information on all populations in contact with the program. Typically, this will mean collecting a profile of demographic information—age, gender, race, family status and structure, educational level, occupation (if any)—on all program participants. In addition, the profile should include: reason (problem or condition) for contact with the host agency, referral source (if any), and agencies and groups referred to (if any) by the host agency.

Just as program staff can describe a specific program participant, individual staff can describe their entire caseload. Similarly, staff collectively can describe the entire program population. To do this—assuming the same data are collected for all participants—univariate statistics can be employed. Such statistics allow for summarizing experiences with participants as well as identifying variations within the participant cohort.

In considering all the clientele with whom an agency and program has contact, it can be useful to break these down into those who merely gain access to a program and those who utilize it. *Access* refers to simply making contact with a program, whereas those who *utilize* it are afforded ongoing benefits of an agency's program.[18]

If examination of accessors and utilizers shows no significant difference between them save for type and severity of problems, one finding is suggested: Program staff might feel that other community resources were more appropriate for dealing with the problem. However, if examination of the two groups shows no significant differences in presenting problems but differences in other variables, then the findings should be examined in light of existing policies and mission. The key questions then become: Should certain variables be so significant in programming decisions? Does the role certain variables seem to play in programming appear to be in keeping with mission and policy statements?

Community Related to the Program

In looking at the cohort of who simply gains access to the agency versus who utilizes its ongoing programs, another question can be asked: What are the characteristics of the community(ies) served by the program? To answer this question, the program staff need only obtain a copy of census reports for the area(s) in question and look at the characteristics for each tract (3,000–6,000 people). Each trait can be profiled individually using the same demographic variables that describe ongoing program participants. Comparisons between participants and tract(s) then can occur.

It may be that a given racial group, say, Asians, constitutes more than 30 percent of the community's population, yet is represented in the program only

minimally. In fact, if the overall service area is multiracial but program participants are overwhelmingly from only one racial group, then this observation
might tell a story. This demographic pattern, however, may not cause operating
problems because clients interact well with staff and there is a waiting list. This
example focuses on race, but any key demographic variables could be used to
determine whether the program is skewed.

Without realizing it, many times program staff do not relate effectively to
all geographical areas within their program radius. In part, a program's physical
location can influence relations. A spatial plotting of the program area, with a
visual depiction of program users, can often reveal a program response pattern
that is top-heavy to one or two geographical areas but unresponsive to one or
two other areas. If so, to what degree are differences in geographical areas
accompanied by differences, perhaps significant, in such considerations as race,
education, family structure, and so on?

Agency and Community Resources: Assessment and Coordination

As the examination process unfolds, questions or thoughts about other resources
in the community begin to present themselves.[19] This is critical for a variety of
reasons. First, if the agency can determine which other programs exist and who
uses them, then the agency's program experiences can be interpreted more accurately. Returning to the example of the program that does not include many
Asians, we can see how this works. Besides knowing that its own program did
not relate to Asians, if the agency also knew that the Asian population had developed its own parallel service system or that Asians were disproportionately using
two other agencies' programs, then the host agency's skewing pattern might
become more balanced. Although the host agency still might be discriminatory,
it could be asserted that Asians were getting service.

On the other hand, if it became known that Asians were not getting program
responses from other possible resources in the community, then the host agency's
response pattern could be seen as quite disturbing. In short, examination of overall
community resources can help a program to assess qualitatively its program
experiences to different groups.

A second benefit of examining community resources affects *coordinating of
programs and avoiding duplication of programs.*[20] Although this benefit helps
people receive programs, it may also involve power issues of agencies relative to
communities and constituencies. Avoiding duplication of services helps promote a
greater range of services and a broader spectrum of recipients.

If we look at two clinics that offer pediatric services, a case can be made that
one of the clinics should relate to preschool children and the other to school-age
children. However, actual examination of clinic *A* might show that 70 percent of
the cases seen were school-age children. Now this might not be problematic if
staff knew that clinic *B* was focusing on preschoolers. If clinic *A* recognized its
pattern of program usage and asked clinic *B* about its utilization pattern, clinic

A could be satisfied or make program adjustments if it thought both clinics were serving primarily the same population. The case becomes even more complicated if both clinics were serving an *identical* population, and, therefore, were overlooking other needy populations.

Agency and Community Resources: Referral Patterns and Gaps

Another positive use of resource examination involves *referral patterns*. If an agency knows the universe of possible referring sources, as well as the universe of possible places to refer clients, then referral practices of the host agency program can be examined. Accurate monitoring of where program users come from can be compared to where they *could* come from. For example, a community mental health adult activity program could be receiving a very large percentage of referrals from a small number of private psychiatrists. Other potential referral sources (public health nurses, public assistance personnel, religious groups, programs sponsored by area offices on aging) might not be referring many (or any) clients. Therefore, a potential problem might be that some physicians are disproportionately able to funnel their clients—especially their "needy" ones— at the expense of others in the community.

This referral process can also work in reverse, which is why inquiry into patterns of program referrals is important. The host agency program may use only a narrow spectrum of other programs in the community, and for good reason: These other resources may offer very relevant services. There may, however, be less satisfactory reasons: Staff may not know about other programs, their requirements, or their possible positive contributions to the host agency's program participants.

It is common and appropriate for programs to refer an individual to an outside body if the host agency lacks the appropriate expertise. In some instances, however, that referral might occur for less noble reasons—for example, the other agency might be willing to serve an uninsured client. For our purposes here, however, we are concerned only with the more noble reason of the referral being the "better fit" between client and provider in another setting.[21] As Greenley and Kirk have suggested, the attrition rate can be rather high with referrals *out* from a program.[22] Possible reasons for this include the following:

- The referred client perceives the referral as a rejection ("You won't help me").
- The program to which the referred client goes assesses the client and re-refers the client for a "better" program-client fit.
- The referred parties cannot negotiate the referral process due to problems of geography, time, transportation, bureaucratic limitations, or diminished motivation.

Nonetheless, almost all programs continue to refer clients daily. Referral can occur with persons making initial contact as well as those who have been "in program'' for some time. In both instances, the host program may not know the outcome of referrals. Although it would require time and money, such a follow-up study could help an agency learn who makes it to other agencies, what happens once they get there, and what happens to cases "lost between agencies." These questions could then be correlated with the demographic and problem profiles (discussed earlier) of people who come to the agency.

If a pattern emerged—for example, that single parents tended not to make it to agency *A*—then the host agency program could explore reasons (location, cost, prior experiences, time) and adjust its referral process or hold single parents longer. Another adjustment might be to make more active referrals, e.g., not just give information but actually work out arrangement difficulties between the other program and the referred client. "Holding" the single parent would mean programmatically doing something more—handling people's fears, talking through the pragmatics of the referral, etc.—before completing the referral.

Keeping in mind the desire to avoid duplication, the loss of referrals to and from the program, and the relation between community characteristics and program client characteristics, another possible issue emerges. This is the problem of the program potentially *not seeing,* much less *addressing, significant unmet needs.* Refer again to the example of the two clinics and their apparent need to coordinate their programs. It was implied that identification of who received responses in the two settings could lead staff to note that in some instances a whole age group was overlooked. A program, while in the process of pursuing efficient use of resources and avoiding duplication, also can detect groups and/or problems that might not be covered adequately by existing programs.

Referral Patterns and Change

Critical examination of the referral process—where clients come from, where the host program sends them, and what happens to referred clients—can lead an organization to consider basic changes in its programming. Program changes might include stepping up publicity of a given program; informing and educating potential referring bodies, especially those bodies not referring *into* the host program; managing cases more aggressively; and encouraging the program staff to invest in the referral process and engage in aggressive follow-up of referrals. Concern with referral patterns can be especially significant in identifying categorries of people and/or needs not being addressed by existing programs and other resources in the community. In some instances, this can lead the host agency to begin programs for groups it may "normally" refer. In other instances, it can lead to an additional program focus and goal(s), such as influencing other programs either to accept referred groups or to reach out more actively to support groups in transition from one agency to another.

USE OF SOCIAL SCIENCE RESEARCH AND THEORY

Figure 5-4 summarizes data that can be routinely collected by staff, individually and collectively, to facilitate ongoing programming. It would be unwise to assume

FIGURE 5-4   Program-Related Particulars for Operationalizing Policy

Population Served	Age
	Gender
	Race
	Education Level
	Occupation
	Family Structure
	Census Tract
	Problem
	Referring Source
	Date of Initial Contact
	Other Programs and Resources Involved
Community Served	Same demographic variables as above but examined for entire community
Resources	Agencies*
	Groups and Organizations*

*To be identifed and coded as experiences occur.

that, as staff compile and work with data, the meaning and possible significance of those data are to be derived only from comparing experiences to the community and to community resources. What an agency knows about its program and the program's possibilities also should be compared to what it knows about certain populations. For example, a considerable body of theory and research (as well as common sense) suggests that one-parent families are more vulnerable to stressors than are two-parent families. The research also suggests that low income correlates with more family stress. Therefore, for a potential client at a family agency committed "to providing necessary services to families and promoting family well-being"[mission], several questions could be asked relative to current programs:

- What are the family structures to which the program relates?
- How does that program compare with the family and living configurations in the community?
- What is the relationship between lower income and family structure in the program?
- What is the relationship between lower income and family structures in the community?

Based on answers to these questions, one scenario might be that the program relates disproportionately to two-parent households with higher income levels. In relating to those households, further analysis might show that a rather limited range of problems or issues is being dealt with—parent-child relationships, affective disorders, and so on. Given these program experiences, staff legitimately could begin to think of additional programs designed to relate to one-parent households or even to one-parent, low-income households. Such programs, which could be directed at the large number of families experiencing stress, might teach coping skills, promote more day care, provide drop-in centers for children on weekends, and so on.

Knowledge derived from the social sciences concerning populations and problems and populations and risk can be brought to understanding a community and the program that relates to that community. If the social sciences report, as they do, that there is a relationship between social class and frequency and severity of mental illness, for example, this relationship should be appreciated by the agency that is oriented to mental health programs. Besides suggesting more therapeutic intervention for the needy, the relationship suggests a range of programming to the larger at-risk populations. It also suggests a focus on cushioning or preventing stress so that it does not produce need. To move in these directions, however, agencies need a working knowledge about the operations of their own programs and the ability to relate that knowledge to existing social science theory and research.

CONCLUSION

Chapters 3 and 4 discussed inquiry and policy. This chapter focused on the positive contributions inquiry can make at the program level. Special attention was given to examining the role of the agency and agency program choices, as well as to examining how agency programs can relate to communities and other agencies. When the products of such inquiry are available, program staff and others at the organizational level may engage more actively in the operationalization and implementation of policy. Figure 5–4 summarizes data that can be routinely collected by staff, individually and collectively, to facilitate ongoing programming.

NOTES

1. P. M. Blau and M. U. Meyer, *Bureaucracy in Modern Society* (New York: Random House, 1971), 18–23; M. L. Miringoff, *Management in Human Service Organizations* (New York: Macmillan, 1980) for a discussion of human service organizations as they relate to characteristics of bureaucracy.
2. T. M. Meenaghan, R. O. Washington, and R. Ryan, *Macro Practice* (New York: Free Press, 1982), 163.
3. E. D. Huttman, *Introduction to Social Policy* (New York: McGraw-Hill, 1981), 137–46.
4. D. Pierce, *Policy for the Social Work Practitioner* (New York: Longman, 1984), 5, 25–38, 159.

5. A. J. Kahn, *Social Policy and Social Services* (New York: Random House, 1973), 149–57, for a discussion of agencies as part of networks.
6. B. L. Gates, *Social Program Administration* (Englewood Cliffs, NJ: Prentice-Hall, 1980), 41.
7. A. Lauffer, *Social Planning at the Community Level* (Englewood Cliffs, NJ: Prentice-Hall, 1979), 71–103.
8. T. M. Meeneghan and M. Gruber, "Social Policy and Clinical Social Work Education: Clinicians as Social Policy Practitioners," *Journal of Social Work Education* 22 (Spring/Summer 1986): 38–45.
9. R. L. Dolgoff and D. Feldstein, *Understanding Social Welfare* (New York: Longman, 1984), 292–93; and R. L. Dolgoff, "Clinicians as Social Policymakers," *Social Casework* 62 (May 1981): 284–92.
10. Meenaghan and Gruber.
11. N. Gilbert and H. Specht, *Dimensions of Social Welfare* (Englewood Cliffs, NJ: Prentice-Hall, 1980), 81–102.
12. M. Bloom, *Primary Prevention: The Possible Science* (Englewood Cliffs, NJ: Prentice-Hall, 1981), 15–16, 26.
13. Ibid., 118–51.
14. J. Walsh, "Prevention in Mental Health: Organizational and Ideological Perspectives," *Social Work* 27 (July, 1982): 298–301.
15. A. Weich, C. Rapp, W. P. Sullivan, and W. Kisthardt, "A Strengths Perspective for Social Work Practice," *Social Work* 34 (July 1989): 350–54.
16. Meenaghan and Gruber.
17. T. Tripodi, P. Fellin, and H. J. Meyer, *The Assessment of Social Research* (Itasca, IL: Peacock, 1983), 163.
18. Gates, 52–58, 150–60.
19. Ibid., 159–60.
20. Meenaghan, Washington, and Ryan, 139–41.
21. J. R. Greenley and S. Kirk, "Organizational Characteristics and the Distribution of Services to Applicants," in H. Resnick and R. Patti (eds.), *Change from Within, Humanizing Social Welfare Organizations* (Philadelphia: Temple University Press, 1980), 57–72.
22. S. A. Kirk and J. R. Greenley, "Denying or Delivering Services?" *Social Work* 19 (July 1974): 439–47.

PART THREE

Need, Risk, and Social Groups

The two chapters in Part Three serve as a bridge between the complex world of policy and inquiry and that of the technology of inquiry, which is the focus of Part Four. Chapter 6 discusses the crucial concepts of risk, need, and levels of possible intervention. These concepts help society choose which concerns to emphasize and which to exclude. Chapter 7 applies the same notion of choice to particular populations at risk.

CHAPTER 6

Crucial Concepts of Human Needs

INTRODUCTION

Social services are responses to human needs or problems. However, not all needs or social problems lead to the development of social services. Some problems become recognized as needing attention, whereas others do not. Issues recognized as problems can be conceptualized or identified in different ways. For example, most people probably agree that a leading problem in the United States today is drug abuse. Yet, despite that widespread agreement, there is a lot of disagreement about what "drug abuse" is and how to deal with it. The fact of public concern does not mean that a problem exists.[1]

Let us look at the problem of drug abuse in more detail. Throughout the history of this country, people have used a variety of drugs. Some substance use (e.g., heroin, cocaine) was not always seen as a problem, and concerns about illegal drug use are largely products of the twentieth century. As a matter of fact, legal drug control did not begin until passage of the Harrison Act in 1914.[2] Prior to that time, there were no such things as "illicit drugs." Now, of course, there is an extensive black market for heroin, cocaine, and marijuna—all of which were readily available in drugstores throughout the country at the beginning of this century.

During the past 75 years, public concern has grown about substance use and abuse. Yet, as Beniger has shown, usage levels have not always been directly related to the level of public concern.[4] What, then, is the problem of drug abuse? Should the concern be with the use of illegal substances, such as heroin or cocaine? What about legal drugs, such as cigarettes and alcoholic beverages, which account for more death and disease than illicit drugs? Should the concern be mainly with addictive substances? What is addiction and how is it best dealt with? For example, some experts still maintain that cocaine and alcohol are not addictive drugs.[5] Is the answer primarily law enforcement, such as quicker trials and more jails, or better interdiction of drugs coming into the country? Or should the focus be on treatment or prevention?

As we can see, many issues need to be addressed whenever we are concerned with human problems or needs; any social problem is a complex matter. Perceptions of the nature of particular problems will vary among individuals, even those who are deemed experts. Furthermore, social and political forces shape perceptions of problems, as well as what are seen as appropriate responses to them.

Broadly speaking, three issues should be considered in coming to grips with a particular problem. First of all, we have to be clear about the nature of the human need or problem, to conceptualize exactly what the problem is—whether it be drug abuse, AIDS, mental health, or poverty. Second, we need to determine the extent of the problem and which individuals or groups are most likely at risk. Here the focus is on epidemiological matters. Finally, we, need to decide where we can best intervene. For example, the intervention might focus on individual drug users in a treatment program or try to steer young children from drug use through educational programs. Or the intervention might bear on changing social conditions, such as poverty and despair, that could lead to drug use. The level of intervention also needs to be addresssed.

HUMAN NEEDS AND SOCIAL PROBLEMS

The Nature of Human Needs

A common activity in our society is talking about what people need; nearly as common is talking about how those needs best can be met. Apparently, then, human needs are self-evident, easily recognized to be those things people generally need to live satisfying lives. This recognition can be taken a step further by identifying who the "truly needy" or "truly disadvantaged are." Although many people are "in need," some are more needy than others.

Maslow's hierarchy of needs is a popular model for conceptualizing human needs.[6] He identified five levels of need; those at lower levels in the hierarchy required satisfaction before needs at higher levels. At the bottom of the hierarchy are basic *physiological needs,* such as food, water, and shelter. At the next level are *safety needs,* which involve security and stability. The third level includes the need for *love and belongingness.* Then comes the need for *esteem*—self-esteem, recognition by others, and dignity. At the top of the hierarchy is the need for *self-actualization,* which is concerned with an individual's ability to express innate talents and potentials.

We can see that some social services focus on needs at all of the levels in Maslow's hierarchy; thus, many social service practitioners find his scheme to be a convenient tool.[7] For example, services that provide welfare benefits— cash, food stamps, and housing—answer basic needs (lowest level). Educational services have as their goal the development of individual talents, which address needs at the top level. At first glance, then, needs seems to be a straightforward notion: We can recognize which needs are most important and who is in need. Hunger, shelter, security, recreation, affection, bonding, esteem, recognition, dignity, poverty, homelessness, neglect, lack of belongingness—all of these concepts are part of our everyday lives.

FIGURE 6-1   Maslow's Hierarchy of Needs

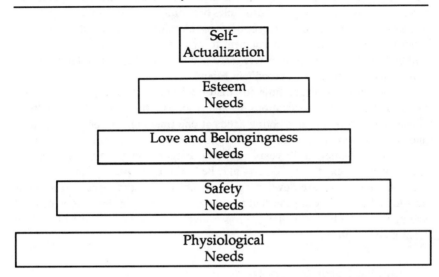

If needs are so self-evident, why are there such intense political disagreements about defining and resolving them? Or about who is "truly needy"? All anyone has to do is watch the news on TV or read a daily newspaper to see just how politicized conceptions of needs are. Needs are ideas, concepts, perceptions, sentiments, and more; they are ambiguous and elusive. In our society, according to Fraser, "we encounter a plurality of competing ways of talking about people's needs."[8] Clearly, there is a great deal of disagreement about what needs exist and which ones require social interventions. The fact that there are competing ways of talking about needs illustrates just how political the intervention process is. She identifies three dimensions (or "moments") to this "politics of need":

> The first is the struggle to establish or deny the political status of a given need, that is, the struggle to validate the need as a matter of legitimate political concern or to enclave it as a nonpolitical matter. The second is the struggle over the interpretation of the need, the struggle for the power to define it and, so, to determine what would satisfy it. The third moment is the struggle over the satisfaction of the need, that is, the struggle to secure or withhold provision.

Needs are a product of a societal context. Even conceptions of basic survival requirements (nutrition, shelter, clothing) will depend on time and place; in other words, what it takes to satisfy a particular need is dictated by culture and history. Our efforts to understand social needs focus on deficiencies, in that the existence of needs implies that something is lacking. If we look at conditions in society, we find a discrepancy between what reality *is* and what we would *like* it to be; in essence, we are dealing with discrepancies between *ideal* conditions (an abstraction based on some set of principles or assumptions) and *actual* conditions. We all need clothing, for instance, but what clothing is considered the minimal requisite varies from one environment to another. A wider range of clothing will be "needed" in Boston, where there is greater fluctuation in daily weather conditions, than will be "needed" in Miami.

In addition to place, time (or historical context) is another important factor in determining perceptions of, and responses to, needs. What might be considered acceptable as meeting needs at one time may not be acceptable at another. For example, what was thought of as an adequate income level for the elderly in America 40 years ago is no longer enough, although there is some concern today that the elderly may be "getting too much," that intergeneraltional inequities are developing.[9] This change in sentiment toward older people and what they are entitled to suggests (again) that definitions of need and need satisfaction can change progressively or regressively over time and from place to place.

Linking Needs to Services

Human services and social needs are intertwined. In fact, the whole point of having social services is to meet particular needs. According to Bradshaw, the history of human services can be seen as society's recognition and organization of ways to meet needs.[10] Linking services to needs, though, poses additional problems in trying to come to grips with the concept of need. As Bradshaw points out, often it will not be clear what is meant by social need in a particular situation. Needs represent perceptions of what should be, whether it is being fed adequately or mastering coping skills in daily living, whereas services represent tangible products or activities, such as food stamps or counseling.

If a person or group is identified as having some need or deficiency, there must be an identifiable factor that distinguishes them from people not considered to be in need. That distinguishing factor or quality is a matter of definition, and it will vary from one situation to another. For the purpose of providing services, Bradshaw describes four ways by which we can try to define social needs: *normative need, felt need, expressed need,* and *comparative need.* The primary differences between these four approaches revolve around two issues: who is making the definition and how it is expressed.

Normative need refers to what experts define as need in a particular situation. By expert, Bradshaw means professionals, administrators, practitioners, or social scientists who are "knowledgeable" in a specialized area as a result of training or experience. The expert first identifies a "desirable" standard (the ideal conditions discussed earlier). Then a comparison is made between that standard and what actually exists. Those considered to be in need will fall below the desirable standard.

As Bradshaw notes, normative needs are not based on definitions of absolute standards; different experts may identify distinct and potentially conflicting standards. Even if they agree, there may be biases in their choice of definition, because most experts and professionals are white, middle class, and male, characteristics of the dominant group in this society. Thus, their values and goals may be in opposition to those of clients in social service programs, especially public programs. The imposition of a dominant group standard on a subordinate group is known as *paternalism*. An example of paternalism is Moynihan's infamous "report on the Negro family," in which he tried to blame most of the problems of blacks on a "disorganized family structure."[11] Wilson continued this tradition in his book on "the truly disadvantaged," in which he identifies a phenomenon called the "male marriageable pool index." If men do not have job opportunities, women will not marry them but will still have babies, leading to a life of welfare dependency.[12] Is the need here for jobs for men or for jobs with equal pay for women and acessible day care for working mothers?

Two major problems arise with identifying need by relying on experts. First, different experts are likely to provide conflicting definitions. Second, no matter what definitions are provided, statements of need follow from value orientations.

Felt need refers to what people identify for themselves as wanted or needed. According to Bradshaw, this approach is inadequate as a measure of "real need." In some cases, individuals may be unwilling or unable to acknowledge a particular need, whereas in other cases they may be too willing to indicate it, thus inflating the number of "truly needy." During the Reagan years, Edwin Meese said that many people used soup kitchens, not because they were needy, but because they could get a free meal. Distrusting the public is another example of paternalism on the part of professionals.

All the same, using felt need as a way of identifying need levels is a common practice, as the use of social surveys in this society illustrates. Surveys of communities often focus on perceptions of local or national problems, such as inadequate police protection, conflicts among different racial and ethnic groups, or drug abuse in the community. When surveys are used to establish felt needs, it is important to examine who is being asked. For example, in a survey about the needs of older people, it was found that the perceptions of older people (those 65 or older) were quite different from those of younger people.[13] That is, younger people tended to identify the needs of older people in a much more simplistic and less pragmatic way than did the elderly themselves.

Expressed need refers to *felt need* turned into action, meaning need is based on demand for a service. Expressed need is not concerned with whether people say that they need a service but with how many people request a particular service. For instance, professionals, in noting that a number of people are interested in a certain type of job training might, as a result, look at how many individuals applied for that training. The total number of applicants is then used as an index of need.

In some cases the focus may be on the difference between how many people request a service and how many are able to receive it as an index of degree of need. In the health area, waiting lists for service often are used as an indicator of the extent of need (the difference between how many people request a service and how many can actually receive it). However, as Bradshaw points out, we must take into account that, for many reasons, not all people suffering from a problem actually request services.

Comparative need focuses on identifying the characteristics of those who receive a particular service. Once that is done, we try to determine how many people have those particular characteristics and use the difference in size between the total population and the service population to arrive at an index of extent of need. This approach has been employed not only to study needs among individuals but also to analyze communities. An example at the individual level is to identify who (in terms of demographic characteristics) is most likely to have nutritional needs, in order to set criteria for who can receive free school meals. Examples at the community level are to compare resources available to different school districts and performance of their students on achievement tests or to identify characteristics of different communities and analyze how those variables relate to crime rates.

Although the comparative approach has some utility, the major problem with it is lack of accuracy in predicting which individuals, groups, or communities are likely to have a particular problem. For example, some social scientists believe that there is a link between genetics and alcoholism. One way to study this possibility is to see whether children whose parents were alcoholics are more likely to have drinking problems than people whose parents were not. Whereas there is a correlation between alcoholism and growing up in a family with alcoholic parents, the correlation here is far from perfect. In fact, children of alcoholics correlate closely to children of non-alcoholics: only a small percentage end up with this problem.[14]

Conceptualizing and Defining Needs

Bradshaw's analysis provides tools for defining and assessing needs in relation to services, but does not provide a place to start. We still need to define the needs with which we are concerned. We have seen that definitions of need are affected by cultural, political, and economic forces; one person's definition may be far different from another's. Even social service planners and providers may disagree substantially over the definition of a particular need.

The problem of determining need would certainly be less complicated if the concept of "need" could simply be treated as self-evident—which, as noted in Chapter 5, is a practice. Many texts on social service practice or social policy and planning assume that their identification of a particular need is valid. Even professional groups have found it easiest to take need for granted. An example of this approach can be seen in *Common Human Needs,* a major statement on needs and services in this society.[15] Originally published in 1945 by the National Association of Social Workers, it has since gone through four editions, most recently in 1987. Nowhere in this document is there an explicit definition of the terms *need* or *common human needs,* except in the context of certain human services. Apparently, the meaning of need is "clear and obvious," because everyone has needs.

Like it or not, however, we must accept the principle that need is a concept that has no inherent meaning. As Kimmel points out, need will have variable meaning, because there is no specific referent for a given need; that is, need refers to nothing in particular, only to a discrepancy between actual and ideal conditions or to something that does not exist.[16] According to Kimmel, all we have to do is look at a dictionary definition for need to see that no boundaries appear to limit what need can mean in a given situation.

Webster's New Twentieth-Century Dictionary defines need in several ways:

1. necessity; compulsion; obligation; as, "there is no *need* to worry now."

2. a lack of something useful, required, or desired; a call or demand for the presence, possession, etc., of something; as, "I feel the *need* for a long rest."

3. something useful, required, or desired that is lacking; want; requirement; as, "what are his daily needs?"

4. (a) a condition in which there is a deficiency of something; a time or situation of difficulty; a condition requiring relief or supply; as, "a friend in need." (b) a condition of poverty; state of extreme want.[17]

Everyday use of the concept of need just seems to add further confusion to arriving at a precise definition. Is something that is useful the same as something that is required? Is something that is required the same as something that is desired? Now necessities and desires are mixed, creating further disagreement over what are "true" needs. Then there are the obligations society has in meeting necessities versus meeting desires, as well as the obligations that recipients of services owe to society.[18]

Even the body of the social services literature does not clarify the concept of need. Trying to focus on conditions that are believed to limit people in meeting their full potential still requires that those limiting conditions be identified in some consistent way that is agreeable to different professionals. Furthermore, the discrepancy between ideal and actual terms will have to be delineated so that services that will diminish that discrepancy can be provided. For example, in looking at health needs, can the conditions of "adequate" health be established? Should the conditions of "adequate" health be what is established rather than those of "optimal" health? Furthermore, are health needs the same for all people—male and female, young and old, pregnant and not pregnant? One option is to set an absolute standard for establishing the level of need, as is done in setting the so-called poverty line. Another approach is to set a relative standard, as is the case in comparing the quality of housing among different cities. Although those methods may provide working standards, the standards are ultimately *arbitrary*. Even if arbitrary standards prove to be workable by achieving a degree of acceptance, they are still arbitrary. As Kimmel stresses, the concept of need "is basically an empty term, one without conceptual boundaries."[19]

NEEDS, PROBLEMS, AND RISK

After arriving at a working definition for a particular need or problem, the next step is to establish the extent of the problem, including identifying which individuals or social groups are most likely to suffer those conditions. Social workers increasingly have found certain epidemiological concepts helpful in assessing problems and designing interventions. Largely this is because the human services model their interventions after techniques employed in the public health field, where epidemiology was pioneered.

As its name implies, epidemiology began as the scientific study of epidemics.[20] The scope of epidemiological concerns has become much broader and, according to Kleinbaum, Kupper, and Morgenstern:

> The range of topics now includes chronic and acute diseases, the quality of health care, and mental health problems. In fact, many health professionals believe that a varity of behavioral and biomedical factors affect the health status of an individual. This belief has enabled epidemiologic research to evolve as a synthesis of knowledge from several health-related disciplines.[21]

They further suggest that epidemiology is concerned with both health and disease:

> "Disease" and "health" are not redundant; the former refers to pathological *processes*, and the latter refers to *states* of well-being. Health or a healthy state may not be equivalent to the absence of disease. Furthermore, each concept has at least three dimensions: biological or physical, perceptual or psychological, and social or behavioral.[22]

From an emphasis on understanding the development and spread of communicable disease, epidemiology has come to focus just as heavily on noncommunicable diseases. A more recent development has been the movement from an emphasis on physical disease states to behavioral pathologies—such as mental illness, alcohol and other substance abuse, eating disorders, and sexual pathologies—where traditional conceptions of physical disease are mimimized.[23] In fact, one might refer to some of these pathologies as *non*-diseases. It might also be useful when the concern is primarily with behavioral rather than physical conditions to distinguish social epidemiology from medical epidemiology. This is especially true because, as Kleinbaum and his associates note, public health professionals apply a conceptualization to their investigations that includes a positive state (health) *and* a negative process (disease). Social epidemiologists, in contrast, tend to focus exclusively on negative processes—alcohol *abuse,* mental *illness*—and to ignore positive states—alcohol *use,* or mental *health.*

As noted earlier, the application of epidemiological concerns to the social services has led social service workers to find certain concepts helpful in determining extent of need and developing intervention strategies. These concepts include risk; incidence and prevalence; methods of counting; and populations and targets. While we shall look at each in turn for the sake of conceptual clarity, these terms are intertwined. That is, the use of one concept will generally bring about the use of one or more of the others.

Risk

When concerned with the development or occurrence of disease, it is necessary to determine the *likelihood* that a particular pathology may come about; any possible condition *could* occur, but some are much more likely than others. The risk of contracting AIDS, for instance, is substantially lower than the risk of suffering a heart attack, and the likelihood of having a heart attack is much lower than the likelihood of catching a cold.

Different human needs and conditions can vary substantially in their probability of occurrence. Although we focus on serious problems, we need to keep in mind that risk is not necessarily associated with the seriousness of a condition. Many relatively minor problems have a great likelihood of occurring; others are unlikely to occur. The same is true for serious problems; some are quite unlikely to occur, whereas others are more likely.

As noted earlier, regardless of how likely it is that a situation will arise, usually there will be more concern with conditions that are seen as serious. It is important to keep in mind, though, that degree of seriousness will not necessarily be associated with perceptions of risk. For example, although drugs are a serious problem in the United States, the extent of use typically has been much less than corresponding public fears. Further, there is evidence that drug use has leveled off, even though political attention increasingly has focused on drug problems.[24]

Risk is mostly concerned with which individuals or groups are most likely either to have a certain condition or be affected at some point. Although it is helpful to have information on suicide or poverty rates, we generally turn our attention to identifying those factors that are predictive of (or distinguish among) which population groups are at greatest risk. In these cases, we would speak of a population-in-need or a population-at-risk, matters to which we will later turn our attention.[25]

Incidence and Prevalence

Risk is a matter of degree and is generally expressed as the likelihood (or probability) that a given case has that particular problem or condition. Most times, we will be concerned with large populations, where we need to know the number of cases with the condition relative to the number of cases in the total population. Obviously, we will first have to define the nature of the condition to observe how many cases have it. We will also have to define the population in which we are interested. Then we will need to know where (geographically) the condition exists, as well as the time frame during which cases occur. Two concepts, developed by public health experts, can help clarify degree of risk: incidence and prevalence.

Incidence refers to the number of *new cases* that develop a particular condition in a defined geographic area during a specified period of time. *Prevalence* refers to the *total number of cases* having a particular condition in a defined geographic area at a specified time.[26] There are more complex technical definitions, but these are the most common in the human services.[27]

The distinction between prevalence and incidence is probably best understood in a health-related context. For example, incidence of flu refers to the number of new cases diagnosed or reported during a certain period (say, a month), whereas the prevalence of flu refers to the total number of people diagnosed with that condition during a particular period, regardless of when they acquired it, or how long it lasted, or even whether they had it more than once.

Treating incidence and prevalence as interchangeable measures can lead to confusion or deliberate distortion of information. For example, there are a number of ways in which state unemployment agencies can report statistics on unemployment benefits. Sometimes, government statistics refer to the total number of beneficiaries receiving unemployment insurance at some point in time (prevalence); at other times, the government uses the number of new unemployment insurance recipients (incidence) as its measure of unemployment.

It may not always be clear, especially in understanding human needs, whether incidence or prevalence is the more relevant measure, but we need to keep in mind how extensiveness of need is determined. Are we interested in new cases arising or in the total number of cases existing? The count will differ, depending on the method used. One guideline in deciding which concept to use is to focus on the nature of our concern. That is, if a particular problem is a stable condition that persists over a long period of time, then prevalence is the more appropriate measure. If the problem reflects rapidly changing but temporary conditions, then incidence is the better measure. For example, if we expect that unemployed workers will be out of work for extended periods because of structural factors in the job market, then prevalence information will help us design appropriate interventions. If we expect unemployed workers to find new jobs quickly, then incidence information is more useful.[28]

Methods of Counting

Identifying risk factors and then measuring incidence or prevalence provides an index of the number of cases that are either in need or at risk of becoming in need. Sometimes this process is straightforward—simply count up the total number of cases in a particular area at a particular time, or count the number of new (reported) cases in that area at that time. For example, we might be interested in knowing how many cases of AIDS have been reported in the United States since such statistics started being kept. Or we might want to look at how many new cases of AIDS were reported during the first six months of 1992.

The same process could be applied to any problem. We could look at how many people were incarcerated in the United States in 1988 (about 689,000). If our goal is to track the trend in imprisonment figures for the 1980s, we could then compare the 1988 figure with the number of people who were incarcerated during 1981 (about 344,000).[29] We could even look at how many people were imprisoned in New York City and compare that count with the number incarcerated in Scranton, Pennsylvania.

Much of the information from the mass media, government reports, various institutes, and private organizations consists of simple counts or comparisons of totals across time or between places. The problem with this is that such information can be limited in value or confusing because of how it is reported. Because they do not take into account changing population sizes over time or different population bases from one locale to another, crude counts can obscure the nature of a problem. We need ways to standardize how counts are presented, so that information is as comprehensible as possible. We also want to limit the extent to which reporting agencies can distort information to fit their own agenda. For example, they may want to paint a problem as worthy of public support because it is increasing or because it has been stable for a long period of time; or they may want to "prove" it is unworthy of support because it is declining or has disappeared altogether. Stating that 1,600 people were arrested last year for drug possession sounds like a lot; it would seem like even more in a small town such as Wabash, Indiana. It might not be such a big number, however, for New York City or for the state of California.

A number of common ways exist for standardizing numbers, especially if the goal is to make comparisons.[30] Among the most common are proportions, percentages, ratios, and rates. To compute a *proportion,* two pieces of information are needed: the number (or frequency) of cases having a particular condition or falling into a particular category (f_i); and the total number of relevant cases (N). Then the frequency of cases is divided by the total number of cases to obtain the proportion (P). Thus:

$$P = \frac{f_i}{N}$$

For example, if we wanted to determine the proportion of people over age 65 who fell below the poverty line in 1985, we divide the number of individuals over 65 whose income fell below $5,156 (for those people living alone) or $6,503 (for couples) by the total number of people over age 65: In this case, the proportion would be .126.[31]

Proportions will range from zero to one and typically be expressed as a decimal value. Because most people find it easier to work with whole numbers than with fractions (or decimals), another common way of standardizing numbers is to use percentages (%). *Percentages* are obtained by multiplying a proportion by 100. In effect, using a percentage gets rid of decimal values (by moving the decimal point two places to the right). For our example on poverty rates among the elderly, we would get 12.6%.

Another option for standardizing numbers is to use the *ratio (R)*, which compares directly two sets of frequencies (f_1/f_2). For example, we might want to compare the number of women over age 65 who are widowed (f_1) with the number of men over age 65 who are widowed (f_2). For 1980, about 8 out of every 100 men age 65 to 74 were widowed, compared with 40 out of every 100 women in the same age group.[32] Thus:

$$R = \frac{f_2}{f_1} \quad \frac{(\text{women})}{(\text{men})} \quad \frac{(40)}{(8)} = 5$$

These frequencies would produce a ratio of 5, meaning that for every man who was widowed, there were 5 women who were widowed.

Epidemiologists and demographers often employ another measure, called the *rate*—for example, birth rate, suicide rate, death rate. This term has become common usage in the human services, where we speak of admission rates, rates of training, and service utilization rates.[33] Rates are essentially the same as percentages in that a proportion or ratio is multiplied by a larger number. (Again, the basic purpose is to get rid of decimal values, because it is easier to express a rate as 800 per 100,000 than as .8%.) For example, the suicide rate in the United States was 12.2 in 1980, which means that for every 100,000 people in the population, 12.2 died that year as a result of suicide.[34] Typically rates are expressed relative to population, usually 100,000. However, the multiplication factor can vary from 1,000 to 100,000, depending on the relative occurrence of the problem.

Populations and Targets

In the discussion on extent of problems, the concept of population was used time and again to refer generally to a group of people. The concept also was used to refer to individuals or groups who may have a problem or be likely to develop it. The term population usually refers to numbers of cases, even when it is limited to a group considered most at risk.

The use of population developed from an interest in survey sampling as a method of obtaining information on large groups of cases spread over broad geographic areas. In epidemiology, as in the social sciences and contemporary human services, the sample survey has become a major data-collection technique.[35]

Although the term *population* usually is applied to a large group, it cannot be applied indiscriminately. A technical term intended to convey certain kinds of information, it is used here to mean a group of people who meet *certain criteria of interest* to a social planner, practitioner or researcher.[36] A population rarely will consist of the world at large. Rather, it is some group in which there is special interest, one that meets designated requirements. For example, if we are interested in examining the drinking practices of American adults, we are not interested in all people, not even all those residing in the United States. Instead, we want to select adults (18 or older), and consumers of alcoholic beverages. In some cases, we might want (or need) to be even more restrictive, perhaps limiting our investigation to those of legal drinking age or to "normal" drinkers. Also, we might omit those in institutional settings (hospitals, prisons, or the military) or who live in "dry" areas. Therefore, populations need to be specified with care, which takes forethought and planning. The appropriate population for a given concern will not be self-evident but must be defined by those interested in understanding that concern.

Accuracy in specifying a population is especially crucial when designing a sample survey for data collection. A satisfactory "representative" sample is random (or probabilistic), drawn only when the nature of the population is known. This is because random samples require establishment of a sampling frame where probabilities of selection of all cases are known. Only under that condition is it possible to determine the extent of sampling error; such knowledge is necessasry to make valid generalizations from the sample to the population that it is meant to represent.[37] Thus, sampling error is a statistical estimate of the margin of error that is likely when inferences are drawn from a sample and applied to the population that the sample is intended to represent. However, computations of sampling error are legitimate only for random samples.

In human services, we often need to focus on very specific populations, perhaps combining the concepts of *at risk* (and perhaps *at need*) and *population*. As a result, we will direct our attention to *target populations* for intervention. According to Rossi, Freeman, and Wright:

> In the identification of targets, the public health concept of *population at risk* may be helpful, particularly in projects that are preventive in character. The term population at risk covers that segment of a population that exclusively or largely is subject, with significant probabilities, to developing a condition. Thus, the population at risk in fertility control studies is usually defined as women of childbearing age. Similarly, projects that are designed to mitigate the effects of natural disasters such as typhoons or hurricanes may define targets as communities located in the typical paths of tropical storms.
>
> The concept of *population at need,* in contrast, centers around the idea of defining targets as units who *currently* manifest a given condition. In projects directed at alleviating poverty, one may define as its target population families whose income adjusted for family size is below a certain minimum.[38]

Specifying a population at risk or at need, then, is simply specifying a target population, the term used in the program planning and evaluation literature. Target specification is crucial because the success of an intervention will likely hinge on how well we have determined who is most likely to be at risk. Keep in mind that the "target" is the focus for intervention, whether that target is an individual, a group, or a geographical or political unit.

Rates for particular problems will be correlated with various demographic and social characteristics to identify differences among population groups. The more accurate rates are in predicting characteristics, then the more carefully programs can be targeted to those with particular levels of risk.

Love and Torrence, investigating the relationship between age and length of unemployment after plant closings, pointed out that research on unemployment typically has ignored older workers, because their unemployment rate is known to be much lower than that of younger workers.[39] As a result, little research has been devoted to older workers, even though some do become unemployed and may have special needs related to reemployment. Upon finding that older workers who lost their jobs after plant closings were unemployed longer than their younger counterparts, Love and Torrence concluded that older unemployed workers needed to be treated as "specific targets" in programs designed to reduce unemployment.

LEVELS OF INTERVENTION AND UNITS OF ANALYSIS

Targets as a Focus for Analysis or Intervention

When specifying program targets, it is important to remember the level at which we are trying to intervene—individual, social group, or some broader target, such as a community or a geographic or political entity. For the social planner or practitioner, level of intervention is analogous to the social researcher's concern with unit of analysis. As Nachmias and Nachmias describe, units of analysis "are entities to which our concepts pertain and which influence subsequent research design, data collection, and data analysis decisions. Does the research problem call for the study of perceptions, attitudes, or behavior? Should we concentrate on individuals or groups? Institutions or societies?"[40] The unit of analysis, then, is the level of aggregation around which the study will revolve. Smith identifies "seven prototype levels" of analysis: aggregative (individual), interactive (group), organizational, ecological, institutional, cultural, and societal units.[41]

Level of intervention or unit of analysis is crucial in identifying target populations; it also has major relevance for the design of social programs. If the level at which the social worker needs to intervene is not correctly assessed, then the intervention may lose a great deal of its potential impact. In fact, if the chosen level of intervention turns out to be inappropriate, the intervention may have no impact (at best) or negative consequences (at worst). The desire to be helpful is an important value premise for the social services, but that sentiment does not guarantee that one will actually be of help. Careful planning of services is essential and includes an adequate assessment of the level for service intervention.

If we are interested in groups, for example—whether for study or as targets for intervention—we need to look at the group as a whole, not just one or a few individuals. We need to be careful not to apply information collected at one level of analysis to another level. In fact, if levels of analysis become mixed, serious problems will arise, one of which is jeopardizing the adequacy of intervention efforts. The term *ecological fallacy* refers to situations where information collected on groups (i.e., in aggregate form) is projected onto individuals. For example, the fact that an individual lives in a high-crime area does not mean that that person is engaging (or is likely to engage) in criminal activity. A similar error, called the *individualistic fallacy,* refers to making generalizations about larger social units based on information from individuals. For instance, the media routinely publicize pictures of drug users in inner-city areas. Yet, those images certainly cannot be generalized to mean that all people living in the inner city are crack addicts. Also, the lack of media focus on middle-class white drug users does not mean an absence of drug use among this population. What people believe about their society and what the actual conditions are often will differ.[42]

Frequently, the information used in planning social services fails to take into account the unit of analysis. In many needs assessment surveys, for example, information about need levels is asked in terms of the household. That is, respondents are asked whether they or anyone in their household has a particular problem. The information collected for identifying target populations, though, generally focuses on the respondents in these surveys. The end result is, at best, a loss in precision, because correlating individual demographic characteristics with household-level needs yields weak associations. Furthermore, it is possible that mixing units of analysis can produce misleading results.

Common Levels or Units

The most popular levels of intervention or units of analysis are the individual, the group, the community, and the societal. As Smith has pointed out, most social research uses data collected at the individual level, but these data are then often aggregated or combined to represent social categories of one sort or another.[43] Interest actually may be in groups, where interaction patterns among individuals define these entities as groups, but the data may be based on only one group member or on limited observations of certain interaction patterns. Focus on social groups, communities, or societal units represents a more global level of interest in collectives that, as Smith put it, "do not derive from an accumulation of individual characteristics." Even in these cases, the raw data may come from individuals, as in analysis of income or wealth or political power.

If the individual is the unit of analysis, the most relevant information is about individual characteristics, attitudes, perceptions, beliefs, and behaviors. When the group is the unit of analysis, the focus generally will be on interaction patterns, relationships, participation in joint activities, and normative expectations and pressures. Groups can vary significantly in size and nature, from informal friendship groups to large bureaucratic organizations. Communities generally refer to geographic and/or political areas, where people live and with which they experience an attachment (either positive or negative). Societal units typically refer to large-scale social organizations, particularly countries, where the focus of attention will be on broad matters, such as the extent of urbanization, type of economic structure, distribution of wealth, and nature of the political order. Information collected at one level may be aggregated or disaggregated and applied at another; the main principle to keep in mind is what the data looked like in the first place and whether they are being mixed appropriately.

In contemporary social services, the individual is probably the most typical level of intervention, although in past decades groups and communities were common targets for intervention strategies. During the 1960s, for example, the community mental health movement concentrated on the ecology of local communities, and counseling services were only one type of activity housed in those settings. The Office of Economic Opportunity funded community organizations that were intended to bring about broad social action, including increasing the level of political participation within the local community and empowering community members. When social theory is used in developing intervention strategies, it is important to keep in mind the ecological fallacy. If a choice is made to work at a particular level of intervention, then the theory that guides such work should apply to the same level.[44] Theory focusing on groups may not be relevant to individuals, or vice versa. Social policy, though, can be applied at any level of intervention. The problem is to decide in advance what is the most appropriate level of intervention for a specific problem. As long as that decision is correctly made, then information can be aggregated or disaggregated accordingly to achieve the most accurate estimates of program targets in terms of their most relevant characteristics.[45] In that the intent of an intervention is to reach the most appropriate clients, designing a program around the characteristics of those individuals most likely to be clients can help achieve that outcome.

CONCLUSION

Coming to grips with the notion of human need is no easy matter. When that concept is used by social planners and human service practitioners, the goal generally is to arrive at an "objective" and "rational" assessment of the level of some need (or needs) for a particular population, by applying some of the thinking that underlies the "scientific method." Yet, as shown in Chapter 5, scientific enterprises take place within a social and political context, which places serious constraints on the extent to which "objectivity" can be realized. Certainly, establishing human needs cannot be removed from this same social and political context. As Fraser so aptly put it, we must keep in mind that we are dealing with a "politics of need."[46]

Sometimes, the language of epidemiology will be used as part of the political process of legitimating a particular need as a recognized problem. However, numbers in and of themselves have no inherent meaning or validity. If we cannot provide a satisfactory conceptualization of the need (or needs) with which we are concerned, then any numbers we generate will likely only add to the confusion or conflict over the acceptability of a dilemma. As we will see in Chapter 8 in a discussion about the technology of needs assessment, one of the weakest elements in this process is adequate conceptualization of the nature and meaning of need.

Generally, the goal in identifying human needs is to find ways of alleviating conditions perceived as adverse. If people are "in need," then programs are needed that will help ameliorate those conditions. At the same time, not all individuals or social groups will have the same likelihood of having a particular problem. In many cases, we will try to identify the distinguishing characteristics of those who are most "at risk," who then will become targets for our intervention.[47] In some cases, that may help us intervene more effectively with certain problems, but identifying targets can serve also as a subtle mechanism for "blaming the victim." It is important, then, to develop a critical understanding of the concept of "populations at risk"—also referred to by contemporary writers as "vulnerable groups"—the topic of Chapter 7.

NOTES

1. J.R. Beniger, *Trafficking in Drug Users: Professional Exchange Networks in the Control of Deviance* (New York: Cambridge University Press, 1983).
2. Drug Abuse Council, *The Facts about "Drug Abuse"* (New York: Free Press, 1980); J. A. Inciardi, *The War on Drugs: Heroin, Cocaine, Crime, and Public Policy* (Palo Alto, CA: Mayfield Publishing, 1986); E. M. Brecher, *Licit and Illicit Drugs* (Boston: Little, Brown, 1972).
3. J. Helmer, *Drugs and Minority Oppression* (New York: Seabury Press, 1975).
4. Beniger.
5. Brecher.
6. A. H. Maslow, *Toward a Pyschology of Being*, 2nd ed. (New York: Van Nostrand Reinhold, 1968).
7. P. Schmolling, M. Youkeles, and W. R. Burger, *Human Services in Contemporary America*, 2nd ed. (Pacific Grove, CA: Brooks/Cole, 1989).
8. N. Fraser, "Talking about Needs: Interpretive Contests at Political Conflicts in Welfare-State Societies," *Ethics* 99 (1989): 294.
9. E. R. Kingson, B. A. Hirshorn, and J. M. Cornman, *Ties That Bind: the Interdependence of Generations* (Washington, DC: Seven Locks Press, 1986).
10. J. Bradshaw, "The Concept of Social Need," *New Society* 30 (1972): 640–43.
11. D. P. Moynihan, *The Negro Family: the Case for National Action* (Washington, DC: U.S. Government Printing Office, 1965).
12. W. J. Wilson, *The Truly Disadvantaged: The Inner City, the Underclass, and Public Policy* (Chicago: University of Chicago Press, 1987).
13. K. M. Kilty and A. Feld, "Attitudes toward Aging and toward the Needs of Older People," *Journal of Gerontology* 5 (1976): 586–94.

14. K. M. Fillmore, "The 1980s' Dominant Theory of Alcohol Problems—Genetic Predisposition to Alcoholism: Where Is It Leading Us?" *Drugs and Society* 2 (1988): 69–87.

15. C. Towle, *Common Human Needs,* rev. ed. (Silver Spring, MD: National Association of Social Workers, 1987).

16. W. A. Kimmel, *Needs Assessment: a Critical Perspective* (Washington, DC: Office of Program Systems, Office of Assistant Secretary for Planning and Evaluation, U.S. Department of Health, Education, and Welfare, 1977).

17. *Webster's New Twentieth-Century Dictionary, unabr.,* 2nd ed. (Cleveland, OH: World Publishing, 1973).

18. L. M. Mead, *Beyond Entitlement: the Social Obligations of Citizenship* (New York: Free Press, 1986).

19. Kimmel.

20. R. G. Smart, "Addiction, Dependency, Abuse, or Use: Which Are We Studing with Epidemiology?" in *Drug Use: Epidemiological and Sociological Approaches,* eds. E. Josephson and E. E. Carroll (New York: Wiley, 1974), 23–42; K. J. Rothman, *Modern Epidemiology* (Boston: Little, Brown, 1986); D. G. Kleinbaum, L. L. Kupper, and H. Morgenstern, *Epidemiologic Research: Principles and Quantitative Methods* (Belmont, CA: Lifetime Learning Publications, 1982).

21. Kleinbaum, 2.

22. Ibid, 20

23. Smart.

24. Beniger.

25. P. H. Rossi, H. E. Freeman, and S. R. Wright, *Evaluation: a Systematic Approach* (Beverly Hills, CA: Sage, 1979).

26. J. McKillip, *Need Analysis Tools for the Human Services and Education* (Beverly Hills, CA: Sage, 1987); Rossi, Freeman, and Wright.

27. Rothman; Kleinbaum et al.

28. E. J. Posavac and R. G. Carey, *Program Evaluation: Methods and Case Studies,* 3rd ed. (Englewood Cliffs, NJ: Prentice-Hall, 1989).

29. "More Americans than Ever Are Crammed into Prisons," *Columbus Dispatch* (April 24, 1989), p. A6.

30. D. Nachmias and C. Nachmias, *Research Methods in the Social Sciences,* 2nd ed. (New York: St. Martin's, 1981), 394; McKillip, 58–59; Rossi, Freeman, and Wright, 82.

31. Villers Foundation, *On the Other Side of Easy Street: Myths and Facts about the Economics of Old Age* (Washington, DC: Villers Foundation, 1987).

32. P. E. Zopf, *America's Older Population* (Houston, TX: Cap and Gown Press, 1986).

33. McKillip.

34. E. Currie and J. H. Skolnick, *America's Problems: Social Issues and Public Policy* (Boston: Little, Brown, 1984), table 9–2, 328.

35. P. H. Rossi, J. D. Wright, and A. B. Anderson, eds., *Handbook of Survey Research* (Orlando, FL: Academic Press, 1983).

36. C. H. Backstrom and G. Hursh-Cesar, *Survey Research,* 2nd ed. (New York: Wiley, 1981).

37. Ibid.

38. Rossi, Freeman, and Wright, 97.

39. D. O. Love and W. D. Torrence, "The Impact of Worker Age on Unemployment and Earnings after Plant Closings," *Journal of Gerontology* 44 (1989): S190–S195.
40. Nachmias and Nachmias, 56.
41. Smith, Strategies of Social Research, p. 373.
42. Nachmias and Nachmias, 56.
43. H. W. Smith, *Strategies of Social Research,* 2nd ed. (Englewood Cliffs, NJ: Prentice-Hall, 1981), 374
44. Nachmias and Nachmias, 57.
45. Rossi, Freeman, and Wright.
46. Fraser.
47. Rossi, Freeman, and Wright.

CHAPTER 7

Understanding Populations at Risk

INTRODUCTION

The language used in describing social problems and designing strategies for intervention changes from one period to another. Looking at such shifts in terminology can provide valuable information about our society. According to Gomberg, our concepts reflect how we understand and deal with problems.[1] Earlier references to particular afflictions or social pathologies—"alcoholism," "poverty," or "child abuse"—now include references to "special populations," "groups at risk," or "vulnerability." In effect, concern has turned from looking not just at the problems themselves but also increasingly to a focus on those who have the problems.

This shift in emphasis has occurred primarily during the past 25 years, along with gradual acceptance of public or social responsibility for the plight of the disadvantaged. Only in the past half century—mainly since the Great Depression—has there been recognition that some problems may need public intervention. Even so, powerful suspicions persist regarding governmental intercessions, especially those at the national level. Indeed, the belief that public programs do more harm than good existed before many programs were created.[2] The original Aid to Dependent Children (ADC) provisions of the Social Security Act, for example, were intended to be temporary measures.[3]

Despite reservations on the part of many policymakers, as well as a significant proportion of the public, the "discovery" of problems such as poverty and child abuse helped increase the legitimacy for broad initiatives in the social services, especially during the 1950s and 1960s. Public awareness of a number of serious social problems grew at that time, and concern centered mainly on determining their extent. Burgeoning social services, modeling themselves in part after the medical professions, came to presume that disease conditions affect all individuals in essentially the same way. For this reason, research emphases in the new field of social epidemiology (as we saw in Chapter 6) focused on establishing operational definitions of specific problems, in order to produce prevalence and incidence rates.

Because one goal of epidemiology is to estimate individual risks (or probabilities) for developing particular conditions or maladies, studies of the extensiveness of social and behavioral problems generally provided demographic breakdowns of rates, based on characteristics such as gender, age, and race.[4] These data demonstrated a simple but unrecognized fact: not all individuals or social groups experienced the same degree of vulnerability to specific difficulties. For example, men were less likely than women or children to live in poverty, and women were less likely to be diagnosed as having drinking problems. As a result, the notion of "special population" (or "group at risk") arose.

POPULATIONS, SOCIAL CHARACTERISTICS, AND VULNERABILITY

In studies on alcoholism, these developments in conceptualizing human needs and social problems can be seen by examining the *Special Reports on Alcohol and Health,* released periodically by the National Institute on Alcohol Abuse and Alcoholism.[5] Although the first report appeared in 1971, it was not until the third volume—which included a chapter devoted to "special populations"—in 1978 that differing degrees of vulnerability were recognized for various population groups. By the time the most recent report was published, this designation had become institutionalized, with coverage including women, adolescents, the elderly, the homeless, and minority groups (specifically blacks, Hispanics, Native Americans, Asian Americans and Pacific islanders).

Underlying a concern with so-called special populations are the issues of vulnerability and "true" need. During the 1970s, the perception grew that, although certain social problems might exist, not all social groups were equally vulnerable to them. That is, some groups—through no fault of their own—were more subject to harm by changes in social and economic conditions and therefore more "deserving" of help. The notion of the "truly disadvantaged" peaked in the 1980s, during serious cuts in funding for many social services.[6] In an era characterized by scarce resources and limitations on the numbers to whom services could be provided, it seemed "reasonable" to focus most attention on those populations that had the highest degree of vulnerability.[7]

As we saw in Chapter 6, risk can be an important factor to look at in the social service planning process, regardless of whether we are developing prevention or remediation programs. We made note of a population at risk as a social group that is more likely than others to develop a certain condition (or conditions).[8] By learning the characteristics of who is most at risk, planners can target programming presumably where it is most needed. Yet, extreme care must be taken in using this concept of risk, especially in labeling certain social groups as "special populations": The implication is that these are groups on which we want to focus special attention, which although preferential can be stigmatizing, especially if individual members are targeted.[9] As we will see, so-called special populations typically are distinguished on the basis of demographic characteristics; they may have little in common besides a racial, age, or gender category that is devalued in our society. Furthermore, the statistical relationships used to identify a group at risk are not likely to be very strong.

RISK, UNCERTAINTY, AND PREDICTABILITY

As an epidemiological construct, risk is concerned with group-level (or aggregate) phenomena rather than with individual experiences. According to Zucker, three factors are crucial to remember in understanding risk. First, risk directs our attention to some "anticipated outcome," usually a negative event. Second, it indicates a "likelihood estimate" in that it provides a statement about the odds of occurrence of that "anticipated outcome." Finally, risk identifies some potential "hazard" or "danger." It does not mean that hazard will occur for a certain individual or that specific individuals are unable to avoid the hazard. Zucker also notes that "risk is an attribute of populations rather than individuals, and is typically inferred on the basis of an observation that some proportion of a group with specified characteristics eventually displays some sign or symptom."[10] It is critical to recognize that risk concerns populations rather than individuals. As Zucker goes on to state: "Elements of risk or danger are inferential in a different sense at the individual level; they are best regarded as signs of covert processes that only some of the time are detectable by their overt display."[11]

Perceptions of Risk

As epidemiologists use the term, *risk* appears to be a relatively objective index of hazard. Yet we have already seen that scientific objectivity is limited. Scientific knowledge is as much a social construction as is our understanding of everyday life, and risk is no different; that is, what we perceive as risk does not necessarily have much to do with "objective" conditions.[12] For instance, many people are frightened to go near someone who has cancer, for fear that it might "rub off" on them; also, reactions to AIDS are often nearly hysterical. Everyday odds of serious injury or death are quite significant for anyone who drives a car, yet that "reality" has had little impact on the number of miles driven in the United States. Because most of us drive, either we live in a constant state of denial or we are remarkably unaware.

Risk implies a degree of uncertainty: something bad could happen. On the other hand: not necessarily. Despite degrees of uncertainty in most matters of daily life, we learn to cope with those vagaries mainly by ignoring them. As Stallings has so aptly described:

> Most of the time people ignore the risks in everyday life. However, when the taken-for-granted outcomes of routine activities fail to occur—a commercial airliner crashes rather than landing safely, the earth trembles violently rather than imperceptibly, a highway bridge collapses rather than conveying vehicles safely from one bank to another—risk and safety often become matters of public discussion and remedial public policy making. Forces that seemed benign, under control, or nonexistent

appear to be malicious, unchecked, and omnipresent in the aftermath of such dramatic events.[13]

It is not just dramatic public events that can shatter one's faith in certitude. For better or worse, we all live in a constant state of uncertainty—we could lose jobs, marriages could fall apart, children might get into serious trouble. All the same, those things do not happen to any one of us every day. In fact, some live much more secure lives than others.

As human service professionals concerned with "vulnerable groups" or "populations at risk," we need to use those concepts with care. Most of us live under circumstances that are much less risky than those of our clients. We have a college or graduate degree, relatively stable jobs and homes, and family incomes that are at the median or higher for this society. We can afford to ignore the riskiness of daily life. Others may, too, but their lives exist on shakier grounds. If clients experience loss of home, job, or family, we need to be careful not to interpret their losses as personal failures or even necessarily as personal responsibilities. Because people like us define what social problems are and create the theories that "explain" them, we have a responsibility to ensure that those definitions and theoretical statements include the perspectives of the people most affected by social conditions.

As we saw earlier, an epidemiological orientation toward risk defines it in terms of the odds or likelihood of some anticipated outcome that can be characterized as a hazard or pathological condition. The terms *likelihood* and *anticipated outcome* imply that we have the capacity to make predictions about hazards. Focusing on populations at risk, then, suggests that we can predict who will be subject to particular problems.

We can predict anything—from which horse will win today's race to whether it will rain during Saturday's football game to which one of a group of young people will become an alcoholic. Some predictions are trivial, whereas others are crucial. Predictions that bear on people's lives definitely are not trivial, so we should be concerned with their accuracy. This may seem like a rather simple issue, but many textbook generalizations on human behavior are based on weak research findings or conjecture.

Correlation and Prediction

Identifying risk factors can be most useful in trying to predict the likelihood of occurrence of particular social or physical conditions. Finding out what variables, such as demographic or social characteristics, are associated with specific social problems or human needs provides valuable information for service planning and delivery. It may also provide insight into the etiology of problems such as alcoholism or mental illness. We noted in Chapter 6 that there is more to epidemiological research than simply counting cases that have certain conditions or identifying the range of services in a particular community. Our goal should also be *analytic,* so as to understand the underlying causes of the problems we are trying to prevent or rehabilitate.[14]

Causal analysis is difficult to carry out effectively in the social sciences, and establishing relationships among variables is only a first step. All the same, it is an important first step. Associations among variables provide valuable information. When we know that a characteristic is statistically related to a particular problem or need, we can use that knowledge to predict future occurrences of the conditions about which we are concerned. For example, we may find a correlation between gender and alcohol abuse, such that men are more likely than women to display alcohol problems. If we know there is a relationship between two variables, we can use information about one of those variables to predict the other variable. In contrast, if there is no association, using one variable as a predictor of the other will yield nothing more than a haphazard forecast. The statistical concepts of correlation and regression, then, are a means by which we can estimate the occurrence of specific conditions under particular circumstances.[15] In this case, the conditions refer to the social problems or human needs with which we are concerned, and the certain circumstances refer to factors (such as demographic or social characteristics) associated with those conditions.

Probability and Accuracy of Prediction.   Keep in mind that the results of correlational research provide information that is probabilistic in nature.[16] Rarely, if ever, will correlations among variables be anywhere near perfect; in most cases, social science research produces outcomes that demonstrate only modest relationships among variables. In statistical analysis, the concept of the *coefficient of determination* (or r^2) can help determine the value of information. This coefficient is an index of the degree of predictability, when we use the values of one variable (X) to predict the values of another variable (Y). For example, if we find a Pearson correlation coefficient of $+.50$ between SAT or ACT scores and freshman grades, those results could be used to predict how well students will do in college. To get an idea of how accurate our predictions will be, we need to square the correlation coefficient, which in this case would yield a value of .25. This value tells us what proportion of our predictions are accurate—in this case telling us we would be accurate 25% of the time.

Predicting Aggregate Risk.   This analytic approach is typically used in identifying populations at risk. Such an approach provides information that is *relative;* as long as our correlations are statistically significant, we know with a certain degree of confidence that those particular factors are associated with specific conditions. However, not all cases with particular characteristics will develop problems. All we know is that there is a higher probability of problems being found among people having certain characteristics. These are group-level or aggregate findings, too. That is, we know that, for this group as a whole, there is a higher likelihood that some individuals will have problems, but we do not know which particular individuals either will have problems or develop them in the future.

Correlation and Causality. Extreme care must be used in drawing causal inferences about relationships among variables based only on the results of correlational analysis. Correlation is a necessary but insufficient condition for establishing causality. That is, for two variables to be causally related, they must be correlated. However, correlation by itself does not establish a causal relationship between two variables.

For example, smoking cigarettes has become linked with a number of serious health problems. In this regard, an important health issue concerns the proposition of an association between cigarette smoking and cardiovascular disease. According to Rothman:

> It is clear that not all cigarette smokers will get cardiovascular disease and equally clear that some nonsmokers will develop cardiovascular disease. Therefore, the proposition cannot prohibit cardiovascular disease among nonsmokers for its absence among smokers. The proposition could be taken to mean that cigarette smokers, on the average, will develop more cardiovascular disease than nonsmokers. Does this statement prohibit finding the same rate of cardiovascular disease among smokers and nonsmokers, presuming that biases such as confounding and misclassification are inoperant? Not quite, since the effect of cigarette smoke could depend on a component cause that might be absent from the compared groups. One might suppose that at least the prohibition of a smaller rate of cardiovascular disease among smokers would be implied by the proposition. If one accepts, however, that a given factor could be both a cause and a preventive in different circumstances, even this prohibition cannot be attached to the statement.[17]

We can see that care needs to be taken in deriving conclusions about social conditions based on correlations among those conditions and factors used to disinguish populations at risk. It is easy to fall into the trap of assuming causal connections that may not exist, as occurred in the 1960s with the culture of poverty thesis and more recently in analyses of the failure of public education in this country.[18,19]

Misrepresenting Special Populations

Although identifying a social group as special or vulnerable may help us to direct services where they are most needed, it can also lead to circumstances in which we simply blame the victim for having the problem. As Ryan has pointed out, social problems generally are described on the basis of existing normative standards, which are not questioned, and any "deviation from norms and standards comes to be defined as failed or incomplete socialization—failure to learn the rules or the inability to learn how to keep them."[20] The individual, then, is responsible for his or her situation and is unable or unwilling to abide by society's conventions. Although Ryan pointed out this tendency to "blame the victim" over 20 years ago, the use of concepts such as "special populations" can provide a subtle and inadvertent mechanism to do precisely that.

During the past decade, there has been a lot of concern with the so-called underclass. America's inner cities are filled with a population that has little or no attachment to society as a whole, where crime and violence run rampant and a significant proportion of the population depends on public welfare (especially AFDC) for subsistence. Publication of William Julius Wilson's *The Truly Disadvantaged* marked the high point of such social analyses.[21] Although discussions of the underclass generally deny it, these analyses are little more than updated variations on the culture of poverty thesis, which posits that the poor become locked into a way of life that reinforces their social status. According to this perspective, certain values and attitudes are learned by the underclass in inner cities or ghettos that are, to some extent, adaptive but that later make it difficult for them to break out of the cycle of marginal work and wages. Dependency on welfare as a primary source of economic support develops and, through socialization, the process becomes self-perpetuating and draws in the next generation. Oscar Lewis, the originator of this theory, took great pains in analyzing how structural forces bring about poverty; however, his ideas were adapted by conservative writers, such as Murray and Mead, and used to attack recent welfare policies.[22,23,24]

Wilson argues that his own analysis of the inner city goes beyond the culture of poverty thesis, but many of his critics believe that he falls into the same trap as the conservatives. According to Marks, Wilson, in ignoring some of the more important social structural factors that affect the lives of ghetto residents, overplays the extent of violence, for example, when other research indicates that rates of homicide are higher among whites in rural areas in the West than among black males in inner cities.[25] His argument that proper role models for black youth can no longer be found in the ghetto belies the fact that the black middle class historically has separated itself from the impoverished. One of Wilson's key concepts, the "male marriageable pool index," is in essence a sexist notion, its point being that black women's only hope for climbing out of poverty is to find a black man who is marriageable (i.e., has a job that pays a living wage), ignoring gender discrimination in salaries and lack of adequate day care in the United States. Furthermore, his analysis does not even portray the facts accurately, as Marks describes:

> Further, the Male Marriageable Pool Index (MMPI) itself does not work in the way that one might expect in two of the four regions of the country examined. In the West, where there is an admittedly small black population, it is shown that the "substantial pool of eligible men does not reverse the trend of female-headed households, although we are told that they are not the same kind of households. In the South, where blacks are known to concentrate in low-waged, low-skilled labor, the finding that families are intact as a result of these "eligible" men is hardly worthy of celebration.[26]

In effect, Wilson's analysis puts the onus on those who live in the inner city: They should stop having babies unless they get married, and it is their lack of proper work attitudes and habits that causes their lives of poverty. As Ryan might note, it is their "incomplete socialization," their "failure" to learn what they should know in order to survive in this society. Discriminatory practices in the economic structure and the lack of well-paying jobs for men and women are not the major concerns in Wilson's type of analysis.

We can see this same process at work in current concerns about the adequacy of the schools in this country.[27] For some time, criticisms have been leveled at the quality of public education. As Ray and Mickelson note, discussion has shifted from an emphasis on schools as the problem to children as the problem:

> By 1987 national reports about educational reform had begun to emphasize "children-at-risk" instead of concentrating primarily on the schools, as in the earlier reports. More recent reports have implied that it was not necessarily schools that needed to be restructured and reformed but rather particular pupils. They referred specifically to working-class and minority students, who are most likely to drop out of school or who, analysts assert, possess "flimsy" high school diplomas.[28]

In sum, once the population at risk has been identified, it becomes defined as the source of the problem itself. Structural factors are no longer considered to be the primary factors; rather, it becomes particular individuals and their skills and attitudes.

Ethical and Value Concerns in Identifying Populations at Risk

Identifying populations at risk does not necessarily mean blaming the victim. Epidemiologically speaking, the intent of identifying a population at risk is to establish which groups or social categories are most likely to have a certain condition. As noted in Chapter 6, Rossi, Freeman, and Wright define a population at risk as "that segment of a population that exclusively or largely is subject with significant probabilities, to developing a condition."[29] As an illustration, they described women of childbearing age as the population at risk in research on fertility control. This conclusion is based on who can get pregnant and who cannot. That certainly does not mean that men should be excluded from fertility control, since there are birth-control devices or sexual behaviors that men can use to avoid causing pregnancy. How we define a population at risk can produce a myopic view of who develops a condition—or even who is responsible.

Even when our focus is legitimately on women (studies on prenatal care, for example), we need to keep in mind that we are dealing with a large population at risk ("women of childbearing age"), most of whom will not become pregnant in a given year. That is, although women are exclusively the group at risk, perhaps no more than 10% of the possible cases will in fact develop the condition. In 1981, for example, the fertility rate for white women was 68 children per 1,000 women, whereas it was 81 per 1,000 for black women.[30] In both cases, pregnancy had a prevalence rate of less than 10% of the relevant populaton. In other words, although no men got pregnant that year, not all that many women did, either.

Often the intent of identifying a population at risk is to be able to target that group for services. Consequently, members of that social category end up being treated differently from others: They are poor, whereas everybody else is not poor, or youths are delinquents, whereas other youths are not delinquents. Targets are perceived as different from others and therefore need to be drawn into programs; thus, in principle we may be promoting a self-fulfilling prophecy. For example, inner-city minority communities are now linked in the public eye to the use of illicit substances, especially crack cocaine. Should we target black male youth? Yet, contrary to media representations, the fact is that young black men are less likely to use drugs than their white counterparts.[32] If we expect young black men to develop conditions that are perceived as negative (whether it is drug use or shoplifting) and we single them out for attention, (as the police and store clerks do), is it any wonder that nearly one out of four black males is in prison or on parole?[33]

Serious ethical and value problems are associated with use of the concept of population at risk. In general, identification of such populations will be overly inclusive (more potential cases will be identified than will actually occur). In many cases, most who are part of a population at risk will never develop the condition. As noted earlier, the vast majority of blacks do not become drug users or alcoholics, just as they do not live out their lives in poverty. It is important to recognize that in this country the condition of the black population is significantly inferior to that of the white. However, it is not poverty that turns its victims into junkies or thieves. If we identify groups as different and then act in accordance with that differentiation, we run the risk of creating those very conditions for people who might otherwise have escaped the problems facing them. By targeting groups, we also engender the possibility of holding the victim responsible for his or her condition, when, in fact, social forces are responsible for particular life circumstances.

Sometimes, the goal in identifying populations at risk is to provide information to determine who should get services and how to select them. This is the concept of *triage*, a term that originated during World War I.[34] Initially, triage was used to "sort" the wounded to determine priorities for medical treatment. Although not usually identified as such, today's concerns about access to medical treatment among older people or among the poor involve triage.[35] Because of cutbacks in social services during the past decade, decisions about who should receive what have become more widespread, although they may not always be as life-threatening as similar decisions about medical care. Of course, lacking food, housing, or income can be dangerous. The guiding principle of triage is to provide services or resources to those considered most likely to benefit, which is no different in principle from identifying those "most in need." Research can identify characteristics of those who "respond effectively" to treatment or intervention, just as it can reveal characteristics associated with particular social problems. Yet we need to keep in mind that we are still dealing with group phenomena that may or may not apply to individual cases.

The point of this discussion is not to reject as improper research that tries to determine what characteristics are most associated with particular problems or conditions. Rather, it is to reiterate the idea that we are dealing with group-level phenomena, from which we can distinguish greater or lesser odds of having problems by identifying relevant social categories. Rarely will we be able to state categorically that nearly everyone in soical group *A* will have a certain problem, whereas the majority of social group *B* will not. Populations at risk refer to broad population groups, and focusing exclusively on the individuals within that group is at best inappropriate and at worst unethical and immoral. As noted in Chapter 6, we must avoid the ecological fallacy, where we generalize from the group level to the individual level.[36]

In most social programs, there is a tension between the goals of research and the goals of intervention. The researcher seeks relationships among variables using statistical methods that provide insight about social conditions or problems. The practitioner needs information that can help guide interventions with individual clients. Probabilistic statements about factors associated with a certain problem rarely will be all that useful to the practitioner when it comes to an individual client. In fact, it may cloud judgment and focus attention on the wrong factors. Epidemiological concepts such as populations at risk may have limited utility for direct service, although they may be extremely valuable on the planning level.

POPULATIONS AT RISK AND REPORTING STRATEGIES

Conventions in Research on Populations at Risk

How information is reported about populations at risk often obscures an understanding of what groups are at risk. Generally, the focus is not really on the population at risk but on specific problems or fields of service. Furthermore, most variables are treated separately. For example, we may look at the relationship between gender and poverty or between race and poverty. In some cases, there may be a little more analytic focus, where two or three factors may be taken into account at the same time. That is, we might compare poverty rates for men and for women, breaking each group down by age or by race, to find areas of overlap among different populations at risk. By and large, though, an unsophisticated orientation to research is taken in such analyses. The most typical analytic strategy is to use contingency tables (or cross tabulation), a technique that implies that the research is primarily for accounting or administrative purposes rather than scientific (i.e., the creation of knowledge).

Rarely are theoretical or conceptual frameworks used to decide what factors are relevant in distinguishing the population at risk. It has become customary to include breakdowns based on certain demographic characteristics, including age, gender, and race. However, little thought enters into these analyses, and the main thrust seems to be on making a "body count." That is, tables are generated that show how many men and women had this problem, how many blacks and whites had this problem, or how many young and old had this problem. In fact, the conventional table produced by the federal government will identify a condition

TABLE 7-1   Families Below Poverty Level: Selected Characteristics, by Race and Hispanic Origin, 1987[1]

Characteristic	Percent below Poverty Level			
	All races[3]	White	Black	Hispanic[2]
Total	10.8	8.2	29.9	25.8
Age of householder:				
15–24 years old	29.5	23.8	56.7	37.8
25–34 years old	15.4	11.4	39.4	28.9
35–44 years old	10.1	8.0	24.4	25.5
45–54 years old	7.0	5.0	20.8	19.6
55–64 years old	7.8	6.2	22.9	19.0
65 years old and over	7.2	5.4	23.7	21.6
Northeast	9.1	7.2	26.3	34.9
Midwest	10.2	7.7	33.6	26.7
South	12.8	8.8	31.1	27.0
West	9.9	8.8	21.3	20.3
Size of family:				
2 persons	8.7	6.9	25.4	20.0
3 persons	10.5	7.9	28.4	24.0
4 persons	10.3	7.7	29.5	22.7
5 persons	14.8	11.1	37.4	33.9
6 persons	22.0	17.1	40.3	35.8
7 persons or more	29.5	23.5	46.6	42.3
Education of householder:[4]				
Elementary: Less than 8 years	28.3	25.4	36.4	40.9
8 years	17.1	14.4	34.9	31.9
High school: 1–3 years	18.8	13.4	42.6	30.6
4 years	9.3	6.9	27.8	16.3
College: 1 year or more	3.7	2.9	11.2	7.8

[1]Source: U.S. Bureau of the Census, *Current Population Reports,* series P–60, No. 161.
[2]Hispanic persons may be of any race.
[3]Includes other races not shown separately.
[4]Householder 25 years old and over.

and then produce a series of frequency distributions combined into a single table. For example, Table 7–1 presents data on families below the poverty level for 1987. In this case, the analysis involved three-way tables by breaking down the percentage of families below the poverty line by crossing race and Hispanic origin with selected other characteristics. Race traditionally is an important correlate of poverty status, but these data could easily be analyzed in a much more sophisticated fashion.

The format in Table 7–1 focuses attention on individual rather than group characteristics. If the intent of the analysis is risk identification, then the data need to be set up in a different manner. As it is, the focus is on identifying a probable level of need and relating that to current or potential services, so that the focus then becomes the field of service or the problem itself. To some extent, this is because of how the data was collected. Most government reporting is based on cross-sectional survey data, which provide a "snapshot" of a subject problem at a single point in time. Some researchers characterize this as capturing a frozen slice of time.[37]

Alternative Methods of Analysis

An alternatiye method would be to concentrate specifically on the population at risk. Ideally, we should follow that population through time, using a longitudinal format in which the same people are contacted periodically. To some extent, we might be able to make use of a replicated cross-sectional format, where, even though different cases are included, data collection takes place at more than one point in time, allowing for different periods to be compared.

The central issue is whether we are concerned with how risk develops over time or with the need for information in the here and now. If we are concerned primarily with administrative matters or with fiscal accountability, then the research will reflect expediency—we will get what we can as quickly and cheaply as possible. However, if we take a more analytic focus, we will be more selective in what we collect and how we collect it. Our purpose will be to get as much information over time as possible, not simply to establish the level of need at a certain point or to test the effectiveness of a particular program.

If our intent is to be analytical and to produce results over a long period, our research needs to be grounded in theory and previous research findings. Why should we corrrelate region of the country with poverty status (as was done in Table 7–1)? Is there some particular reason, other than administrative convenience and tradition? Should we separate Hispanics from whites or blacks, and can we do so with precision? Are we interested in finding trends or making projections about future levels of risk? What assumptions do we need to make about the data at hand?

Unfortunately, much of the epidemiological research carried out in the social services is atheoretical and nonanalytical, following certain traditions that have developed during the past half century without a great deal of thought given to the adequacy of those strategies. Although the focus is ostensibly on identifying populations at risk, the underlying goal seems to be to produce immediate information that can be applied to existing programs. In most cases, emphasis is on the individual as the unit of analysis or level of intervention. Intervention strategies tend to be small in scale, with reform and amelioration of individual condition as the driving forces. In effect, there is a firm belief in the workability of the system and a limited willingness to challenge conventional approaches to dealing with social problems.

WHY IDENTIFY POPULATIONS AT RISK?

Identifying populations at risk should focus our efforts in a much different way. Because the concern is with broad population groups and their problems, the emphasis in research and planning should be on producing data that can guide the development of large-scale interventions. The condition of the group as a whole needs to be changed, not just the condition of some of the individuals in the population at risk. Analysis should focus on the impact of social structure on the condition of the population group, as well as assessing the range of problems it experiences. Many social problems are intertwined; that is, poverty, health, housing, transportation, and such, do not stand alone.[38] Those conditions, in fact, probably are correlated within the population at risk. If we concentrate on large groups where we anticipate that those at risk have multiple problems, then social services need to take into account the political and economic structure as a point of intervention, in addition to the more traditional individual-oriented programs.

The first task is to identify empirically or theoretically what characteristics could be used to define the population at risk.[39] For example, the relationships between race and a variety of social conditions, such as poverty, educational attainment, occupational attainment, access to medical care, and contact with the criminal justice system, have long been established. The thrust of the analysis, then, should be on establishing the extent to which certain racial groups experience various social problems. In this case, a different orientation would be taken in carrying out the analysis, as illustrated in Table 7–2 where the intent is to document the range of problems experienced by the population at risk. Other distinguishing characteristics can also be included, with multivariate analysis the most useful analytic strategy.[40]

If the goal of analysis is prevention, then it is essential to clearly distinguish the population at risk, including the development of risk over time. The philosophical question here is, are we mainly interested in prevention or in remediation? If the concern is prevention, then we need to focus on the structural conditions that lead to risk and to examine changes in risk levels over an extended period. If the concern is remediation, then we will concentrate on individual factors associated with particular conditions or problems. We may speak of groups at risk, but the concept is applied only in a partial sense, where the goal is to identify cases that need treatment. This is the traditional pattern in the social services, where the single case is often the standard unit of intervention. Although prevention frequently is looked on as a valuable alternative to remediation, it is seldom put into practice. Perhaps part of the problem has been an inability to appreciate fully such epidemiological constructs as population at risk.

CONCLUSION

Concepts such as "special populations," "vulnerable groups," and "populations at risk" not only tell us about social problems but also about how we relate to those

TABLE 7-2   Selected Social Conditions, by Race and Hispanic Origin, 1987

Social Condition	Race and Hispanic Origin			
	All	White	Black	Hispanic
Money Income of Familes, 1987 (Median)	30,853	32,374	18,098	20,306
Persons Below Poverty Level, 1987 (Percent)	13.5	10.5	33.1	28.2
Familes Below Poverty Level, 1987 (Percent)	10.8	8.2	29.9	25.8
Household Net Worth, 1984 (Median)	32,667	39,135	3,397	4,913
Occupational Distribution of Employed Persons, 1983 (Percent):				
White-collar workers	55.4	56.0	39.5	NA
Blue-collar workers	28.2	27.7	33.1	NA
Service workers	13.7	12.5	24.5	NA
Farm workers	3.7	3.8	3.0	NA
Unemployment Rates, 1985 (Percent)	7.2	6.2	15.0	11.2
Home Ownership, 1983 (Percent)	NA	67.7	46.2	NA
Source of Physician Care, 1983 (Percent):				
Doctor's Office	55.9	57.4	44.1	NA
Emergency Room	14.9	13.4	26.5	NA
Hospital OP Clinic/Phone	15.5	16.2	9.7	NA
Life Expectancy at Birth, 1984:				
Male	71.1	71.8	65.5	NA
Female	78.3	78.8	73.7	NA
Infant Mortality Rates, 1983 (per 1,000 live births)	11.2	9.7	19.2	NA
Admissions Rates to Public and Private Psychiatric Services, 1980 (per 100,000):				
State and County	163.6	136.8	328.0	NA
Private	62.6	63.4	57.5	NA
Duration of Placement for Children in Foster Care, 1982 (Percent):				
1-6 months	NA	26.7	18.0	22.7
7-12 months	NA	15.5	13.4	7.9
13-24 months	NA	20.2	13.6	15.8
25-48 months	NA	18.3	20.1	19.7
49-59 months	NA	3.9	8.2	20.2
60 months or more	NA	13.8	26.4	11.8
Unknown	NA	1.5	0.3	1.9

ADAPTED FROM: Statistical Abstracts of the United States; S. M. Rosen, D. Fanshel, and M. E. Lutz, Face of the Nation 1987: Statistical Supplement to the 18th Edition of the Encyclopedia of Social Work. Silver Spring, MD: National Association of Social Workers, 1987.

problems. Our underlying concern is to distinguish "true" need. The political atmosphere of the past two decades focused increasing attention on the costs of social programs that many critics argued were ineffective at best and part of the problem at worst.[41] Because of serious cuts in the funding for human services during the 1980s, the notion of the "truly disadvantaged" emerged. Identifying populations at risk seemed like a useful way of determining who was "truly" in need and therefore deserving of assistance. Yet, there are at least three important ways in which the concept of population at risk can be misapplied.

First, as noted above, this term can serve as a subtle means of "blaming the victim." Ryan alerted us to this issue some two decades ago, and we obviously need to remain vigilant.[42] It is an easy step to go from identifying a group as being at risk of a particular condition to interpreting their behavior or attitudes as being responsible for their problems. For example, in a case study of school reform in a southern city, Ray and Mickelson found that explanations based on fundamental problems related to social structure often give way to facile explanations of individual responsibility. In this study, erosion in the quality of education was largely because the school system became overburdened by rapid urban growth. However, the issue of school reform became identified in terms of "children-at-risk"—certain children seen as the core of the problem because of their lack of "correct" school work habits and attitudes. According to Ray and Mickelson:

> The business-led school reform movement, nationally and as it was manifested in Sunbelt City, has become institutionalized; business intervention in education on behalf of business goals has been legitimated. Moreover, the emphasis on low-income families as the source of the problem neatly blames the poor for U.S. corporate leaders' relative weakness in world markets, allowing the latter to escape examination of their role in exacerbating domestic poverty through the expansion of unstable jobs that offer low annual wages, no security, and few advancement possibilities.[43]

Second, the concept of population at risk implies that we can clearly distinguish who is at risk and who is not. There are, then, serious ethical and value principles to keep in mind when applying this notion. In most cases, we take two chances with the people we identify as being in the risk group: misclassifying them and stigmatizing them. Our ability to predict who has what problems is seriously limited, and most statistical relationships reflect modest levels of association at best. Although children of alcoholics, for example, have been found to be more likely to develop alcohol problems as adults than children whose parents have not been diagnosed as alcoholic, by no stretch of the imagination do most— or even a majority—of the former develop drinking problems.[44] Specifications of populations at risk generally will be overinclusive. As a result, when applying such information based on group-level analyses to individual situations—especially if our identification is negative (labeling someone "alcoholism-prone")—we need to avoid committing the ecological fallacy.

Finally, even if the concept of population at risk is applied as a framework for research and social planning, its value is limited. For example, epidemiological studies of groups at risk often are descriptive in nature, with little theoretical or conceptual orientation guiding the design. The characteristics used to distinguish who is at risk often are based on traditional rather than theoretical issues, and analysis of data typically is simplistic.

NOTES

1. E. L. Gomberg, "Special Populations," in *Alcohol, Science & Society Revisited,* eds. E. L. Gomberg, H. R. White, and J. A. Carpenter (Ann Arbor: University of Michigan Press, 1982), 337–54.
2. C. H. Murray, *Losing Ground: American Social Policy 1950–1980* (New York: Basic Books, 1984).
3. E. A. Segal, "Welfare Reform: Help for Poor Women and Children?" *Affilia* 4 (1989): 42–50.
4. R. G. Smart "Addiction, Dependency, Abuse, or Use: Which Are We Studying with Epidemiology?" in *Drug Use: Epidemiological and Sociological Approaches,* eds. E. Josephson and E. E. Carroll (New York: Wiley, 1974), 23–42.
5. There have now been seven Special Reports to the U. S. Congress on Alcohol and Health, from the Secretary of Health and Human Services (or previously the Secretary of Health, Education, and Welfare), published and disseminated by the National Institute on Alcohol Abuse and Alcoholism. The first report appeared in 1971, followed by the second in 1974, the third in 1978, the fourth in 1981, the fifth in 1983, the sixth in 1987, and the seventh in 1990.
6. M. R. Burt and K. J. Pittman, *Testing the Social Safety Net* (Washington, DC: Urban Institute, 1985).
7. Whether resources were as limited during the Reagan era as many politicians and social analysts argued is debatable. Resources being put into human services were certainly restricted, but the United States engaged in one of the most massive military buildups in history during the 1980s. See, for example, Kevin Phillips, *The Politics of Rich and Poor* (New York: Random House, 1990).
8. P. H. Rossi, H. E. Freeman, and S. R. Wright, *Evaluation: A Systematic Approach,* 3rd edition (Beverly Hills, CA: Sage, 1979).
9. A. Walsh, "Twice Labeled: the Effect of Psychiatric Labeling on the Sentencing of Sex Offenders," *Social Problems* 37 (1990): 375–89.
10. R. A. Zucker, "Is Risk for Alcoholism Predictable?" *Drugs & Society* 3 (1989): 70.
11. Ibid., 71.
12. R. A. Stallings, "Media Discourse and the Social Construction of Risk," *Social Problems* 37 (1990): 80–95.
13. Ibid., 81.
14. Smart, 24.
15. S. K. Kachigan, *Statistical Analysis* (New York: Radius Press, 1986).
16. Zucker.
17. K. J. Rothman, *Modern Epidemiology* (Boston: Little, Brown, 1986), 16.
18. Classic statements on the "culture of poverty" include O. Lewis, *Five Families: Mexican Case Studies in the Culture of Poverty* (New York: Basic Books, 1959) and D. P. Moynihan, *The Negro Family: the Case for National Action* (Washington,

DC: U. S. Government Printing Office, 1965); this proposition has recently seen a resurgence, e.g., W. J. Wilson, *The Truly Disadvantaged: the Inner City, the Underclass, and Public Policy* (Chicago: University of Chicago Press, 1987).

19. C. A. Ray and R. A. Mickelson, "Corporate Leaders, Resistant Youth, and School Reform in Sunbelt City: the Political Economy of Education," *Social Problems* 37 (1990): 178–90.

20. W. Ryan, *Blaming the Victim* (New York: Pantheon, 1971), 13.

21. W. J. Wilson.

22. O. Lewis, "The Culture of Poverty," in *On Understanding Poverty: Perspectives from the Social Sciences,* ed. D. P. Moynihan (New York: Basic Books, 1968), 187–200.

23. Murray.

24 L. Mead, *Beyond Entitlement: the Social Obligations of Citizenship* (New York: Free Press, 1986).

25. C. Marks, "Occasional Laborers and Chronic Want: A Review of William J. Wilson's *The Truly Disadvantaged,*" *Journal of Sociology and Social Welfare* 16 (1989): 57–68.

26. Ibid., 58–59.

27. Ray and Mickelson.

28. Ibid., 183.

29. Rossi et al., 97

30. H. R. Rogers, Jr., *Poor Women, Poor Families* (Armonk, NY: Sharpe, 1986), 44.

31. P. L. Berger and T. Luckmann, *The Social Construction of Reality* (New York: Doubleday, 1966); C. I. Waxman, *The Stigma of Poverty* (New York: Pergamon, 1977).

32. Parents' Resource Institute for Drug Education (PRIDE), *National Survey Shows Black Students Less Likely to Use Drugs than White Students* (Atlanta: National Parents' Resource Institute for Drug Education, Inc.).

33. "More Americans than Ever Are Crammed into Prisons," *Columbus Dispatch* (April 24, 1989), p. A6.

34. M. A. Strosberg, I. A. Fein, and J. D. Carroll, eds., *Rationing of Medical Care for the Critically Ill* (Washington, DC: Brookings Institution, 1989).

35. E.g., C. L. Estes, "Aging, Health, and Social Policy: Crisis and Crossroad," *Journal of Aging & Social Policy* 1 (1989): 17–32.

36. D. Nachmias and C. Nachmias, *Research Methods in the Social Sciences,* 2nd ed. (New York: St. Martin's, 1981).

37. E. Babbie, *The Practice of Social Research,* 5th ed. (Belmont, CA: Wadsworth, 1989).

38. R. O. Washington, *Program Evaluation in the Human Services* (Washington, DC: University Press of America, 1980).

39. Rothman.

40. Kachigan.

41. E.g., Mead, Murray, Wilson.

42. Ryan.

43. Ray and Mickelson, p.187.

44. R. J. Biedler, "Adult Children of Alcoholics: Is It Really a Separate Field for Study?" *Drugs & Society* 3 (1989): 133–42.

PART FOUR

Technology, Decision Making, and Human Services

This section of the book extends the discussion of the use of inquiry in the social and political world. In particular, two forms of inquiry are presented: the technology of needs assessment and the technology of program evaluation. The technology is seen as being directly related to choices relative to certain major concepts—need, risk, and prevention (presented in Chapters 6 and 7). Discussion of choices relative to these major concepts is presented in the overall context that such choices reflect interests and values in the larger society, and perhaps in the human services professions.

Even though detailed discussion of the technology of needs assessment and program evaluation will be presented in Chapters 8 and 10, choices, values, and interests are seen as proximate to the "pure technology." In fact, Chapters 9 and 11 identify some of the major questions and issues inherent in the selection and use of specific technologies. This section of the book emphasizes that technology—including technology in the social welfare arena—is shaped and influenced by political, organizational, and professional interests.

CHAPTER 8

The Technology of Needs Assessment

INTRODUCTION

Twenty-five years ago, a request for a "needs assessment" would have met with bewilderment. Now its meaning is clearly understood throughout the health, education, and human services fields, and it is readily seen as a particular application of social research methods and a means of acquiring information for specific purposes. Needs assessment has achieved legitimacy as a kind of social research in the usual ways by which scientific activities receive acceptance (see Chapters 2 and 3). Descriptions of research using these techniques have become commonplace in the books, journals, and reports that make up the professional literature of the human services and applied social sciences. In addition, courses or segments of courses in university curricula in many applied fields introduce these methods to novice professionals.

Whereas similar earlier research could probably be identified, the term *needs assessment* was first used in the 1960s. This was a dramatic time, especially in the social service and education arenas. For the first time in America's history, broad governmental involvement in matters of health and well-being came about. Problems such as poverty entered public awareness, and a nationwide consensus emerged among policy-makers and decision-makers, as well as social critics, that these problems could be ameliorated through public intervention. As a result, existing social services were expanded and new services were mandated by Congress.[1]

At the same time, another sentiment was emerging. Throughout the twentieth century, science and technology had demonstrated a profound capacity to modify the environment and to alter the circumstances under which we live. As noted earlier, professionals in the social services and education, partly to legitimate their activities, adopted precepts of the positivist version of science. However, this enthusiasm for applying science to social services was not simply self-serving; social service professionals also had a sense that research could help establish the adequacy of social interventions. Rather than relying on the perceptions and beliefs of the authorities who established and managed them, social programs, it was felt, should be examined to establish concretely their success or failure. Consequently, the legislation that authorized these new and expanded services required that assessments of the extent of problems or needs be done as part of program planning and development and to serve as a basis for evaluating their effectiveness. Since that time, a number of methods for doing needs assessments have been developed, with an increasing emphasis on objectivity and quantification.[2]

Initially, methods for doing needs assessment grew out of the philosophical orientation that came hand-in-hand with the call to action by the social activists of the 1960s. As Summers notes:

> Needs assessment is far more than a matter of choosing techniques for gathering information about citizens' preferences or discovering failures in the delivery of public services. It is a special case of citizen participation, and participation issues are essentially questions of value.[3]

Needs assessment, then, was originally seen as a mechanism for giving the people a voice in decisions about what needs existed and what services should be provided. If there was a problem with the process of making public policy, it was that this decision-making power was monopolized by the professionals and the politicians. As Summers stresses: "In the United States we are taught that citizens have a right to be heard and to expect that elected leaders and other officials will be responsive."[4] By asking the people what their problems and needs are and then incorporating that information into policy decisions, the social policy process could be democratized. Concerns and goals of the elite would have less influence on the outcome of public policy.

During the early years of needs assessment practice, this philosophy was common: Communities were brought into the decision-making process, and efforts were made to orient social programs around the needs and desires of clients. A "community action" orientation was advocated in many areas of human services (e.g., welfare rights and community mental health movements).[5] As needs assessment developed and became more refined as a social research technology, this original aim was overshadowed by positivistic science, which, as we have seen, requires rationality, the province of "experts" whose credentials demonstrate competency. As a result, most current discussions of needs assessment focus mainly on its mechanical or "how-to" aspects.[6]

THE PURPOSE OF NEEDS ASSESSMENT

The primary goal of needs assessment is not simply the production of information, especially in contemporary applications. Rather, its goal is to produce information that can be used in concrete and relatively objective operations. According to Siegel, Attkisson, and Carson:

> Assessment provides one important informational input to a much broader planning process that leads to (a) the selection of and priority setting among problems and target populations to be addressed; (b) the selection and operationalization of specific

community program activities; and (c) the evaluation of these program activities. Assessment information helps to assure that there will be additional inputs to prevent sole reliance on professional formulations of service needs and/or to prevent overriding influence by the most vocal or powerful community groups in program planning.[7]

To provide information for those purposes, a clear grasp is required of what are the appropriate needs. Yet, as discussed in Chapter 6, the nature and identification of human needs is a complex and potentially confusing matter. Although we may feel intuitively that needs are pretty unmistakable and indisputable, disagreement over their nature and extent will be found in any practical situation.

Conceptual Frameworks and Human Needs

Much of the difficulty in establishing the "right" needs revolves around the conceptual framework used to understand a particular problem area. If, for example, the problem area is drug use/abuse among young people, a variety of options are available to determine need, one of which is to ascertain who is using how much of what substances. Presumably that information will help establish what programs might be needed. Yet, it would probably give extremely limited information—unless the research was guided by some framework that could help determine what variables should be measured and how they relate to needs and services.

A basic research methods text would advise that research be developed within the context of a theoretical or conceptual framework.[8] Unless the research is grounded in existing theory and empirical findings, we run a serious risk of selecting inappropriate variables or inadequate research designs that consume a lot of time and resources while producing little of value. Remember, research is not done in a vacuum of simply collecting "facts and figures." Sanders and Pinhey, in comparing the work of a detective and a scientist, point out that detectives do not work without a theory that guides them in looking for particular facts:

> Take for instance the investigation of a criminal homicide, and the eternal question of detective fiction, "Who done it?" Without some kind of theory, everybody in the entire world could be a suspect, but since detectives operate with theory, not only do they focus their investigation on certain people, they are able to center it around key questions. In the case of the typical homicide, detectives theorize that the killer is someone related to the victim. Such a theory is based on their past observations and experiences. As a result of this theory, they closely question husbands, wives, business partners, friends, and others who are related to victims. Now it may turn out that the murderer was a total stranger, but because of the assumptions of the detectives' theory, they begin their inquiry with friends and relatives of victims. As can be imagined, without *some kind of theory* to guide an investigation, literally billions of people could be suspected of a single murder.[9]

In similar fashion, theory assists the social researcher in deciding what information is relevant and what information should be anticipated. The facts obtained may or may not be consistent with our theory, but at least they establish a starting point. Otherwise, how can we decide what questions are relevant in our survey of drugs? Do we just ask people what they do, or do we also focus on friendship patterns and family relationships? Do we presume that *all* substance use is problematic?

By far, the weakest link in most needs assessment research—regardless of the problem area of concern—is the application of a conceptual framework.[10] Needs are taken for granted (as are those factors that identify populations at risk); yet, without adequate conceptualization of the nature of the problem and of those most at risk, it is unlikely that the needs being assessed will be framed so that sound indicators can be identified. For example, we might be concerned with job training for older people with inadequate retirement incomes that need to be supplemented by working. Yet, without examining the local labor market, we may end up with information that is limited in utility. The result might be that many older people who want to work may be found to lack certain skills or may face discriminatory hiring patterns.

At the very least, we need to identify three categories of variables before attempting a needs assessment: (1) predisposing variables, (2) need or problem variables, and (3) enabling variables.[11] Problems and services do not exist in isolation. People often have particular characteristics that put them at risk (*predisposing variables*); they possess varying economic, social, environmental, and personal resources (*enabling variables*); and various dimensions exist on which needs can be defined, such as physical health, income security, or housing adequacy (*need variables*). Selection of variables within each of these three categories should be guided by theory relevant for the particular problem area. There is no social problem for which valuable theory does not exist, and practitioners and planners in the human services do themselves a disservice if they ignore social science theory.

Identifying Needs or Conditions

Most needs assessment research is concerned with identifying who has what needs or problems. Finding the appropriate indicators for those social or physical conditions is problematic, but determining the extent of problems and the characteristics of those most in need is essentially what needs assessment is about. Doing so suggests talking to someone, and a variety of options are available as to who is asked what questions.

In Chapter 6, we discussed Bradshaw's four categories of social needs: normative, felt, expressed, and comparative.[12] By and large, these different ways of identifying human needs focus on particular groups who have the appropriate information. Normative need is defined by what *experts perceive* as need, whereas felt need refers to what *people themselves* say they need or want. Expressed need focuses on service agencies, because need is identified in terms of requests for service. Finally, comparative need elicits an analytic approach, where we first determine the characteristics of recipients and then establish the total population sharing those characteristics. In all of these cases, we try to develop an index of need based on the perceptions, reports, or records of a particular group, whether that group be experts, the community at large, service providers, or those who not only have problems but who also request services. Even if we focus on the use of services, we need to distinguish among those who are aware of particular services, those who indicate that they might use services, and those who actually use services.[13]

By far, the most common research method in the contemporary social sciences is survey research, the purpose of which is to obtain relevant data by talking to people.[14] "Talking" can be done in a variety of ways: face-to-face interviews, phone surveys, group-administered surveys and questionnaires, and self-completed questionnaires. The goal in each is to compile data by posing appropriate questions directly to an audience. Because most needs assessment research is carried out in this way, it should come as no surprise that this technology has drawn heavily from social survey methods. In fact, as we will see, one of the most common methods for doing needs assessment is the large-scale population survey, whether it is focused on a general population or a specific target group.

Factors Influencing the Conduct of Needs Assessment

In previous discussion of science and the creation of knowledge, we saw that scientists operate within a social, political, and economic context. Social science is not value-free, and social researchers are members of a culture who share beliefs, attitudes, perceptions, expectations, and values. Nowhere is this more evident than in applied social research such as needs assessment and program evaluation.

Ostensibly, application of research to the human services is intended to have beneficial outcomes, ultimately enhancing the impact and effectiveness of those services. Many factors are cited as being responsible for the increasing emphasis on the need for social service research, including:

- Recognition of consumers' or clients' perceptions of services by decision-makers and service providers;
- Improvement in effectiveness of service administrators and providers;
- Acknowledgment of limited social resources and the need for information to assist in their equitable and efficient allocation; and
- Legislative mandates on the provision of public funds for human services.[15]

Eliminating Politics: Rational Allocation of Resources.   Advocates argue that one of the major benefits of needs assessment is its potential as a mechanism for making rational choices for resource allocation. In this way, the political character of needs assessment can be eliminated or substantially reduced. In discussing the application of needs assessment to mental health concerns, Goldsmith and his associates make this argument:

> Stated from the perspective of state mental health authorities (currently the key organizations concerned with needs assessment), needs assessment allows one to allocate scarce resources in a rational manner. It can indicate if sufficient potential clients (persons with unmet needs) warrant establishing an outlet for one's product (in this case, mental health services).[16]

To allocate resources rationally, decisionmakers need to know not only a population's needs but also its potential demand and use for those services. Therefore, market factors can be considered in the provision of social services (just as they are in the provision of general consumer goods). In this sense, social services may be seen as a commodity for which supply and demand factors apply, as they do in the provision of health services.[17] In fact, critics have complained that market researchers long ago established effective ways for determing need and demand, especially in the pursuit of "rational resource allocation."[18]

Accepting the Reality of Politics: Roles and Actors.   The question becomes one of *who* interprets information and decides *what* resources are allocated *where* (who defines "the market" and what it should provide for whom). In recent years, these decisions more and more have come to be made within large organizations that provide particular mass services. As Hobbs has pointed out:

> Vesting greater control and responsibility for satisfying human needs in the hands of bureaucratically organized agencies does more than reflect a more active role of society. It also drastically alters the relationship between those having needs and those allocating resources pertinent to satisfying those needs. It introduces roles— those with needs become "consumers" or "clients"; the service/resource agencies become "providers."[19]

Carrying out a needs assessment is a political process, and a variety of actors may participate, depending on the scope of the problem and the nature and extent of the service providers. Hobbs's distinction between "clients" and "providers" is crucial, but it also is necessary to delineate other roles as well, including distinguishing among different kinds of "providers." In Ohio, for example, the Department of Human Services, in administering public welfare for the state, allocates resources and defines rules. Yet, the rules are applied in all 88 counties by local departments, which have a degree of autonomy or discretion. Aside from this, various layers of politics affect perception of problems and allocation of resources. These layers range from local community leaders to state officials; journalists to professors; local entrepreneurs who contract for job training, drug treatment, or day-care services to large businesses such as health services or supermarket chains. It is within that context that needs assessment takes place.

    It is critical to grasp the political and social nature of needs assessment and how those forces interact with the research process. Specific factors that influence the conduct of needs assessment center on identifying the relevant actors:

- Who chooses what problem is looked at;
- Who identifies what information is to be collected and how;
- Who analyzes and interprets that information;
- Who establishes the time constraints under which the needs assessment is conducted;
- Who controls access to and dissemination of the information; and
- Who controls the extent to which potential recipients will be included in the process.

Summer's concept of "democratic governance" may be an ideal in our society, but it is questionable how democratically governed public policy actually is in the United States.[20,21] Such are the issues to confront before turning attention to the technology of needs assessment.

NEEDS ASSESSMENT TECHNIQUES

While there is a wide variety of techniques for carrying out needs assessments, there is little or no consensus or preference about which particular method is best or most useful. In fact, some critics say that the diversity in methods has created confusion and problems because they lack apparent logic or conceptual order.[22] It is true that, to a large extent, categorizing needs assessment procedures is an arbitrary process, but this is just as true of any typology of research methods. More often than not, the research design used in a particular study will draw elements from more than one type of design. Only where research design might be characterized as experimental or as a survey are we likely to identify a single study design. Actually there *is* an underlying logic for characterizing the methods used in specific studies, most of which, as already noted, are a variation on survey research. Again, differences in design revolve around who does the asking, who does the answering, and what the question format is.

The balance of this chapter will examine six common approaches to needs assessment:

- Primary surveys;
- Social indicators analysis;
- Secondary data analysis;
- Examinations of institutional records;
- Service inventories and resource identification; and
- Informal and group techniques.

Surveys and Populations

The social survey is by far the most common method for doing research in the contemporary social sciences, whether that research is basic or applied. The scope of the survey enterprise in contemporary American society is enormous. According to Rossi, Wright, and Anderson:

> Accurate measures of the current total size of survey research activities are simply nonexistent. The fragmentary data that do exist suggest an industry composed of five subsectors that only partially overlap in activity, and who together each year contact 32 million households, conducting 100 million interviews. Assuming that each interview is priced on the average at $25, the total income of the industry is about $2.5 billion. Assuming a higher per interview price, closer to $50, doubles the estimated gross income of the industry to about $5 billion. Since survey interviewing varies widely in cost depending on sampling design, length of interview, method (face-to-face or by telephone or by mail), the toal gross of the survey research industry is probably between these two estimates.[23]

The five subsectors referred to include:

1. The federal government (e.g., Bureau of the Census, Bureau of Labor Statistics)
2. The academic sector (e.g., National Opinion Research Center, Institute for Social Research)
3. The private sector (e.g., A. C. Nielson, Louis Harris and Associates, the Gallup Organization)
4. The mass media (e.g., CBS–New York Times poll, ABC and Washington Post poll)
5. Ad hoc and in-house surveys (e.g., AT&T polls of employees or customers, local community planning groups doing community needs assessments)

The goal of most surveys is to collect information about individuals, groups, households, or larger social groups in a systematic and standardized way. Typically, individuals chosen for the study will not comprise all of the people about whom the researcher is interested.[24] The cases that are surveyed are a sample that has been selected in such a way that it cannot represent any larger group, which is generally referred to as a population.

The needs assessment literature distinguishes four types of surveys, based on the nature of the population being surveyed: general population, target population, service provider, and key informant.[25]

General Population Surveys.   Probably most common among social service practitioners, a general population survey draws the sample from a specified population, which typically will be geographically delimited. For example, we might be interested in the student body at the Ohio State University; individuals residing in the Columbus, Ohio, metropolitian area; persons living in the state of Ohio; the population in the North Central region of the United States; or, perhaps, the adult population of the country. General population surveys, then, focus on broad population groups, although regional or national studies may specify who is included (for example, persons of legal drinking age or noninstitutionalized persons). Criteria for who is included depend on the nature of the study.

In Bradshaw's terms, one goal for a general population survey is to identify felt need.[26] That is, the information can be used to describe what problems are recognized or acknowledged by members of the sample. If respondents are asked to report in terms of themselves or their families, individual and household characteristics can be correlated with indicators of needs or problems to identify what kinds of individuals or households are most (or least) likely to have specific problems.

In most general population surveys, a large body of information is collected so that the research is reasonably efficient in terms of cost, time, and labor. As a result, depending on the specific information obtained, general population surveys can be used for much more than identifying incidence and prevalence rates. They can be used to identify relationships between different needs or problems; the extent to which people are eligible for services within the population as a whole; the extent to which eligible cases make use of services; perceptions of barriers to the use of services as well as attitudes toward and perceptions of service providers (practitioner groups and agencies); and perceptions of the magnitude of particular social problems in the community.

Washington points out several issues that should be considered so as to ensure optimal use of data from a general population survey.[27] First, we need to identify carefully what needs are to be assessed. Otherwise, our results are likely to be vague and thus open to challenge. Second, the sample must be defined and selected with precision. Because the goal is to generalize findings to the population within the limits of sampling error, a random sample is needed. To estimate sampling error, we must use random sampling methods. Third, it is important to include questions that ask respondents about their behavior as well as their attitudes. In many needs assessments, the focus tends to be on attitudes, under the presumption that those attitudes will be related to behavior. Yet, in many cases, attitudes are not good predictors of behavior.[28] Finally, data should be included about service eligibility, because not all those with a problem will be eligible. If the findings are intended to provide projections about the need for services, then information is needed on how many cases in the population are eligible rather than simply how many have that problem or need.

Because of the prominence of survey research, a large body of professional expertise can be drawn on in designing and carrying out such research. When carefully done, sample surveys can provide extremely valuable information. At the same time, they pose serious disadvantages as a tool for conducting needs assessments. For example, although they appear flexible (because almost any question can be asked), they can be quite rigid, especially when questions are designed to maximize standardization. In most cases, response categories as well as questions will be standardized. If problems or needs are poorly conceptualized, then response categories and questions may yield confusing, vague, or misleading information.

General population surveys also are expensive, not just in terms of dollar costs but also in time and staff effort. Rarely is it possible to complete one involving a sample size of, say, 1,500 to 2,000 cases in less than six months to a year. More work may be involved than was recognized when a project was proposed—needs defined, instruments designed, interviews or questionnaires completed, data processed, extensive analysis completed, results interpreted, and a report prepared.

Another problem is lack of skilled staff. Although in some cases work can be contracted out, agency personnel still are needed, especially in the concept and design stages. In-house staff are needed to help in interpreting results. As noted earlier, quantitative social science provides "facts," but those "facts" need to be given meaning before they can be applied to policy or service delivery.

Target Population Surveys.   In certain circumstances, general population surveys are inefficient for finding individuals with specific problems—those "at risk." This is the goal of a *target population survey.* For example, if our concern is with people who have drinking problems, we will probably find only a handful of such cases in a general population survey. This is because, although about two-thirds of the U.S. adult population drinks, only some 10 percent are expected to display a drinking problem. In a sample of 1,000 people, then, although 650 would probably acknowledge that they are current drinkers, only about 65 would be found to have a drinking problem. Such a small sample would seriously limit the analysis.

In principle, then, this target population survey technique is not really different from a general population survey. The nature of the target population will still need to be carefully delineated and a random sample of the relevant population drawn, if our goal is to generalize the results from the sample to the target population with any degree of confidence. Drawing such a random sample may be no easy task. In our example, finding the population with drinking problems from which a random sample might be drawn could be extremely difficult in that we may be unable to identify those with the condition unless they are in treatment. Yet, if we use individuals in treatment, we will probably get a biased sample. More than 10 million people are estimated to have drinking problems, whereas no more than a half million are in treatment.[29] Generalizing research results based on a sample of alcoholics in treatment to the total population of alcoholics could produce erroneous conclusions.

Specifying the target population accurately is crucial, a process that, according to McKillip, begins by determining eligibility criteria and the missions of social agencies:

> Human service agencies have income, disability, and geographic restrictions for their clients. Agency mission statements may limit services by sex, or by religious and ethnic group membership. Target population descriptions should identify the number of potential clients within each of the eligibility and mission restrictions. For example, if an agency is targeting senior women with incomes of less than $5,000 a year, it is the population with this combination of characteristics that needs to be described.[30]

In addition to eligibility factors, McKillip also suggests that important demographic characteristics (income or age) be taken into account. In some cases, eligibility criteria will include demographic factors (age or income limits).

As Washington notes, target population surveys provide certain kinds of information beyond that obtained in general population surveys.[31] With the target population survey, the focus is still on felt need but now in terms of those who are most likely to be in need. One can, of course, make comparisons between perceptions of needs among target populations and among general populations, as long as both kinds of data are available. In addition, target population surveys allow the researcher to focus attention on perceptions of barriers to receiving services, needs for services that are currently unavailable, and service effectiveness and client satisfaction.

Obviously, the results of a target population survey cannot be generalized beyond that particular population. If we are interested in documenting the extent of need, regardless of service eligibility limitations, then a broader population would have to be sampled. One also needs to guard the rights of respondents who are either eligible for or are receiving services. Their survey participation should be completely voluntary, and their responses should in no way jeopardize their receipt of services. If an agency needs to monitor its clientele, as is the case with recipients of AFDC, then that monitoring would be unethical and immoral if carried out in the guise of research.

Service Provider Surveys.   Questions in general population and target population surveys may be quite sensitive or negative, and people may have difficulty in answering them accurately because of embarrassment or fear of losing services. Consequently, *service provider surveys* offer another way of getting information about such issues because, as Washington notes, they can provide "a valid and rich source of information about such unmet needs for service and can complement information provided by other respondent groups."[32] They are another potentially valuable source of information about community problems and barriers to service—a source directly from the service provider community itself.[33]

Information from service providers can be used to collect data about agency and community resources; characteristics of those using various community resources; and problems and needs for service that are not either widely recognized or socially acceptable (teen pregnancy, sexually transmitted disease).

In most cases, provider surveys can be carried out quickly and easily because the population of providers is relatively limited in most communities, and a sampling frame (or list of relevant individuals) can be established without much difficulty. For instance, a researcher can identify agencies or organizations concerned with child welfare, day-care provision, or mental health services. These surveys often focus on direct service staff but can include supervisors and administrators as well. In fact, it may be quite useful to compare the perceptions and concerns of different kinds of practitioners; comparing mental health workers with practitioners in the field of mental retardation and developmental disabilities, for example, might provide valuable information concerning awareness and understanding of dual diagnosis.

Because most service providers are professionals in terms of educational backgrounds, licensing provisions, job descriptions, and so forth, such surveys address what Bradshaw calls normative need; i.e., what "experts" define as need in a particular situation.[34] Although that information may be of value, it must be recognized that such data may also reflect certain biases. Rather than identifying client problems accurately, the data may reflect cultural and class biases on the part of service providers—especially if client and provider differ demographically (race, age, gender, socioeconomic status). Used alone, service provider survey results could be open to charges of paternalism, or the agency's mission could bias service providers perceptions. Because providers are likely to have a vested interest in the continuation of their agencies, they may tend to identify problems that relate to the services provided by their agencies. In most cases, it is probably best to use service provider surveys in conjunction with target population and/or general population surveys. Biases can arise in any type of survey, and comparative data can help unravel these biases and provide more useful information.

Key Informant Surveys.   All communities have individuals who can be identified as leaders or as representatives for particular community groups or constituencies. These "key informants" can be questioned for needs assessment purposes, because they are in key positions and, presumably, can provide relevant information about the community's needs and problems. According to Rothman and Gant, "Such key informants may be formal leaders such as agency board members, elected officials, or ministers. However, informal leaders should also be contacted." These are grass roots individuals, whom people seek out for advice or assistance even though they hold no formal positions.[35]

In the needs assessment literature, key informant surveys generally are characterized as a quick and inexpensive method for collecting data. One needs mainly to identify "opportunistically connected" individuals who are likely to be knowledgeable about their communities.[36] Although that sounds relatively straightforward, it may not always prove to be so, particularly if key informants are drawn largely from individuals holding formal positions within their communities. Their "expert" opinions can be as biased as those of social service practitioners or planners. In fact, they may have their own political agendas. In Chapter 6, we noted the political nature of the "drug problem" in America, where massive public attention is focused on the problem when most kinds of licit and illicit drug use are, in fact, declining.[37] If our key informants were police officers or elected officials, then we would probably find that our community had an enormous drug problem. As with the other three types of surveys, key informant surveys are probably most useful as a data source if used to complement other kinds of information.

Key informant surveys can be as complex and large in focus as any other type of survey. In many cases, however, they are "quick and dirty." A handful of cases may be interviewed, using an in-depth, qualitative approach rather than a standardized, quantitative format. But they can be carried out in the traditional survey form. Several years ago, the Ohio Department of Mental Health carried out a study on the mental health problems of the homeless. A target population of more than 1,000 homeless was surveyed in one phase of the project. In another phase, several hundred key informants (local officials, service planning representatives, members of advocacy groups) throughout the state were also surveyed, using a standardized interview format.[38]

Key informant surveys may have their most value outside of their application as a method of collecting data. As we have already seen, the planning and provision of social services is just as political a process as any other social activity. In that context, key informant surveys provide a means for developing support for the modification of existing services or the creation of new services. They can be used to build a constituency or identify pockets of resistance. By including formal and informal community leaders, the democratization of community governance can be facilitated.[39]

Social Indicators Analysis

Many public and private organizations collect vast amounts of information on the health and well-being of various populations, ranging from local communities to the nation as a whole. In most cases, the data would not measure particular needs or social problems directly, but some of the measures might provide "indicators" (or "proxies") for human needs. Identifying appropriate social indicators for particular problems within this wealth of information could then provide another way for projecting levels of need. As Bell and his associates pointed out, the use of social indicators makes certain critical assumptions:

> The underlying assumption of the approach is that estimates of the needs and social well-being of those in a community can be made by examining selected social and demographic descriptors that have been found to correlate highly with service utilization. In other words, some social indicators are accepted as empirical predictors of need.[40]

Two assumptions are involved in using social indicators to determine need. First, there is the assumption that social and demographic factors will be *highly correlated* with service utilization; second, there is the assumption that service utilization rates by themselves are indicators of level of need.

As Bell and colleagues document, there is a tradition in the American social sciences "to relate the quality of human environments to dysfunctional manifestations."[41] In many cases, the focus is on establising how environmental and social conditions relate to individual problems, especially in identifying populations at risk. Although demographic factors are certainly correlated with many problems, the main concern is the strength of those correlations. As Bell and colleagues pointed out, using social indicators to estimate need levels presumes that such relationships are strong.

Limits of Statistical Analysis.   Unfortunately, strength of association is a matter of interpretation, and most correlations between social and demographic variables and various kinds of social problems are, at best, modest. This is true, in fact, of most associations between variables in social science research: empirical relationships are generally far from perfect.[42] Is a correlation of .40 moderate or strong? What about a correlation of .60? Of .80? We know that the closer a correlation is to + or − 1.00, the stronger it is. Rarely are the results of social research strong and unequivocal, and, in most cases, they demonstrate weak to moderate relationships. In fact, we generally have to use statistics simply to establish the existence of relationships. That is, statistical analysis is used as a means for establishing the level of confidence we can have in our results, with that level of confidence expressed in probabilistic terms. Often, the statistics used (such as the t-test or the analysis of variance) only tell us whether there is a "statistically significant" relationship without providing direct information about strength of association, as the correlation coefficient does.

The fact that social science empiricism is imperfect does not mean it cannot be used.[43] Rather, it means that we need to take care in how we apply research findings, and nowhere is that more evident than in the use of social indicators.

The Broad Nature of Social Indicators.   During the past 20 years, the use of social indicators has increased substantially, and the federal government periodically releases large compilations of such social statistics. Most of the variables in these analyses focus on "quality of life" issues, including:

- Population characteristics (gender, age, racial composition);
- Economic factors (income levels, assets of households, expenditure patterns);
- Employment characteristics (occupational patterns, unemployment rates, amounts of work);
- Family patterns (marital and divorce rates, single-parent status);
- Educational characteristics (attainment, school drop-out rates);
- Housing (condition of housing units, overcrowding, type of structure);
- Physical and mental health (long-term disability, causes of death, prevalence and incidence rates of illnesses);
- Crime indicators (crime rates, contacts with law enforcement agencies, fear of crime);
- Fertility and child-care patterns (number of children, expectations about having children, child-care expenses);
- Recreational patterns (leisure activities, participation in sports); and
- Life-satisfaction indexes (measures of happiness and well-being or of community solidarity).[44]

This sort of information provides a broad picture of a particular community or geographic area. However, by itself it is unlikely to lend insight into specific program issues or particular needs. Do high unemployment rates, for example, mean there will be greater utilization of mental health services? Will average weekly earnings, the death rate from cirrhosis of the liver, suicide rates, or divorce rates predict mental health utilization rates? Even if they do, how accurately will those factors predict such rates? Can we project utilization rates for next year, based on the average unemployment rate for this year? Will the same characteristics predict different rates from one period to another?

Utility of Social Indicators.   As we have stressed, social indicators used to assess needs should be carefully chosen. Need levels cannot be measured accurately unless we can clearly conceptualize those needs. Social indicators analysis has the appearance of simplicity and convenience for conducting needs assessments, in that data are compiled regularly by governmental, regulatory, or private organizations. Yet, that apparent ease can be misleading in that the value of this method hinges on the ability to document a strong link between the selected indicators and the needs they are supposed to represent.

Where the analysis of social indicators can be especially valuable is in identifying trends over time.[45] Because such data generally are collected as part of a continuing process, they can depict how particular conditions may be changing. For example, was drug use more prevalent in 1990 than in 1985? Has the violent-crime index increased, remained constant, or decreased during the past five years? How does life expectancy today compare with 1950 or 1900? What proportion of older people were below the poverty line last year, compared with five years before? Has there been an increase in the number of single-parent families, and what projection can we make for the future?

Limitations of Social Indicators.   Where the use of social indicators is most limited is in applications to local program decision-making. Data are often based on national sample surveys of large populations or compilations of utilization rates over broad geographic areas. If information is disaggregated to the local level, there may be relatively small samples left on which to base projections. Statistical estimates, then, may be unstable because of very high error rates. Furthermore, questionable assumptions may need to be made in order to make projections to future years (e.g., predicting the size of the elderly population based on current fertility rates).

Another serious problem with social indicators lies in the ecological fallacy.[46] In predicting group-level phenomena, we need to be careful about projecting those findings to individuals. That is, when we find statistical relationships between particular social and demographic characteristics and specific problems, those results are based on aggregate or group data. Such findings cannot tell us *which* individuals will have problems. For example, we may find that certain characteristics, such as gender or age, are related to the use of particular chemical substances. That does not tell us,though, that specific person with those characteristics will suffer from the particular problem—only that people with those particular characteristics are more likely than others to experience a problem. We need to be extremely careful in generalizing from group-level phenomena or relationships to actual individuals.

Secondary Data Analysis

Collecting data is a costly and time-consuming activity. In many situations, it also is unnecessary. We noted above that many organizations, especially governmental bureaucracies and academic institutions, are responsible for compiling data on a regular basis. A number of archives (e.g., the Inter-University Consortium for Political and Social Research at the University of Michigan) now contain literally thousands of sample surveys. These data, available for nominal or modest fees, are accessible by means of appropriate computer facilities, including statistical software and programming expertise.

The goal of secondary analysis is to use existing data to answer particular questions. In contrast to the use of social indicators, the intent here is to find data that were originally compiled for other purposes but that can be reanalyzed because they have clear relevance to the mission of a particular organization.[47] In other words, secondary data analysis involves manipulating existing data, whereas social indicator analysis often is done as a primary activity or uses data in an existing form without further analysis.

Secondary analysis can range from simple, where a handful of variables are enumerated, to complex, where a large number of variables and their interrelationships are analyzed using multivariate statistical procedures. Whether simple or complicated, two factors—access and relevance—need to be taken into account in deciding whether this is an appropriate method of needs assessment. If suitable data are readily available, then this can be a quick and direct needs assessment strategy to apply.

The first problem to resolve is access—determining what is available and in what form. As mentioned, archival services specialize in providing the results of large sample surveys in so-called machine-readable form, which generally means making raw data files available on nine-track tapes that can be used on mainframe computer systems. The data are called "raw" because they are provided as numeric data that are not structured by a statistical or data base program. In other words, they can be read by many computers, but the data will have to be programmed before an analysis can be done. In addition to data, then, the archival service will provide documentation for the data base—identifying what variables are located where so that they can be programmed and analyzed.

More important than access is relevance. The fact that data are readily available does not mean that they will be germane to the research questions being posed. Unless data unquestionably relate to the research objectives, a secondary analysis may end up being little more than an exercise in futility.

If applicable data can be found, then it is important to document their reliability and validity; not all data bases are equally sound. Some organizations and institutions are more careful than others in conducting their research. Consequently, the documentation provided with the data needs to be examined in terms of the rigor with which the sampling plan was carried out (if a survey was involved), as well as the adequacy (i.e., the reliability and validity) of the instruments used in the data collection. Rubin has identified several guidelines for assessing quality of data:

- Determine the social, political, or organizational circumstances that define how the data-gathering agency chose to maintain the data series (i.e., data are not simply "neutral" collections of facts but were collected by an organization for some purpose where political, social, and economic factors influence the research process).
- Check the professional reputation of the source of the data.
- Check the continuity of the data series (i.e., how long the data have been compiled by a particular organization).
- Examine the internal consistency of the data (i.e., its reliability).
- Examine the operationalizations of the terms used by the data-collecting agency (i.e., measurement validity).[48]

If data appear to have relevance and if the quality is satisfactory, then secondary analysis can provide useful information. As with the other methods discussed, it is probably best to use secondary analysis in conjunction with other techniques, because the weaknesses of a particular method can be offset by the strengths of other approaches.

Examination of Institutional Records

In many situations, reviewing administrative or managerial records can provide valuable information.[49] These materials can be used to identify client characteristics, the volume of services and to whom they are provided, requests for services that are unavailable from reporting agencies, and referral patterns between different organizations. Examining institutional records is an activity that any given agency can do for itself, or a survey may be conducted by a particular organization or by an outside body of the various agencies and programs located in a geographically defined area. Even if other needs assessment strategies are intended, this process should probably be done as well. As Washington has suggested, "Every needs assessment process should begin with a review of management data. This is relatively simple to do and provides important clues regarding apparent needs reflected in demand for services, trends in services delivered, target populations or areas requiring special study."[50]

In a sense, this procedure is similar to secondary data analysis, in that existing information is analyzed for a different purpose than that for which it was originally designed. It differs from secondary analysis in the nature of the information used and the source from which it is drawn: organizational records. A good way to conceptualize this process is to look at it as an examination of rates under treatment, where we are trying to identify the size of the group at risk based on knowledge of the characteristics of those receiving services at a specific agency or agencies. According to Rossi, Freeman, and Wright: "The assumption underlying this approach is that the characteristics of the desired target population and its size will parallel closely the attributes of those who have already received treatment."[51] This can provide information about expressed need and comparative need, in Bradshaw's terms.[52] By identifying the numbers and characteristics of those receiving treatment, we get information about expressed need—what Bradshaw calls "felt need turned into action." Then, by determining the characteristics of those receiving services and then comparing the client group with the total population having those same demographic and social characteristics, we can ascertain comparative need, which is the extent of people in need who are not receiving services.

Examining administrative records is probably easier now than in the past, because of the extent to which records have become automated in social service agencies during the past decade.[53] Although some agencies still have not computerized their records, many have, especially larger organizations. As a result, getting data on rates under treatment not only has become simpler but more comparable from one agency to another. In the past, records were maintained in file folders, and many organizations designed their own forms (or at least decided what information would be recorded on face sheets), which allowed only limited comparability from one agency to another. Automation has led to more conformity in record keeping, because many organizations use either the same or similar software packages in processing records about clients, staff, and agency activities.

The problem with these data probably will be accuracy. Once basic information has been entered into computerized systems, records are seldom checked or verified. Information entered inaccurately is likely to stay that way, and updating of files is also likely to lag, because in most agencies data entry is not a priority task. In addition, decisions about what information to keep are based on administrative needs, and data that could have research value may not be seen as relevant or important and therefore may not be included in the design of a data base.[54] As Washington notes: "In order to maximize the use of administrative data in ascertaining needs, care should be taken to define data needs as reporting systems are developed."[55]

Service Inventories and Resource Identification

A service inventory identifies what resources exist in a community. It may be focused simply on determining what agencies provide which kinds of services, or it may supply information on how many units of service are provided to how many clients with what specific characteristics.[56] In most cases, the information on service providers and their programs can then be compiled, published, and disseminated as a community resource in its own right.

Generally, a service inventory will take the form of a survey, where agencies are contacted and asked to supply the following details:

- What services they offer (including definitions of services);
- What constitutes a unit of service;
- Descriptions of their service areas;
- How many units of service they delivered during a particular time in their service areas; and
- The characteristics of clients to whom they provided services during a given period.

Analysis of such data can be used to identify not only extent of need but also overlap and gaps in service delivery. Determining duplication and gaps may be the most valuable outcome of a service inventory.

The major problem with service inventories is comparability of definitions of service types and units from one agency to another. Some time ago, the United Way attempted to develop a typology of services that would reduce the ambiguity in resource surveys. The typology was called *UWASIS: A Taxonomy of Social Goals and Human Service Programs* (UWASIS is an acronym for United Way of America Services Identification System).[57] This system, which has gone through several editions, has been applied by a number of researchers but is rather cumbersome and has met with limited success.

Informal and Group Techniques

Techniques described so far often require specialized skills or significant amounts of time and resources. In addition, they provide highly structured and quantitative information. However, there are certain methods (described below) that are simpler and quicker to carry out: some of these alternatives also provide more qualitative information or more directly acknowledge the role of politics in analyzing human needs.

Delphi Panels and Nominal Groups.   The Delphi panel, which dates back to the early 1950s, was one of the first procedures used.[58] About a decade later, a method now called the nominal group technique (a group ''in name only'') was developed.[59] Both approaches involve groups of people but limit actual interaction among them, in order to control for some of the factors considered to be potential biases for group-generated products. The nominal group approach was designed deliberately to provide a mechanism that would promote brainstorming while offsetting personal and social factors known to influence the creation of ideas in group settings.[60]

The Delphi panel eliminates all interaction. According to McKillip: ''The procedure is flexible and combines anonymous gathering of quantitative estimates, feedback to respondents, and the opportunity to alter responses because of the feedback."[61] The process begins by focusing on what needs are relevant and who can provide that information. After a questionnaire has been constructed, it is distributed, usually through the mail, to a panel of "experts." Each respondent completes the questionnaire in isolation, so there is no group interaction, although variation in opinion and fact can still be generated. Panel size can range from a handful to several hundred experts, depending on time, resources, and the nature of the problem.

After the initial round of questionnaires has been compiled and analyzed, the panel is provided with a new copy of the questionnaire that includes the distribution of responses elicited from the panel for each question. The panelists are then given an opportunity to change their responses based on the feedback. There may be several more rounds, until the investigators feel that they have realized as much agreement as possible on the various questions. Clearly, the goal of a Delphi panel is to achieve consensus. It has the strength of a group approach, where a large number of people are asked to provide information or opinions. Yet, by eliminating contact, it controls for the typical dynamics of group interaction, where a small number of people may have undue influence because of personalities or communication factors.

For a Delphi panel to be effective, two elements are critical. First, a questionnaire design must provide valid and reliable information. That is, a good deal of structure and standardization may be involved in the questionnaire, but, if important questions are posed in an open-ended format, a high level of writing ability may be required from the panel. Second, the method requires a significant amount of time—a questionnaire must be designed, distributed, collected, and then compiled during each succeeding round. A *minimum* of 45 days is generally recommended for a Delphi panel.

The nominal group approach allows more of a group process to take place. A working panel is physically brought together, and, if more than a dozen or so people are present, they will be separated into several small work groups. According to Miller and Hustedde, the nominal group "can be viewed as a brainstorming technique where people work in each other's presence but write their ideas independently."[62]

Typically, a small group will be presented with a question or problem. They will be asked to write down any ideas that come to mind within a limited time, usually 5 to 10 minutes. Each person in turn will be asked to present an idea, until no one has a new idea to offer. Those ideas will be written on a flip chart or chalkboard, so that everyone in the group can see each one. Next, the ideas will be clarified in terms of agreement and disagreement; argument, however, is discouraged, although the group will be encouraged to combine what comes to be seen as similar ideas. After that process, group members are asked to prioritize the ideas on a sheet of paper. Votes are then tallied and recorded alongside the ideas as listed on the flip chart or chalkboard. Finally, the group reaches a consensus on the listing of priorities by discussing and rating the various concepts.

If several small groups are working independently, the same process is followed to arrive at a final set of prioritized ideas.

The nominal group process is much quicker than that of the Delphi panel. Even with complex issues, the intent is to complete the process within a single working day or no more than two or three days. In certain respects, the nominal group approach simply takes a routine staff or public meeting and structures it toward accomplishing a particular goal. As Miller and Hustedde point out: "It differs from routine meetings in that it attempts to maximize the input of every individual present and minimizes the domination of the most vocal people as well as the noninvolvement of the most reticent participant."[63] At the same time, participation in a nominal group can be rather cumbersome and tedious.

Public Forums.   Public forums provide members of the community with an opportunity to participate in an open meeting where they can voice their concerns. Success depends on the nature of the forum and the extent to which the public is invited. Some forums are likely to have widespread notice and involvement, whereas others may be restricted to groups with particular agendas or vested interests. Regardless, public forums are probably the most direct method of mixing needs assessment with political process; at least, it is in this context that politics are most readily apparent. Some critics argue that a public forum is not "scientific" or at least "not representative." It certainly does, however, harken back to the goal of citizen participation.[64]

McKillip distinguishes between what he calls the "public hearing" and the "community forum."[65] The public hearing is generally a formal process, involving a committee that takes testimony from "expert witnesses," who are likely to be questioned and cross-examined. Attorneys may be present to assist witnesses representing different groups or to direct the committee's questioning of witnesses. Most presenters are likely to represent an interest group and may be paid to participate. As a result, community representation is apt to be limited to formally recognized groups. After the hearing is completed, the committee may prepare and publish a summary report.

The community forum is intended to include the community more broadly. Published notices will indicate where and when the forum will be held, and attendees will be given a chance to make a brief statement. Although less formally structured than the public hearing, the community forum will need to establish and enforce presentation rules, one of which is length. The goal in this case is not so much to collect data but to build public support for a particular issue or public program. Names and addresses of attendees usually are requested, so that follow-up contacts can be made, especially to encourage further political participation by those in agreement with forum conveners. If adequate notice is made and the issue deemed important, this technique can provide invaluable information about public sentiment—especially that segment of the public that is most likely to act.

CONCLUSION

A wide variety of methods exist for doing needs assessments, each providing different information. Depending on the circumstances, we can probably acquire useful data from any one of these methods. A rule found throughout the needs assessment literature is to use as many approaches as possible rather than relying on a single one. The weaknesses of any one technique can be offset by the strengths of other methods, and different approaches often provide complimentary information.

Note, however, that most of the techniques discussed have some elements of similarity, and most are a variation on survey research methods. Survey types include general population, target population, service provider, and key informant surveys. Social indicators and secondary data analysis draw generally on surveys of a particular population group or geographical area. Social indicators specifically deal with well-being, whereas secondary data analysis simply means borrowing someone else's data and applying them to another set of issues. In both cases, we work with "proxies" for our concerns with social problems or human needs; hopefully we selected those indicators wisely. Examination of institutional records is another kind of survey of existing information. In this case, the material surveyed is collected from administrative or managerial records. Next, we turned our attention to service inventories and resource identification, another kind of survey. However, in this case, the focus is on what services are available in a community and to whom those services are provided. Finally, we looked at group techniques and public forums; both approaches are concerned with who participates (who is sampled) and what is asked.

The social survey is a common and well-established research method, but it has some important limitations.[66] First, a number of potential sources of error or bias are inherent in the methodology, including the adequacy of the sampling frame, the representativeness of the actual sample, and the nature of the questions asked (e.g., content, form, order). Second, information of interest to the researcher may be difficult for people to recall accurately. For example, in surveys on health, questions often concern how many days of work were missed last year or how many times a respondent visited the doctor. Such questions are difficult to answer accurately without making a time-consuming check of personal records. Third, questions about attitudes often are important elements in surveys. Yet, attitudes may not be highly related to behavior, which is of most concern in needs assessment. Finally, most surveys are cross-sectional, carried out at only one point in time. As a result, they give information only about that historical point and present a nondynamic view of the world.

In addition to these broad shortcomings of survey methods, there are some specific limitations relative to needs assessment that have to be addressed as well. Who is involved and their roles affect outcomes. We should also be concerned with the limited use of conceptual frameworks in needs assessment studies and ought to assess the application of findings from needs assessment research. These issues will be addressed in the next chapter.

NOTES

1. D. Hobbs, "Strategy for Needs Assessments," in *Needs Assessment: Theory and Methods,* eds. D. E. Johnson, L. R. Meiller, L. C. Miller, and G. F. Summers (Ames, Iowa: Iowa State University Press, 1987), 20–34.
2. B. R. Witkin, *Assessing Needs in Educational and Social Programs* (San Francisco: Jossey-Bass, 1984).
3. G. F. Summers, "Democratic Governance," in Johnson et al., 3–4.
4. Ibid., p. 4.
5. E.g., F. F. Piven and R. A. Cloward, *Regulating the Poor: the Functions of Public Welfare* (New York: Vintage, 1971); W. A. Kimmel, *Needs Assessment: a Critical Perspective* (Washington, DC: Department of Health, Education, and Welfare, 1977); G. J. Warheit, "Past Trends and Future Directions," in *Needs Assessment: Its Future,* eds. H. F. Goldsmith, E. Lin, R. A. Bell, and D. J. Jackson (Washington, DC: Department of Health and Human Services, Mental Health Service System Reports, Series BN No. 8, 1988), 6–12.
6. Witkin; J. McKillip, *Needs Analysis: Tools for the Human Services and Education* (Newbury Park, CA: Sage, 1987); K. A. Neuber, *Needs Assessment: a Model for Community Planning* (Newbury Park, CA: Sage, 1980); P. H. Rossi and H. E. Freeman, *Evaluation: a Systematic Approach,* 4th Ed. (Newbury Park, CA: Sage, 1989), Chapter 2; L. M. Siegel, C. C. Attkisson, and L. G. Carson, "Need Identification and Program Planning," in *Evaluation of Human Service Programs,* eds. C. C. Attkisson, W. A. Hargreaves, M. J. Horowitz, and J. E. Sorensen (New York: Academic Press, 1978), 215–252; R. A. Bell, T. D. Nguyen, G. J. Warheit, and J. M. Buhl, "Service Utilization, Social Indicator, and Citizen Survey Approaches to Human Service Need Assessment," in R. A. Bell, pp. 253–300; W. J. Reid and R. R. Friedman, "Needs Assessment" in *Research in Social Work,* eds. W. J. Reid and A. D. Smith (New York: Columbia University Press, 1981), 295–309; J. P. Hornick and B. Burrows, "Program Evaluation," in *Social Work Research and Evaluation,* 3rd ed., ed. R. M. Grinnell, Jr. (Itasca, IL: Peacock, 1988), 400–420.
7. Siegel et al., 221–22.
8. E. Babbie, *The Practice of Social Research,* 5th ed. (Belmont, CA: Wadsworth, 1989); N. K. Denzin, *The Research Act,* 3rd ed. (Englewood Cliffs, NJ: Prentice-Hall, 1989); B. S. Phillips, *Social Research: Strategy and Tactics,* 3rd ed. (New York: Macmillian, 1976); H. W. Smith, *Strategies of Social Research,* 2nd ed. (Englewood Cliffs, NJ: Prentice-Hall, 1981).
9. W. B. Sanders and T. K. Pinhey, *The Conduct of Social Research* (New York: Holt, Rinehard, and Winston, 1983), 19–20.
10. Z. Harel, L. Noelker, and B. F. Blake, "Comprehensive Services for the Aged: Theoretical and Empirical Perspectives," *Gerontologist* 25 (1985): 644–49.
11. Harel et al.; H. F. Goldsmith, D. J. Jackson, and R. L. Hough, "Process Model of Seeking Mental Health Services," in Goldsmith et al., 49–64.
12. J. Bradshaw, "The Concept of Social Need," *New Society* 30 (1972): 640–43.
13. Harel et al.

14. P. H. Rossi, J. D. Wright, and A. B. Anderson, "Sample Surveys: History, Current Practice, and Future Prospects," in *Handbook of Survey Research,* eds. P. H. Rossi, J. D. Wright, and A. B. Anderson (Orlando, FL: Academic Press, 1983), 1–20.
15. E. J. Posavac and R. G. Carey, *Program Evaluation: Methods and Case Studies,* 3rd ed. (Englewood Cliffs, NJ: Prentice-Hall), 16–18.
16. H. F. Goldsmith, E. Lin, D. J. Jackson, R. W. Manderscheid, and R. A. Bell, "The Future of Mental Health Needs Assessment," in Goldsmith et al., 80.
17. P. Starr, *The Social Transformation of American Medicine* (New York: Basic Books, 1982); J. H. Ehrenreich, *The Altruistic Imagination* (Ithaca, NY: Cornell University Press, 1985).
18. R. C. Kessler, "A Critical Evaluation of Mental Health Needs Assessment," in Goldsmith et al., 75–78.
19. Hobbs, 21.
20. Summers.
21. For example, see G. W. Domhoff, *Who Rules America Now?* (Englewood Cliffs, NJ: Prentice-Hall, 1983); T. R. Dye, *Who's Running America?* (Englewood Cliffs, NJ: Prentice-Hall, 1976); C. W. Mills, *The Power Elite* (New York: Oxford University Press, 1956); F. F. Piven and R. A. Cloward, *Why Americans Don't Vote* (New York: Pantheon, 1988).
22. Kimmel.
23. Rossi, Wright, and Anderson, 9–10.
24. Denzin; Babbie; Sanders and Pinhey.
25. R. O. Washington, *Program Evaluation in the Human Services* (Washington, DC: University Press of America, 1980).
26. Bradshaw.
27. Washington.
28. W. P. Archibald, *Social Psychology as Political Economy* (Toronto: McGraw-Hill Ryerson, 1978).
29. Secretary of Health and Human Services, *Sixth Special Report on Alcohol and Health* (Washington, DC: U. S. Government Printing Office, 1987).
30. McKillip, 44.
31. Washington.
32. J. Rothman and L. M. Gant, "Approaches and Models of Community Intervention," in Johnson et al., 35–44.
33. Washington, 149.
34. Bradshaw.
35. Rothman and Gant, 38–39.
36. McKillip, 81.
37. D. B. Heath, "The New Temperance Movement: Through the Looking Glass," *Drugs & Society* 3 (1989): 143–68; M. Fraser and N. Kohlert, "Substance Abuse and Public Policy," *Social Service Review* 62 (1988): 103–26.
38. D. Roth, J. Bean, N. Lust, and T. Savenau, *Homelessness in Ohio: a Study of People in Need.* (Columbus, Ohio: Ohio Department of Mental Health, Office of Program Evaluation and Research, 1986).
39. Summers.
40. Bell et al., 266.
41. Ibid., 267.
42. Babbie, 59–60.

43. M. E. Spenser, "The Imperfect Empiricism of the Social Sciences," *Sociological Forum* 2 (1987): 331–72.
44. Bell et al.; Washington.
45. Rossi and Freeman.
46. Bell et al..
47. Washington; T. M. Meenaghan, R. O. Washington, and R.M. Ryan, *Macro Practice in the Human Services* (New York: Free Press, 1982).
48. H. J. Rubin, *Applied Social Research* (Columbus, OH: Merrill, 1983), 314–16.
49. McKillip; Rothman and Gant.
50. Washington, 153.
51. P. H. Rossi, H. E. Freeman, and S. R. Wright, *Evaluation: a Systematic Approach,* 3rd ed. (Newbury Park, CA: Sage, 1979), 105.
52. Bradshaw.
53. K. M. Kilty and C. Dilday, "The Humane Use of Information Technology in the Social Services," paper presented at the First International Conference on Human Service Information Technology Applications, Birmingham, England (September, 1987).
54. M. L. Gruber, R. K. Caputo, and T. M. Meenaghan, "Information Management," in *Human Services at Risk,* ed. F. C. Perlmutter (Lexington, MA: Lexington, 1984), 127–46.
55. Washington, 153.
56. Washington; United Way, *Needs Assessment* (Alexandria, Virginia: United Way of America, 1982).
57. United Way.
58. L. C. Miller and R. J. Hustedde, "Group Approaches," in Johnson et al., 91–125.
59. Witkin, 133.
60. Miller and Hustedde, 112.
61. McKillip, 90.
62. Miller and Hustedde, 112.
63. Ibid., 112.
64. Summers.
65. McKillips, 91–92.
66. Babbie.

CHAPTER 9

Crucial Issues in Needs Assessment

INTRODUCTION

The limits of objectivity and rationality are no more apparent than in applying the social sciences to an understanding of human needs. Many early advocates of needs assessment realized just how limited that process was. In fact, their goal was not simply to generate data that could be used in making decisions about priortizing problems and allocating scarce resources. Rather, it was to lead to greater citizen participation in (or democratization of) the public policy process.[1] As they saw it, policy choices are not made in a vacuum devoid of values and ethics but within a social, political, and economic context, where different social groups vie with each other.

Traditionally, many social analysts have argued that the American political structure is pluralistic in nature, where power (or influence) is broadly distributed throughout the various segments of society. However, studies of the dispersion of power in the United States—whether at the local or national level—clearly show that some groups have substantially more influence than others, especially on the development and implementation of public policy.[2] Class, race, and gender have been among the most important factors that distinguish the more powerful from the less powerful. Although these divisions have not always been blatantly apparent, they have surfaced and led to serious social unrest at various points in time, including the middle to late 1960s. Those most affected by policy choices— generally the vulnerable and oppressed—often have the least influence on the policy process. Needs assessment was seen as a pivotal means for changing the policy equation by giving the powerless a voice.

CITIZENS, EXPERTS, AND TECHNOLOGY

To understand the purpose of a needs assessment project, one must look beyond the focus or topic of the study to two other equally important matters: who is doing the needs assessment and for whom it is being done. By looking at the evolution of this technology over the past 25 years, we find dramatically different answers to the questions of who is doing the research and who is using the results.

More and more, the importance of the role of the citizen—including the citizen who is also the client—has been eroded by an expansion in the role of the expert. This becomes evident by examining the popularity of various methods of acquiring information about human needs.

"Objective" versus "Subjective" Identification of Need

According to Summers, there are two intrinsically different ways of doing needs assessment: "the social indicators approach and the self-report approach."[3] As we have seen, the social indicators approach focuses on identifying variables that can be used as proxies for needs. If needs are clear, then we simply identify factors that can "stand in" for them, especially "objective" indicators (unemployment rates, infant mortality rates, cirrhosis of the liver deaths, and so on)—measures that do not require asking people directly about their problems. How well the system is functioning can be determined from the difference between what we define as satisfactory levels of social functioning and what is empirically observed. If the "acceptable" unemployment rate is 5 percent, then any discrepancy between that standard and observed unemployment rates that is greater than zero implies that there are problems. The point, then, is that there is no need to ask people themselves about the problems they may be experiencing. Needs are self-evident, and identifying their extensiveness or the nature of the groups at risk is merely a question of finding appropriate gauges, especially by using standard vital statistics or statistical series.

In contrast, what Summers calls the "self-report" approach is based on a much different set of assumptions, in this case the presumption that decision-makers probably do *not* know people's needs. In effect, so-called objective indicators in the form of existing statistical materials will be neither self-evident nor necessarily valid; rather, the best source of information about needs is people themselves. This approach to needs assessment implies that its purpose is not just to serve in collecting data, which in fact may be a minor activity. From this perspective, the role of needs assessment is to provide citizens with a way of making their needs *known* to those in decision-making roles. Surveys of community groups (especially target populations) and the use of public forums and group processes (where community members make up the groups) are instrumental in giving the public a voice. In fact, Summers argues that the main focus here will be articulating needs to decision-makers, since community groups already will know what needs should be addressed.

Methods and Citizen Input versus Expert Input

In considering the methods reviewed in Chapter 8, we can easily sort them into Summers's two general categories, because we are really dealing with "felt need" versus "normative need," that is, either needs identified by those potentially in need or by those in decision-making positions—citizens versus experts.[4] In this

TABLE 9-1 Conceptualizations of Need and Techological Choices

Technological Choices	Conceptualizations of Need	
	Citizen Input	Expert Input
	[felt need]	[normative need] [expressed need] [comparative need]
Surveys		
General Population	X	
Target Population	X	
Service Provider		X
Key Informants		X
Social Indicators Analysis		X
Secondary Data Analysis		X
Surveying Institutional Records		X
Service Inventories and Resource Identification		X
Informal and Group Techniques Nominal Groups/Delphi Panels		X
Public Forums	X	

regard, we can classify expressed need and comparative need as variations on normative need. In the final analysis, both types of need are based on expert opinion or analysis and do not necessarily take into account the perceptions of the community or of those actually in need. In effect, the public can be ignored in the need identification process, just as it is when needs are conceptualized within the framework of normative need.

Table 9-1 summarizes the technological choices that have developed for doing needs assessment during the past quarter-century, contrasting them in terms of whether needs are identified based on citizen input or on expert input. By and large, most of the methodological options fall into the "expert input" category. Experts identify what issues or questions to include (in the case of service provider or key informant surveys and group methods), the types of indicators that will be the focus of analysis (in the case of existing data), or what to look for (in the case of reviews of administrative records). Only general and target population surveys and public forums provide direct citizen input. Yet, even with these surveys, the methodological issues of question content and sample selection probably will fall mainly to experts.

As mentioned, previous concern with including clients and other community representatives in the needs assessment process has become less common. The relevance of what is measured or identified as indicators of community well-being or satisfaction have been eclipsed by a focus on effect. At one time, citizens' groups or private individuals were included in the review bodies that oversaw the development of methodology, but even that practice has faded. Now experts do everything, from conceptualizing what issues to include to identifying the populations that should be surveyed or what indicators will stand for what needs. These experts will often be removed from the communities they are assessing, bringing different perspectives on the problems of that community than would its residents themselves. In most cases, the experts and the citizens will have had very dissimilar life experiences. The experts are likely to represent a privileged social group; they are generally well-educated white males with high incomes and stable jobs. In contrast, the citizens—especially if they are clients or potential clients—will probably represent disadvantaged social groups (minorities of color, poor or single heads of household, or individuals with combinations of these characteristics).[5] Obviously, their perceptions of problems and means for coping with them may differ.

The central issue here is not whether differences exist in perceptions about problems and services. Needs assessment is a technology that is presumed to benefit social service organizations and their clients by providing information that can be used in program planning and service delivery. Presumably, then, the service clientele benefit most from that technology, but is that really the case? Who are the main beneficiaries—those who need the services or those who apply the technology?

Technological Development and Decision Making

As technology develops, it places more and more stress on rationality and objectivity. After all, isn't the goal in applying the scientific enterprise to human services to provide a sound basis for practice, to legitimize the social services as professions?[6] Scientific method—particularly the positivist tradition—forces us to be logical and dispassionate, focusing our attention on demonstrating effectiveness by operationalizing our goals and creating suitable empirical referents. We study certain "objects" using reliable and valid "instruments." In effect, we need to separate ourselves as researchers from the people whom we study. Ideally, the instruments we design should not rely on self-reports from clients (although in some cases, we may want such data), but should lead us to identify sources of information that are independent of the subjects of our research—employment records, school participation rates, medical reports. As a result, recipients of social interventions become literally "objects"—both for service delivery and for research.

We should not be surprised by this objectification of people—after all, is "social engineering" any different from other kinds of engineering by which we manipulate the environment to modify certain conditions by intervening to change certain elements? In the case of the human services, that manipulation revolves around introducing particular interventions (social programs) with the goal of bringing about change in certain objects (individuals or groups of people). Welfare clients, for example, are presumed to lack basic work skills and habits, as well as proper motivation to hold down a job and "better" themselves. Therefore, we design a program, with certain incentives and sanctions (receipt or loss of services), that will produce the desired outcome (holding a "steady" job and/or leaving the welfare rolls) in those objects (welfare recipients).[7]

To a large extent, rationalization and objectification are seen as a means of simplifying the planning and decision-making process. That is, they make the job of the planner and administrator much easier by providing a set of guidelines requiring certain expertise for those who participate in that process. In general, allocation of social and economic resources is responsive to a variety of forces within a community, including the political structure, the business leadership, and the professional social service community. Introducing the citizenry into the planning equation only complicates an already confusing political process, especially if the goal of this process is to arrive at a consensus on what needs exist and what services should be provided. A pluralistic political process is generally regarded as unlikely to lead to carefully reasoned decisions. According to MacRae:

> When professionals, service bureaucracies, and their clients bargain about needs, there are risks that each set of professionals and bureaucrats will unconsciously exaggerate the efficacy of their own services and the extent of their clientele's needs, that client representation will be biased toward persons associated with the professions, and that taxpayer interests will not be adequately represented. For these reasons among others, a systematic analysis of the values expected to result from serving these needs, if introduced into the political process, may lead to better social results than political bargaining alone.[8]

In other words, social services decision making needs to be shifted from the political arena to one of "reasoned argument," particularly in examining what outcomes are intended. Decisions about public policy need to be made on a rational basis. How better to do so than by introducing procedures that emphasize objectivity and limit the range and number of actors to be included?

Technology, Participation, and Consensus

The goal of policy-makers is to bring about a consensus concerning needs and interventions. However, if there are competing constituencies, the likelihood of reaching agreement is reduced. What we need, then, is a basis for promoting consensus among the groups that participate in the decision-making process. One option is to find a mechanism that produces "rational" decisions. Decisions based on reason should be cogent and readily acceptable. According to Hill and Bramley:

> The attractions of consensus are obvious if you are in the business of making policy prescriptions. There is a solid foundation of agreement about ends, the political heat is taken out of the debate, and attention can focus on the technical, professional and administrative tasks of selecting the best means. It seems that need is a concept which has been seen as consensual, a basis for agreement and action, whether because of the idea of objective necessity or because of some shared values born of common humanity.[9]

Bringing experts into the policy equation simplifies the process, presumably by making consensus more likely. If we carefully design research that will provide quantitative indexes, then all can plainly see the extent of the problem and agree on a solution. There is no need to rely on a competitive political process, where vested interests and differing values can clash. Even if citizens groups become involved, they can also be provided with those unequivocal data, typically in the form of tables and graphs. If objective facts are laid out on the table, dissension and disagreement evolve into reasoned argument and, ultimately, to discussion and agreement. Anything else would be irrational.

Two distinct issues underlie the discussion thus far. First, we need a means for obtaining clear and unequivocal data; at this point, the most attractive solution to that problem is the scientific method. Second, only certain people have the backgrounds and skills to apply the scientific method properly; that means we need experts to obtain the necessary information. As we discussed earlier, science is still typically regarded as a purely intellectual and dispassionate activity, one that can provide a means for making decisions largely unaffected by subjective factors such as values or political orientations.[10] Therefore, the public can be better served by restricting the collection of information to the "scientific" experts. Then, the "planning" experts can apply that information to their decision-making activities. How can there be legitimate disagreement with cold, hard "objective facts?"

Technology Serves Whose Interests?

The next question is to what extent can needs assessment as a research tool produce objective results? Restricting who participates in the process certainly reduces conflict, but mainly it serves the interests of those who control the resources. In effect, it limits who looks at the problem, which means that it limits *how* the problem is looked at. A problem can be examined in a variety of ways, in terms of what issues are considered relevant and how the data are interpreted. The danger here is that few alternatives will be examined if participants in the decision-making process share similar value orientations and perspectives. By rationalizing decision-making, we limit the range of alternatives that can materialize.

Assume we are designing a program to assist older workers in making the transition to retirement. Because program resources are limited, priorities will have to be established in terms of the range of services and the potential clientele for whom those services will be targeted. As professionals trained in the conventional wisdom of gerontology, we will probably focus our attention primarily on men. Yet Beeson has pointed out, "Retirement has received more attention than any other issue related to later life because of assumptions about its salience for men. Women who retire have been neglected because of parallel assumptions about the relative unimportance of work in their lives."[11] Yet, women are affected by retirement just as much as men.[12] Narrowing the range of life experience among those who ask the questions, then, limits the kind and scope of questions addressed.

Science and the Limits of Discourse

Rationalization is partly the product of bureaucratization.[13] In modern bureaucratic organizations, technical competence is an important element in defining organizational positions and the hierarchy among those positions. Within this context, then, technology serves primarily the needs of those who carry it out. Furthermore, because researchers will be hired by bureaucrats at higher levels in the organizational structure, it is likely that those hired will share the values and goals of those who do the hiring. In social service agencies, the interests of the organization will take precedence over the interests of the clients. In effect, the values and perspectives of those who work for the organization will dictate the issues that get addressed by research. A profound faith in the scientific method is an important element in the worldview of the modern technocratic bureaucrat.[14]

Perhaps we are interested in identifying what factors affect learning. If we are conventionally trained social scientists, one way of looking at that general issue would be to think about making various comparisons. We might hypothesize that more learning takes place in smaller classes. For the sake of argument, assume that classroom size is found to have no demonstrable impact on objective, standardized tests of learning. Is the number of bodies in the classroom the critical issue? Have we measured learning adequately? What if larger classrooms produced higher test scores? Perhaps what is more important is the form of education.[15] In this country, we are most accustomed to the didactic, lecture format, an approach that might not be thought of as a matter for research by most researchers. Actually, if we challenged that issue, we might end up calling into question nearly every school building in the United States. Are we prepared to do away with that structure and all the jobs it provides, any more than we could the social security system or the public welfare system?

As we saw in Chapter 3, the questions raised by social scientists are a function of their education and worldview. Because of experimental design, researchers are oriented toward making comparisons, a strategy that can lead to strange research questions. In recalling Morrell's description of a research proposal by the RAND Corporation on desegregation in the public schools, comparisons were to be made between segregated and desegregated schools.[16] Was that the real point? In effect, the research question became whether segregation was preferable to desegregation. Can we ask fundamental questions by the traditional canons of the scientific method? Will those fundamental questions even be seen as questions, or will our ideologies lead us to ask certain questions over others? In sum, can needs assessment or any other form of social research, whether basic or applied, provide objectivity and rationality that transcend value and ethical assumptions? We must keep in mind that positivism and scientific realism are aspects of Western cultural thought. Furthermore, culture imbues one's worldview with a sense of naturalness that makes it extremely difficult to challenge basic assumptions.[17]

We are not arguing that needs assessment should be avoided. However, if the goal is to get factual information that will provide an unequivocal set of priorities that can be applied to allocation of resources,[18] then one is likely to be sorely disappointed. In fact, that sentiment may be a primary reason for so much concern about the limited use of needs assessment data.[19] Use of a rational, scientific model for doing needs assessment does not necessarily produce consensus. More than likely, it produces the *appearance* of consensus among the administrators, planners, and researchers who are directly responsible for the research. In many cases, that appearance will be subject to challenge by other vested interests among the political and professional social service communities. The results of such research can be used to justify decisions, but that does not mean agreement on those decisions will be widespread, nor does it guarantee the soundness of those decisions. Even if they are indeed rational, such decisions can be quite arbitrary.

CONCEPTUAL FRAMEWORKS AND NEEDS ASSESSMENT

As noted in Chapter 8, one of the most serious deficiencies in needs assessment research concerns the application of theoretical and conceptual frameworks. In most cases, objectives may be stated, but they will often be broad and vague. A methodology will then be selected but without necessarily being linked to the purposes of the research. Although a variety of methodological options are available, in most cases what might be appropriate for a certain situation will not be readily apparent. According to Kimmel, the reason a rationale is seldom used in choosing a method is probably because of the appearance that needs assessment methodologies "are many, heterogeneous and without practical or conceptual links or unifying logic."[20] As we tried to show in the last chapter, that statement is not entirely accurate, in that most needs assessment methods represent a variation on survey research approaches. At the same time, the point that Kimmel made concerning "conceptual links" and "unifying logic" is a major issue that only now is beginning to emerge.

Research Questions and Frames of Reference

Research design is obviously related to the nature of the problem. If we have carefully identified what research questions or hypotheses we want to investigate, then they should guide us in selecting appropriate methodologies. In addition, it will be necessary to determine what kinds of research are feasible and practical. Although a large-scale general population survey might appear the "ideal" way for answering particular questions, resources may not allow such a time-consuming and costly project. Keep in mind, though, that there will never be a single design that is best for studying any particular problem.[21] The background and experiences of the researchers will have a significant impact on what they see as reasonable options. Just as important, though, is having a conceptual or theoretical orientation as a point of reference for framing research questions or issues.

Again, "need" is not self-evident; defining the problems of particular population groups involves value preferences. Even distinguishing the most vulnerable or at-risk population groups is influenced by individual ethical and moral perspectives. At the heart of needs assessment is a concern with particular social problems and the social groups who suffer most from those problems, which means we need to examine carefully our own perspectives. What problem are we trying to understand? Can we identify the conditions, theoretically or empirically, that brought about that problem? Can we identify the characteristics of those most likely to experience that problem?

We do not necessarily need a well-developed theoretical model that can be applied to a particular social problem. However, if we do not apply a framework, we risk producing research of limited utility at best and of questionable validity (due to hidden biases) at worst.

A General Conceptual Framework

In recent years, the need for a conceptual framework has been recognized in needs assessment literature, and attempts have been made to develop general frameworks for particular purposes. In looking at research on service utilization among older people, Harel and his associates proposed a framework that classifies potentially relevant variables into three categories: "These are predisposing variables (demographic and socioeconomic), need variables (physical health, mental health, functional status), and enabling variables (economic resources, living environment, social resources, and personal resources such as life perspective and coping skills)."[22]

Their proposal is certainly a good starting point, for it identifies some factors that may affect certain problems as well as suggests some interrelationships that empirical analysis may find among the variables. The proposal also is extremely limited in that it is intended as a general model independent of substantive issues; that is, it can be applied to any problem area.[23] As a result, the main purpose of the model is to sort variables into three broad classes (predisposing, need, and enabling), but, because the typology is content-free, no conceptual limits constrain those categories. As Harel and his associates go on to say; "Despite this conceptual advance, there is still no agreement among researchers about the most appropriate operational referents for these variable categories."[24] What this means is that choices of variables intended to represent any of those three categories will differ from one researcher or planner to another. In fact, there probably will be disagreement about which category a variable falls in. For example, with AIDS, is life-style (which involves life perspective and coping skills) a predisposing factor or an enabling factor? Could it even be identified by some analysts as an indicator of a need variable?

It is critical to recognize that research is never truly atheoretical; whether we realize it or not, we operate on implicit assumptions about particular problems and the conditions that lead to them. Because of diverse and competing theories of human behavior, social services professionals tend to consider themselves "eclectic," to draw on theory only when it holds promise in practice situations. That orientation certainly sounds good, but it obscures the propensity of most practitioners for relying on certain frameworks more than others when addressing particular clients or problems. Not applying a conceptual framework to a research problem, then, really begs the issue. At best, it might be excused as intellectual laziness, but this can be extremely dangerous. At worst, it can mean imposing a value and ethical frame of reference that goes unacknowledged. Choosing variables, research designs, and study subjects can be fraught with peril, and the application of biased research results can have profound positive or negative impacts on the well-being of service recipients.

APPLICATION OF FINDINGS FROM NEEDS ASSESSMENT RESEARCH

There is a common sentiment among human services professionals that in general the results of needs assessment research have been ignored. In the past, this rejection largely was due to a perception of poor quality surrounding this type of research. For example, in analyzing adequacy of needs assessments of the elderly, Lareau and Heumann concluded that most of the research they located was of such dubious quality as to render it practically useless as a source of information for planners.[25] Similar concerns have been voiced in other fields of social service practice. One might conclude, then, that ignoring the findings of needs assessments has been done with good reason.

Even where the merit of the research was not challenged, still a sense of futility has surrounded needs assessments. In many cases, significant effort was put into projects, only to have the results recorded in a report that no one read. According to Robins:

> While there have been a small group of vocal proponents of the activity who see it as integral to an effective human service planning process, they have been outnumbered by critics who view needs assessment requirements as burdensome, ill-defined and difficult to implement. Even among these critics, none were so fiercely opposed as those who had carried out mandated studies only to find them unused and sitting on a shelf.[26]

A number of matters need to be considered before using findings from needs assessment research. Practitioners sometimes may fear that results will be used against them, especially if an outside group or agency conducts the project. In an era of scarce resources, such fears are certainly not groundless; in fact, if the needs assessment is meant to provide information for establishing priorities in resource allocation, then the findings could be used as "evidence" that particular programs are "less necessary" than others.

In community-wide needs assessments, the group responsible for the project may be viewed with suspicion by other members of the social service community.

Most programs have their own concerns and vested interests, which they may feel were slighted during development of instrumentation as well as data collection and analysis. For example, a series of needs assessments were carried out in the late 1970s in Columbus, Ohio, under the direction of a newly created planning council, which had not yet established its legitimacy. Consequently, the results of these projects became embroiled in controversy and were largely rejected by social service practitioners. Many criticisms dealt with technical matters, but it was clearly a political controversy within the human service community.[27] In general, acceptance or rejection will be contingent on acceptance or rejection of the body (or bodies) responsible for designing and implementing the project. As Robins found, utilization of needs assessment increases substantially when organizations carry out their own projects.[28]

As already seen, it is important to take into account the various actors involved in needs assessments, because they bring to the process a variety of perspectives—some of which will produce conflict. At least six broad categories of actors need to be considered: clients, the community at large, staff, administrators, boards, and researchers. The most likelihood of divergence in perspectives lies between clients and agency staff and administrators. As Sun points out:

> Traditionally agencies and care-givers have been offering services which reflected their interest and specialty. Consequently their services are planned and evaluated based largely on data supplied by program personnel themselves, whose reports reflect some measure of self-protection and self-interest. In many cases, however, the consumer population in question may view its own needs as something other than what the provider normatively views them as.[29]

In some cases, there may be considerable similarity between the perspectives of clients and those of the community as a whole. However, if the client population represents some disvalued group, then there may be little sympathy and concern on the part of the community, which in fact may share the sentiments of the agency staff and administrators. By and large, there is likely to be considerable convergence in perspectives among the agency personnel, including both staff and administrators. They are also likely to display compliance with the views of their boards and their funding agencies, which may lead to perspectives that are sharply divergent from those of their clients or potential clients. Results of needs assessment research, then, are most likely to be used when they are consistent with the prevailing perspectives of community leaders, especially those who serve on boards or control funding resources.

METHODOLOGICAL CHOICES AND SOURCES OF POTENTIAL BIAS

Survey research methodology is well established, and a large body of evidence supports both its scientific soundness and practical utility. Because needs assessment technology draws heavily on the survey method, it can use the strengths of this tradition to provide itself with a degree of legitimacy. When carefully followed, survey procedures can provide valuable and accurate data, although they can not guarantee validity or reliability. A classic example was the failure of the Literary Digest poll, which predicted a victory by Landon over Roosevelt.[30] In recent years, we have grown accustomed to the ubiquitousness of surveys, and we rarely challenge their credibility. Yet, even when done carefully, they do not always provide trustworthy information. In the recent elections in Nicaragua, nearly all polls predicted a convincing victory for Ortega over Chamorro, whereas the outcome was just the opposite.[31]

Several issues can affect the adequacy of survey research, causing biased or inaccurate results. Four critical factors—sampling methods, response rates, instrumentation, and types of surveys data-collection techniques—will be reviewed in the following sections.

Sampling

Populations, Samples, and Sampling Error.   Most survey research seeks to obtain relevant data for a broad *population* of individuals with common characteristics. Ideally, we should include every person in our research, but often that is impractical, especially if the subject population numbers in the hundreds of thousands or millions. Consequently, we must depend on information obtained from a subset—or *sample*—of that population. The goal of sampling, then, is to find a group of cases that can serve as a miniaturized version of the population. If the sample is representative, then its basic characteristics should be nearly the same as those of the population it is intended to represent. Under certain conditions, we can compute a statistic called *sampling error*, which will indicate the *maximum amount of error* likely to occur for that particular sample.[32]

The first step in sampling is to determine the nature of the population. Rarely will we be concerned with all the people living in a particular geographic area. Even most general population surveys eliminate persons under age 18 and institutionalized groups, thus limiting the scope of the population. If our focus is on a target population, we need to select relevant characteristics that identify the population—poverty status, age, race, marital status, or some combination of several characteristics.

Sampling Frame.   Once we decide on the nature of the population, we need to identify potential cases. In other words, we need to establish the *sampling frame*, which we can think of as an "empirical representation" of the population. Ideally, the sampling frame should be a list identifying every relevant case (such as a voter registration list if our sample is to consist of registered voters, or the phone book if it is to consist of phone subscribers, or street addresses for households as the unit of selection). How accurately our sampling frame represents the entire population is a critical matter. For example, if using the phone book, significant numbers of people (perhaps 20 percent or more nationwide) do not have listed numbers; thus, this approach to devising a sampling frame is likely to produce a biased sample, regardless of how we draw the actual cases.

Sampling Methods.   To ensure as representative a sample as possible, most sampling experts recommend use of *probability* or *random sampling methods* (or strategies). It is only with the use of probability or random samples that we can legitimately compute sampling error for a particular sample and then generalize from the sample to the population (i.e., apply inferential or decision-making statistics). Sampling error informs us about the level of bias in the sample; that is, the maximum amount of error that is likely to occur when we generalize results from the sample to the population. In this case, bias does not imply a value statement; rather, it provides us with information about the representativeness of the sample.

Probability Samples.   To serve as an adequate probability sample, a sample must fulfill two conditions: The *chances of selection* for any given case must be *known,* and they must be *greater than 0 percent* and *less than 100 percent.* That is, all cases must have a probability of being included, which probability can be determined without guaranteeing automatic inclusion or exclusion. For a true random sample, all cases would have to have an equal chance of selection, but that is not necessary for a probability sample. The odds of selection can differ, as long as they are known for each case. Sometimes we will want to draw stratified random samples, where certain populations are overrepresented and others are underrepresented. As long as the bias is known, it can be corrected statistically when making population projections.

Problems in Sampling.   A satisfactory sampling frame can be difficult to construct if the population of interest is a group that is socially devalued, or if the problem with which we are concerned is a hidden behavior or event (drug abuse, criminal activities, mental incapacity). If we cannot develop an appropriate sampling frame (one that identifies all relevant cases), then it is impossible to draw a probability sample, which means an inability to generalize from the sample to the population. If the sample is selected using nonprobability (or purposive) sampling methods, sampling error cannot be estimated with precision, and the amount of bias is unknown. Recent efforts to identify methods for studying "hidden populations," have not yet met with complete acceptance by the social science community.[33] Some authors of research reports present computations of sampling error, but with the caveat that such statistics would apply if "this were a truly scientific sample," a caveat that, unfortunately, would be lost on the naive or untrained.[34]

Concerns about sampling may surface whenever the focus of attention is on service populations. Recall the example from Chapter 8, where the concern as with drawing a sample of alcoholics or problem drinkers. Because this is a largely hidden population, trying to create a sampling frame would be quite difficult. At one time, the National Institute on Alcohol Abuse and Alcoholism estimated that, of 9 million alcoholics and problem drinkers in the United States, about 300,000 received services through formal treatment programs and perhaps another 600,000 were members of Alcoholics Anonymous.[35] Even assuming that those two groups do not overlap, less than 10 percent of those having a problem with alcohol receive some sort of treatment. If we then develop a sampling frame based on individuals who are in treatment, will it be representative of those who have the problem? That would seem unlikely, considering how few people are in treatment in proportion to the estimated size of the population. Probably there are serious differences between those in treatment and those having the condition in general, which raises the specter of serious bias. The use of biased samples may also account for the contradictory findings among studies on alcoholism.

Of course, alcoholism is not the only area where sampling bias is a problem and perhaps a major reason for conflicting findings. Studies of homelessness or poverty might also yield nonrepresentative samples. Even in studying the elderly, we could encounter problems in establishing an adequate sampling frame and may have to rely on devices such as membership lists from senior centers. If we *can* identify a sampling frame and try to draw a probability sample, it will be effective only if we have selected the correct population characteristics. Once again, we must confront the extent to which we have properly conceptualized the nature of the problem and the social conditions that led to it. In effect, we must confront the adequacy of our research, i.e., the validity of our research design. Did we get sound answers, or are they open to challenge?

Response Rates

Adequacy of sampling method is only one consideration in deciding on the soundness of a research project. Of equal importance is the *response rate,* which, interestingly enough, is probably one of the most neglected issues in survey research. *Response rate* refers to the extent to which potential cases in a survey are either available or willing to participate. Contact will not be made with every case drawn, and some of the people contacted will refuse to be interviewed or to fill out questionnaires. Although this is seen as a problem, it is not one to which most discussions of survey methods give much attention. For example, although Backstrom and Hursh-Cesar acknowledge that "nonresponse" means that information is lost and the resulting sample may lose some of its representativeness, they dismiss the critical nature of this issue by stating:

> These limitations are not to be interpreted as failures that could be overcome with better survey management. They are instead inherent features of this type of research, which must be kept in mind so that we temper our reliance on the resulting data.[36]

Other writers make note of increasing problems with response rates in recent years but do not provide actual figures.[37]

Statistical projections from samples to populations are based on the assumption that all cases contacted actually participated in the research. Any degree of

nonresponse, then, suggests the possibility of bias. Often ignored, this nonresponse is an essential factor in assessing the validity of survey research. In many
needs assessment projects, the extent of nonresponse may be quite high, calling
into question the generality of the findings. For example, if in a telephone survey
6 out of 10 people respond, that means that 4 out of 10 did *not*. That is a sizeable
refusal or noncontact rate, implying the likelihood of systematic bias in terms of
who was not contacted or who refused to participate. Basing projections on such
a sample to a specific population is a risky venture.

Instrumentation

Surveys are made up of questions, some of which will stand alone and others
which will be grouped to create scales and indexes. Survey content—whether an
interviewer-administered form or a self-administered questionnaire—is another
important threat to the integrity of the information. When assessing this element
of a survey or needs assessment project, several issues should be considered,
including question type, format, content, and sequence.

We want questions and statements that are valid and reliable. If concerned
with instrument validity, we seek to establish the extent to which the instrument
measures what it was intended to measure. In other words, do the questions
tap the issues and problems in which we are interested? Reliability refers to
consistency, where the goal is to create questions that will yield the same answers
from one time to another or that will yield similar answers when the questions
relate to specific topics.[38]

Designing an interview schedule or questionnaire is one of the more problematic tasks in doing survey research. According to Sheatsley:

> Unlike sampling and data processing, questionnaire design is not a science or technol-
> ogy but remains an art. Given the same research task and the same hypotheses, six
> qualified questionnaire writers will be likely to come up with six instruments that
> differ widely in their choice of items, line of questioning, use of open-ended questions,
> and length of time the interview takes. Frequently, a good a priori case can be made
> for any of them. Furthermore, all researchers know that when they start analyzing
> their data, they are sure to find that some of the questions are useless to the task,
> whereas others that are sorely needed were somehow omitted from the design. There
> are no pat or simple rules for questionnaire writing. Most texts and articles on the
> subject are pitched on a vague general level, such as "Decide what information you
> need," or they consist of highly specific admonitions, such as "Be sure alternatives
> are mutually exclusive." The authors of these instructions are experienced research-
> ers who know their field, but it is very hard to tell someone how to design a useful
> questionnaire.[39]

In a sense, the problem here is also one of sampling: Have we covered the
required content in as many ways as are necessary to provide useful information?
Because questions can be asked in ways that bias responses, we should probably
try to ask the more significant questions in more than one way, using more

than one type or set of response categories. It is in the design of the instrument where we need to ensure including as broad a range of ideas and perspectives as possible. Leaving the design in the hands of a researcher or a small group of individuals who have similar orientations can produce an instrument that yields limited or misleading information. Advisory councils can be an especially useful check and balance on instrument construction in needs assessment surveys. Proper instrumentation may require additional time and energy, but the central issue is whether we want useful information or "data" that are potentially misleading or otherwise inadequate.

Types of Surveys

There are three common ways of conducting surveys: face-to-face interactions, phone interviews, or mailed questionnaires. Response rates tend to be highest with face-to-face surveys and lowest with mailed questionnaires. Because face-to-face interview costs are extremely high,[40] advocates for phone and mail surveys have emerged, along with a substantial body of research devoted to demonstrating their efficacy, especially in comparison to face-to-face surveys.[41]

To a large extent, the central issue revolves around response rate. Face-to-face surveys, although less cost-effective, still produce higher response rates and presumably, less biased results than the other methods. Mailed questionnaires require respondents that have fixed addresses, and phone surveys, of course, can only reach people with telephones. If our concern is with individuals suffering from a variety of personal and social ills, we reduce the likelihood of including them in our surveys if done by phone or mail. Face-to-face interviews can take place anywhere—shelters, parks, streets. We need to ask ourselves one simple question: Whom do we need to reach with our questions? The answer will guide us in choosing the method most likely to provide valid information.

CONCLUSIONS

Needs assessments can provide useful information for social service professionals, but only if extreme care is taken in how that information is acquired. There are a variety of ways in which the values and ethics of those who carry out the research can affect the results obtained. In the early years of needs assessment, the intent was often to bring the public into the public policy equation by providing them with a mechanism for making their needs known directly to decision-makers.

As the technology of needs assessment has evolved, there has been more emphasis on this research approach as a means for bringing objectivity and rationality to the policy-making process. The scientific method was seen as a way of obtaining "clear and unequivocal data" that could be applied to dealing with social problems and human needs. However, carrying out this method was seen as requiring a great deal of "expertise" in its own right. As a result, expert input came to supersede public input. In fact, the public—especially those who use or are eligible for services—have become "objects" of inquiry rather than actors in public policy.

Lack of adequate conceptual frameworks in needs assessment research was identified as another element that could bias project outcomes. In addition, several factors inherent in survey research methods are capable of biasing the information obtained, including sampling, response rates, instrumentation, and survey type (or the way in which data are collected).

NOTES

1. G. F. Summers, "Democratic Governance," in *Needs Assessment: Theory and Methods,* eds. D. E. Johnson, L. R. Miller, L. C. Miller, and G. F. Summers (Ames: Iowa State University Press, 1987), 3–19.
2. C. W. Mills, *The Power Elite* (New York: Oxford University Press, 1956); G. W. Domhoff, *Who Rules America Now?* (Englewood Cliffs, NJ: Prentice-Hall, 1983).
3. Summers, 16–17.
4. J. Bradshaw, "The Concept of Need," *New Society* 30 (1972): 640–43.
5. H. J. Aaron, *Politics and the Professors: the Great Society in Perspective* (Washington, DC: Brookings Institution, 1978).
6.. J. H. Ehrenreich, *The Altruistic Imagination: a History of Social Work and Social Policy in the United States* (Ithaca, NY: Cornell University Press, 1985).
7. Much of this section draws on material from a paper by K. M. Kilty and A. Jackson, "Social Science as Big Business: the Case of Welfare Reform," which was presented at the annual meeting of the Society for the Study of Social Problems, San Francisco, August, 1989.
8. D. MacRae, Jr., *Policy Indicators: Links between Social Science and Public Debate* (Chapel Hill: University of North Carolina Press, 1985), 64.
9. M. Hill and G. Bramley, *Analysing Social Policy* (New York: Basil Blackwell, 1986), 56.
10. S. Restivo, "Modern Science as a Social Problem," *Social Problems* 35 (1988): 35.
11. D. Beeson, "Women in Aging Studies: a Critique and Suggestions," *Social Problems* 23 (1975): 52–59.
12. V. Richardson and K. M. Kilty, "Adjustment to Retirement: Continuity vs. Discontinuity," *International Journal of Aging and Human Development* 33 (1991): 151–169.
13. R. W. Mack and J. Pease, *Sociology and Social Life,* 5th ed. (New York: D. Van Nostrand, 1972).
14. Aaron.
15. D. S. Eitzen, *Social Structure and Social Problems in America* (Boston: Allyn and Bacon, 1974).
16. E. S. Mornell, "Social Science and Social Policy: Epistemology and Values in Contemporary Research," *School Review* 87 (1979): 295–313.
17. R. A. LeVine, *Culture, Behavior, and Personality,* 2nd ed. (New York: Aldrine, 1982).
18. United Way, *Needs Assessment* (Alexandria, Virginia: United Way of America, 1982), 37–38.

19. B. J. Robins, "Local Response to Planning Mandates: the Prevalence and Utilization of Needs Assessment by Human Service Agencies," *Evaluation and Program Planning* 5 (1982): 199–208.

20. W. A. Kimmel, *Needs Assessment: a Critical Perspective* (Washington, DC: Office of Program Systems, Office of Assistant Secretary for Planning and Evaluation, U.S. Department of Health, Education, and Welfare, 1977), 14.

21. E. A. Suchman, "General Considerations of Research Design" in *Handbook of Research Design and Social Measurement,*4th ed., D. C. Miller (New York: Longman, 1983), 50.

22. Z. Harel, L. Noelker, and B. F. Blake, "Comprehensive Services for the Aged: Theoretical and Empirical Perspectives," *Gerontologist* 25 (1985): 644.

23. E.g., H. F. Goldsmith, D. J. Jackson, and R. L. Hough, "Process Model of Seeking Mental Health Services: Proposed Framework for Organizing the Literature on Help Seeking," in *Needs Assessment: Its Future,* eds. H. F. Goldsmith, E. Lin, R. A. Bell, and D. J. Jackson (Rockville, MD: Division of Biometry and Applied Sciences, National Institute of Mental Health, U.S. Department of Health and Human Services, 1988), 49–64.

24. Harel et al., 644.

25. L. S. Lareau and L. F. Heumann, "The Inadequacy of Needs Assessments of the Elderly," *Gerontologist* 22 (1982): 324–330.

26. Robins, 199.

27. R. O. Washington, *Program Evaluation in the Human Services* (Washington, DC: University Press of America, 1980).

28. Robins, 205.

29. K. Sung, "Converging Perspectives of Consumers and Providers in Assessing Needs of Families," *Journal of Social Service Research* 12 (1989): 3.

30. D. A. Dillman, *Mail and Telephone Surveys: the Total Design Method* (New York: Wiley, 1978); P. H. Rossi, J. D. Wright, and A. B. Anderson, "Sample Surveys: History, Current Practice, and Future Prospects," in *Handbook of Survey Research,* eds. P. H. Rossi, J. D. Wright, and A. B. Anderson (Orlando, FL: Academic Press, 1983), 1–20.

31. "Pollsters Humiliated in Forcast for Ortega," *Columbus Dispatch* (February 27, 1990).

32. E.g., E. Babbie, *Survey Research Methods* (Belmont, CA: Wadsworth, 1983); C. H. Backstrom and G. Hursh-Cesar, *Survey Research, 2nd ed.* (New York: Wiley, 1981); R. M. Jaeger, *Sampling in Education and the Social Sciences* (New York: Longman, 1984); G. Kalton, *Introduction to Survey Sampling* (Beverly Hills, CA: Sage, 1983).

33. E.g., J. K. Watters and P. Biernacki, "Targeted Sampling: Options for the Study of Hidden Populations," *Social Problems* 36 (1989): 416–430.

34. E.g., D. Roth, "Homeless in Ohio: a Statewide Epidemiological Survey," in *Homelessness in the United States,* ed. J. A. Momeni (Westport, CT: Greenwood Press, 1989), 145–163.

35. Secretary of Health, Education, and Welfare, *First Special Report to the U.S. Congress on Alcohol & Health* (Rockville, MD: National Institute on Alcohol Abuse and Alcoholism, U.S. Department of Health, Education, and Welfare, 1971).

36. Backstrom and Hursh-Cesar, 7.

37. Rossi et al., 9.

38. E. Babbie, *The Practice of Social Research, 5th ed.* (Belmont, CA: Wadsworth, 1989); N. K. Denzin, *The Research Act,* 3rd ed. (Englewood Cliffs, NJ: Prentice-Hall, 1989); B. S. Phillips, *Social Research: Strategy and Tactics,* 3rd ed. (New York: Macmillan, 1976); H. W. Smith, *Strategies of Social Research,* 2nd ed. (Englewood Cliffs, NJ: Prentice-Hall, 1981).
39. P. B. Sheatsley, "Questionnaire Construction and Item Writing," in Rossi et al., 200.
40. Backstrom and Hursh-Cesar, 41–46.
41. Dillman,; R. M. Groves and R. L. Kahn, *Surveys by Telephone* (New York: Academic Press, 1979); S. Sudman, "Applied Sampling," in Rossi et al., 145–194.

CHAPTER 10

The Technology of Program Evaluation

INTRODUCTION

The impetus for program evaluation can have many sources, each of which has shaped the meaning and process of program evaluation. This chapter first identifies some of the major forces that contributed to the movement of program evaluation. Second, it discusses the methodology and design of program evaluation, with special attention to the issues of implementation in the human service area. Third, the chapter presents the logic behind the experimental design, as well as some of the major conditions that affect the validity of findings. Finally, the chapter evaluates several major variants of the experimental design.

POLICY BACKGROUND TO PROGRAM EVALUATION

In the 1960s and early 1970s there was an increased focus in the larger society and in the human service profession upon clients as consumers of services.[1] This focus raised two important issues:

1. Were programs *relevant* to the consumers; that is, did they address what consumers wanted?
2. Did the programs *achieve* what they were supposed to; that is, did they achieve what the consumers had wanted?

These two issues were extensions of the social and political climate of the 1960s.[2] This was a climate marked by an emphasis upon a new strategy—the War on Poverty—with its emphasis upon the community, organizational development of neighborhoods and community, and the physical and sociopolitical arrangements in and impacting on the local community. The more traditional casework strategy of working with individuals and families, which utilized a heavy personal and psychological focus, was eclipsed.[4] The phrase "maximum feasible participation" in time came to represent not only a new focus upon the community, but a new range of roles for people as clients and consumers of services.[5]

Consumer and Community Involvement

In the 1970s, the concept of expanded roles for citizens spread beyond the confines of impoverished areas and came to be accepted as a right by many different populations. Citizen involvement soon became the norm for health planning groups, county and area offices on aging, Title XX planning and funding processes, and so on.[6] In short, the social and political climate of the 1960s affirmed new roles for "consumers" of social services and created structures that required the involvement of community members.

This period of consumer and community involvement introduced the expectation that programs and services should be accountable to the groups they serve or could serve. The push for broader involvement legitimized the perceptions, aspirations, and needs of the people, rather than those of the experts, and reinforced that what is offered ought to be what people in communities see as important.[7]

Thus, the key terms in program evaluation are accountability and relevance. *Accountability* is a condition of a relationship wherein at least one of the parties feels obligated to answer in some way to the other party.[8] Program evaluation may be a way in which the obligation is played out. *Relevance* is a condition wherein someone or some organization does something that is in keeping with what a person, group, or community perceives is needed.[9]

It is clear that the consumer/community movement developed a normative expectation that services and professionals should be accountable to the community and that the substance of such accountability should be in keeping with community needs and expectations. Early attempts at program evaluation emphasized the fit between services and population and community characteristics. This early program evaluation also was influenced by programming designs (pilot and demonstration projects) that emphasized the need to learn more about communities.[10]

Evaluation Literature

Another significant factor in the emergence of program evaluation was the development of a body of literature on evaluation research. In a fairly quick order this literature became very significant within the social work and human service communities as they grappled with issues of professional focus, credibility and sanctions.[11] These issues were in no small part raised initially by the climate of the Johnson years of the mid to late 1960s but were exacerbated by the Nixon years—though for different reasons.

One of the major works that influenced program evaluation was Suchman's *Evaluation Research,* published in 1967.[12] Without making much reference to the very broad concept of accountability, Suchman made a crucial distinction between evaluation and evaluative research. According to Suchman, evaluation suggested judgments based on logic and reason, whereas evaluative research required scientific research methods and techniques.[13] In program evaluation, evaluative research came to dominate because of forces within the helping professions and in the larger social order. Evaluative research was very compatible with the human service professions' increasing call for science and scientific testing. It also allowed for products that had a specificity and clarity that could assist political decision-makers in their efforts to curtail or to expand human service programs.

The practice of evaluative research often was considered to be the same as accountability. Not only was this incorrect conceptually, it also shifted the emphasis away from program relevance and the role of citizens and communities and towards the experts and professionals who had the skills to conduct evaluative research—the methodologists. This shift can be seen in Rossi, Freeman, and Wright's *Evaluation: a Systematic Approach,* which first appeared in 1979 and is now in a fourth edition. This book focuses on the mechanics of evaluation, and the language of the book has become more "scientific" with each edition. It is clearly written for the methodologist who will carry out the evaluative research. Discussion of the influence of the political, economic, and social context of the social program is severely limited, if not absent.[14]

Planning, Budgeting, and Political Climate

How the evaluative research emphasis actually played itself out in the human service field as well as in the political context of the larger society, relates to another factor that contributed to the rise of program evaluation: The federal government's initiation of new planning and budgeting strategies.[15] In the early 1960s the Department of Defense initiated the Planning, Programming and Budgeting System (PPBS). Subsequent to this came the Program Evaluation and Review Technique (PERT) which was widely used in many federal government agencies.[16]

PPBS and PERT basically are ways to consciously tie the budget of any organization to the organization's planning activity. In a sense, the budget, seen in an integrated organizational context, represents an implementation statement. In an ideal sense, both PPBS and PERT allow for consideration of such things as program effectiveness and efficiency within a budgetary system. Evaluative research became linked to both of these developments as an instrumental way to critically examine costs, to reduce costs, and to require programs to serve more people at lower cost per unit.

In short, effectiveness came to mean cost effectiveness, and really effective programs often meant lower costs. In the 1970s, a political and fiscal period that was becoming conservative, evaluative research often served as an instrumental and allegedly scientific way to achieve less fiscal involvement in human services. Thus, program evaluation during the Nixon years and thereafter was characterized by a struggle between efficiency and effectiveness.

More specifically, the possible purposes of policy were reflected in the questions that government agencies asked: Is the problem and/or problem population such that government response is *necessary;* if so, how much response? Are services *efficient;* do they operate within resource constraints? What *other fiscal and social payoffs,* if any, can result from the investment of resources? Can the *desired social stability* be purchased at cheaper costs?[6]

When these kinds of political questions became dominant in government, possible policy and program concerns with organizational relevance and reduction of risk in selected racial and economic groups were ''lost.'' ''Good'' welfare rapidly became reduced welfare that focused on the individual and was determined by demonstrated need. Substitute arrangements and services, counseling, training, and other person-related responses took precedence over community-focused responses. Interventions now became almost exclusively focused upon persons. The emergence of program evaluation and program evaluators was in part to facilitate the elimination of responses that were questionable; that is, that did not produce demonstrated payoffs for valued constituencies, or that focused upon populations and groups that were not valued, but that merely were in need. In short, program evaluation, allegedly designed to focus upon effectiveness, helped contribute to a decision-making environment that was primarily interested in efficiency.

Thus, program evaluation moved from looking at programs from the perspective of an accountability to communities and consumers, with a stress upon relevance, to striving for both efficiency and effectiveness, with an emphasis upon the role of methodologists and system analysts. In this context, evaluative research was contaminated by the changes in values that accompanied the shift in the larger society from consumerism to cost containment. The call for program evaluation as a full accounting of the use of resources came to suggest marked differences in the areas of accounting to whom (from recipients and communities to taxpayers), and from relevance and effectiveness in the eyes of consumers and affected communities to cost reduction and cost minimization.

Somewhat inadvertently, as discussed in Chapter 1, social work and other human services in this period were just beginning to aggressively use scientific inquiry.[16] This encouraged professionals to apply measurement and objectivity to the critical examination of programs. For social workers, evaluative research of programs often became interchangeable with evaluation and accountability. Yet, in pursuing the path of technical development and technical competency, such larger issues as the purposes of programming, and social/political values and issues were ignored. Because program evaluation was influenced by and was part of the larger political process, many concerns and questions relative to groups and communities were not raised. These included: Why do certain groups continue to have disproportionately higher rates of certain needs? What is being done to reduce risk for certain groups? What is an appropriate amount of reduction in the risk-need relationship for certain groups?

PROGRAM EVALUATION:
LOGIC AND EXPERIMENTAL DESIGN

The rest of this chapter focuses on the logic and technology of program evaluation.

The Logic of Program Evaluation

Putting aside for the moment the situational context of program evaluation, it is relatively easy to describe the logic or spirit of program evaluation.[18] Basically, programs should be evaluated according to how well their results meet expectations.

To answer this question, program evaluators should ascertain that whatever results occur after a program is delivered are indeed attributable to that program. Thus, program evaluators should ensure that people whose needs are the focus of the program being examined are compared with people who represent what would have happened if the program being examined did not exist. And to make the comparison really inclusive, it would be logical to define precisely the circumstances of both the program participants and the comparison group before the onset of the program. Similarly, the program participants and the comparison group should be examined after the program. Looking at participants and nonparticipants at two points—before and after the program—can help program evaluators determine the program's actual results.

In more technical terms:

- There is a group of people who are subjects in the sense that they receive an *intervention,* i.e., a program;
- The intervention has specific desired *effects*;
- There is a *comparison group* that does not receive the intervention;
- Both groups need to be *measured before and after* the program intervention to see whether the groups show the intended effects; and
- *Inferences* about program's success can be made after completing this measurement and comparison.

Target Population, Samples, and Measures

Other terms and issues are important to the logic of program evaluation. First there is the issue of whom to study—which groups should be compared. This highlights the critical issue of the relationship between *target population* to be studied and *sample* actually studied. The target population to be studied, in most cases in the human services, is rarely representative of any larger population. For example, an agency may have on its waiting list more than 500 sexually active young women who have become pregnant. But it is very hard to say that these 500 women "represent" some definable population group beyond the agency. In fact, in many programs the people who actually are in contact with an agency's program may be quite different from the general population of the community. People may be in the program precisely because they are so different—because, for example, they are so ill or so poor, or because they are so motivated or have such good personal resources.

Despite the serious difficulty in viewing groups of people who participate in social programs or services as representative of the larger community, program evaluation can ascertain the characteristics of the participants and can always consider these characteristics in light of what is known about the larger population and community. In actuality, in conducting the program evaluation, the logic and steps of program evaluations stated on the previous page must be rigorously pursued to the degree possible.[19]

To ensure comparability of groups, evaluators should first identify the target population. In the previous example it is the 500 pregnant women. From that target population, evaluators draw a *sample*. A sample is some smaller portion of a population. Instrumentally, a sample allows program evaluation to reflect some level of statistical inference; in other words, to move from facts to inference.

The ideal sample is a miniature version of the population. However, there is really not much likelihood of ever fully knowing the population in terms of all possible characteristics. Therefore, sampling is usually an attempt to eliminate systematic biases so that the sample studied reflects a strong approximation of the population from which it is drawn.

There are a variety of sampling procedures that can be employed in program evaluation so that statistical inferences can subsequently be present in the evaluation. If the goal is to generalize from a sample to a population, the most appropriate sampling procedure is random sampling. Another sampling procedure, purposive sampling, is sometimes employed, but it has serious drawbacks, which are noted below.

Random sampling refers to the manner in which the sample is drawn. It does not have to do with any of the characteristics of the population itself. In a simple random sample, every member in the population has the same probability of being chosen to be in the sample. It also means that the selection of any one member or case cannot systematically affect the selection of any other. Use of a table of random numbers is often employed in conjunction with assigning numbers to members in the population to actually draw a sample. A variant of the simple random sample is the systematic random sample which uses some natural ordering of the population. This type of sampling could involve taking every Nth case to achieve the sample desired.

Another variant is stratified random sampling. Evaluation is more likely to draw a sample in this fashion where there is knowledge about various key characteristics or strata that make up the population. These known characteristics can be used to categorize the population into some specific subgroups, such as by gender or by level of education. Once the population is divided by the selected categories, the evaluation effort would determine the percentage of the total population that falls into each category. The evaluation would then attempt to ensure that the sample would show each category in the same way or percentage as occurs in the population. For example, if 70 percent of the population were under twenty-one years of age, then the sample would have the same percentage of members who were under twenty-one. The sample then becomes a mini version of the population. However, in attempting to get a stratified sample, the principle of randomness within strata or categories must be maintained.

An alternative to random sampling is a strategy that focuses upon selection of a sample according to some criteria that are known to be relevant such as income. This is called a purposive sample. It clearly violates the principle that every case or member should stand an equal chance of being included. For this reason, such samples are considered non-probability samples, and, as such, their use can adversely affect the legitimate use of statistical inference in program evaluation.

After the sample is drawn, it is divided into two groups—the intervention/ program group and the control group—making sure that the factors, exclusive of the program, that influence the results have, if not an equal, at least a comparable chance of occurring in both groups. Using the earlier example of a target population of 500 pregnant women, 25 women from the waiting list are *randomly assigned* to some program intervention whereas 25 others who are also on the waiting list do not receive the intervention. Measurements called *baseline measures* are taken before program intervention. For the example being discussed here, measures may be on such things as frequency of intercourse, number of partners, use of prophylactics, etc. Critical measures would be on matters that the program was designed to influence in some direction, the notion being that the program modified people's behavior in some specific way(s).

Using this process, evaluators can make several kinds of assessments. First, they can examine the intervention/participation group both before and after the program intervention. Second, they can compare the control group with itself before and after the program intervention. Third, evaluators can compare the intervention program group with the control group at the point of base-line measures—called Time 1—and at the point of repeat measures—called Time 2.

Thus, this process enables program evaluators to infer that whatever change, if any, that occurred among program participants did so because of the program intervention.

Figure 10–1 shows how all of these concepts—target population, sample, experimental group, control group, baseline measures, program intervention and follow-up measures interrelate within what is called the *experimental design*.

Inferring Causal Relationships

For many social scientists, experimental design is the ideal research design. This is especially true in psychology, where experimental design, especially in the laboratory setting, is considered to be the most powerful methodology for doing social research, especially when coupled with analysis of variance as an analytic strategy.[20]

The value of experimental design derives from its use in the physical sciences, where there has been a great deal of success in manipulating and controlling the environment.[21] The goal of research in the physical sciences is to establish *causal* relationships between variables: To examine whether Variable A *caused* Variable B to change; that is, to examine whether Variable B would have changed if Variable A had not been introduced.[22]

FIGURE 10-1   Ideal Study Design for Making Comparison*

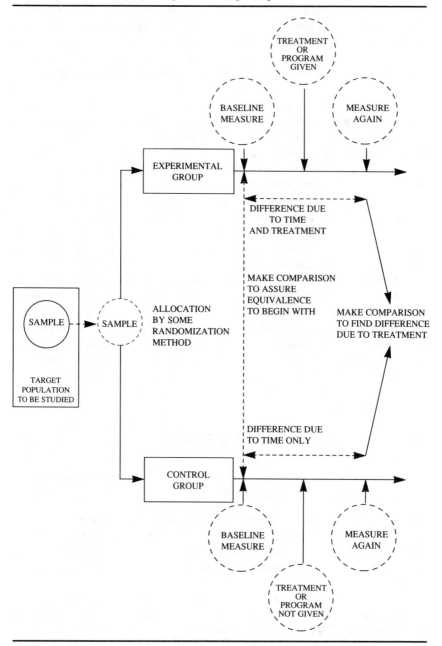

*Reprinted from *Evaluation Handbook,* second edition, Office of Program Evaluation, USAID, MC 1026.1 Supplement II, Washington, D.C. 20523.

Taken alone, statistical analysis cannot demonstrate causal relationships; it can only document associations between variables. An association shows that, as one variable changes, so does another, but it does not tell which variable needs to come first. Unless a time sequence can be established, it cannot be concluded that a causal relationship exists; in order for one variable to cause change in another, the causal variable must precede in time the variable that changes. What is needed, then, is some means of establishing unequivocally that one variable affects the other, and not the other way around.

Experimental design provides a means for establishing causal relationships. First, we identify the *independent variable*—the variable that we expect to bring about change. Then we identify the *dependent variable*—the variable that we expect will display change after the independent variable is introduced. Finally, the logic of experimental design provides documentation for the *time sequence*. In program evaluation, the independent variable is the intervention, which the experimental group receives but the control group does not. After the intervention, we measure the dependent variable for both groups. If the dependent variable changes, that change can be attributed to the introduction of the independent variable, because the independent variable preceded the dependent variable in time. The length of time is irrelevant; the critical factor is the sequence of events. As long as the experimental and control groups were randomly assigned (in order to control for differences between them), the experimental design provides a powerful means for making causal inferences. That is, it provides a *plausible* explanation for change. In sum, the three elements of experimental design are (1) the manipulation of one or more independent variables; (2) the use of experimental and control groups; and (3) the random assignment of cases to groups.

Doing Program Evaluation: Dealing With Validity and Programming Constraints

In reviewing the ideal program evaluation format, one might correctly say that it is impossible to randomly assign clients to either receive or be denied interventions; people's real-life needs, rights, demands and a general sense of ethics often interfere with carrying out classic experimental design. These factors limit program evaluators' ability to infer that results and changes are attributable to program intervention alone.

The concept of *validity* highlights possible contaminants to the inference process. Campbell suggested that several types of variables can significantly threaten internal validity.[23] *Internal validity* refers to correct conclusions about the people and groups who are actually studied. Among the major factors that can affect internal validity are:

1. Some specific event or events occurs between measurements, besides and in addition to the experimental variable. For example, the experimental variable

might be a counseling group or support activity focusing on making decisions about sex. But in addition to this, there might be some new event that is not the experimental variable, which could affect the conclusions about the program's effectiveness; e.g. there may have been the introduction of prophylactics in public high schools, or changes in policy and/or programming concerning whether pregnant high school students can stay in school.

2. Some developments or processes within the subjects occur as a result of the passage of time, e.g., they grow older, they develop new friends.

3. Getting baseline measures affects in some way the subsequent measurement(s) after the program has been initiated, e.g., the subjects behave differently because they know they are being studied.

4. The measurements at different times are not really the same because of such factors as changes in the conditions in which the evaluation instrument is administered, changes in the instrument itself, or use of different observers or raters.

5. The groups selected for examination are very different, skewed in one or more directions.

6. There are biases in the selection of particular subjects in the study relative to their placement in the experimental and control groups.

7. There is significant loss of subjects from the groups being studied.

8. Some combination of the above phenomena produces an effect or change that is incorrectly attributed to the program being examined.

To handle these possible events that could affect the internal validity (i.e., the ability to draw accurate conclusions about the people and programs being studied), the design of the program evaluation is critical. In essence, internal validity measures how confident we can be that our own program intervention brought about any observed changes in the cases participating in the intervention.

Similarly, external validity may be a concern if certain factors are not accounted for in the design of the program evaluation. *External validity* refers to the degree to which we can confidently generalize our findings to other groups, locations, or situations. Factors that can affect external validity include:

• Selection biases in possible program group assignments. For example certain kinds of clients or problems are funneled to the experimental program group simply because the "new" program or the experimental group looks appropriate for the given population or problem.

• The reaction of the people assigned to the experimental program to the measurement process before the program is actually implemented, such that this group or members of it actually respond to the programs differently than will people from the same population who do not receive the program.

- The reactive effect of the program setting and the procedures associated with the experimental program.
- The cumulative effect of prior programs on experimental groups participants.

Variants in Experimental Design

In the context of the methodological concerns raised above, it is useful to look at some of the major variants of experimental design that are used in the human service field. The variants will be examined in relation to how they deal with the issues of internal and external validity. However, validity issues are not the only concerns that should be kept in mind when evaluating a program. In any case some of the major designs are:[25]

- case design
- pretest-posttest no-control design
- time-series no-control design
- group comparison design
- equivalent time-samples design
- nonequivalent control-group design
- posttest-only control-group design
- pretest-posttest control-group design
- four-group design

Case Design. Case design focuses on a group that receives some program intervention: counseling, job training, schooling, and so on. While called a case design, it is really a study of a cohort of people who have received a common program/intervention. With case designs, there is no control group. Typically, this design evaluates program group members at some point after the program has been initiated. Program evaluators may interview program participants and evaluate them according to certain reference points relevant to the program—securing employment, staying married, and the like. Evaluators can also assess participants' behavior or attitudes that are assessed relative to the program.

The case design approach has major problems with internal and external validity. It is not possible, using case design, to infer convincingly that the alleged changes, if any, associated with a program were indeed the effect of the program; such changes could theoretically have occurred without the program. Without an appropriate comparison group, this design cannot ascertain whether or not factors extraneous to the program affected the people receiving the program. This design also precludes generalization to the larger population.

Thus, with case design, one cannot accurately say (1) that changes are attributable to the program intervention; or (2) that if this program were offered to others in the larger target population, the same or similar results would be likely.

Despite these very serious limitations in internal and external validity, case design is useful when the purpose of the evaluation is to get beginning knowledge about people or groups and about what seems to relate with which people and/ or conditions. Such a design possibly allows the evaluator to gather beginning information on how program participants are feeling and reacting to the program as well as securing some relatively accessible information on which components of the program seem to be working. However, case design should not rely on a single point of measurement done after the study, but should make fairly frequent measurements of the very *process* of program interaction with participants. Such frequent intervals of data collection can help the program staff to make ongoing adjustments or changes to the program.

In using case designs in this way to collect information and to make adjustments in programs, the design could call for professionals to rate program participants along some dimension after the program experience, such as ability to perform well in employment interviews. It could also call for periodic feedback from participants concerning their willingness to use certain interviewing strategies that are raised in counseling sessions. In sum, the evaluation can be designed to make the program fit the participants, for them to learn from the program experience. The rule here is to not have so many "feedback" opportunities that the program is dominated by them, yet have enough to learn pragmatic program concerns of participants' receptivity, perceptions, attitudes, and so on concerning the program.

Pretest-Posttest No-Control Design

In this design a program is offered to a group, but, before the program is implemented, the program staff collects information about participants (the pretest). The program is then offered, and, after its conclusion, the participants are studied again (the posttest). There is no control group. Following are some examples. A group of high school students are tested about knowledge or behavior before a drug awareness program and then after the actual program. A group of battered women are tested on self-image and survival skills/strategies before and after participating in a program focusing on these areas. In both examples, results prior to and after the program are compared.

This design has appeal precisely because it does not require a control; therefore it is simple to conduct. When one factors in practice imperatives and professional obligations to be of service to those in need, one can see why many professionals at the program level can appreciate this design. They can respect the professional obligation to provide service in a timely fashion. They do not have to get involved in controls, sampling or even issues of who is in greater need of the service.

Although very workable for many problems and people, this design does not completely address the major validity concerns. Other factors in the lives of the students and women may have contributed to differences in test results between the pretest (Time 1, or T1) and the posttest (Time 2, or T2). Similarly, if considerable time elapses between T1 and T2, increased maturation and experience may affect T2 scores.

Other concerns are not addressed by this design. Without a control group, it is very difficult to assess what role, if any, the very process of pretesting might have had on the posttest study. The pretest influence rather than the actual program may account for much of the change. With specific respect to external validity, this design does not control for possible contamination between the pretest and the program. For example, the students and the battered women may have "learned" by taking the pretests how to focus or process the program offered subsequently. Thus, it cannot ascertain whether any changes reflected in posttest are purely a function of the program.

In addition, the actual program offered might be shaped by the nature and results of the pretest scores. In actual practice, the pretest is not always a pretest but often is actually a component of the overall intervention.

Time-Series No-Control Design

In this design there are several pre-and posttest measurements. A group of clients, for example, those on a waiting list, could be examined several times before they actually participated in a program, and then several times afterwards. This design is an improvement over the pretest-posttest no control design because it takes into consideration the possible effect of the testing process. If testing before the program has an impact, then several tests before the program should reveal this, especially the impact of cumulative testing.

The issue of maturation is also addressed when there are several tests. Maturation refers to developments or processes within the subjects as a result of the passage of time. Maturation effects could be identified as distinct from program effects if the total spacing of time between pre- and posttests measures is at least as great as the period of program intervention.

However, some of these very strengths concerning internal validity can be related to difficulties in external validity. It is possible that a series of measurements prior to a program being fully offered can influence how the program is received by program participants. Similarly, a series of measurements after a program can promote reinforcement of effects of the program. In both instances, the exact role of the program itself may be difficult to assess.

Conventionally, this design is seen as being most applicable when the evaluation design can or will have only one group. Since it has multiple points of measurement, it theoretically addresses, in part, the issue of maturation, but it is less successful in addressing the issue of test contamination on the participants.

Group Comparison Design

In the group comparison design, the group that participates the program is compared afterward to a group that has not participated. Examples include a program group whose members voluntarily undergo counseling in a drug program in addition to detoxification being compared to a group whose members undergo only detoxification. Both are studied at the same point after the program.

Obviously the big issue in this design is that the two groups must be equivalent; unfortunately this design does not ensure that. In other words, even if there are changes between the detox-plus-counseling group and the detox-alone group, it is difficult to ascertain that the changes between the groups are attributable to the counseling. The groups may have been different to start with, and/or the program may interact with preexisting differences.

When this design is used, researchers will generally try to demonstrate similarity between the groups by comparing them statistically according to key characteristics and then controlling for any differences in analyzing the results. The problem with this strategy is that the key characteristics identified by researchers may not actually be the major factors that account for any initial differences. Such differences might be explained by unknown factors. Further, if people are used as judges or to score participants and they know which participants have received counseling, differences may be produced from this information.

With respect to external validity, as long as the comparison group and the program group are from the same population, generalizations may be considered. But generalizations can only be made to the specified population. If only one of the groups is drawn from a specified target population, generalization to the group not drawn from the specified population is not possible.

Equivalent Time-Samples Design

This design has only one group, but at some points in the study the program experimental variable is present, while at other points it is not. The classic example of this is a study in which sometimes the participant is given a placebo, whereas at other times the participant receives actual medication. Typically, the timing of the placebo administration would be random. Researchers rate participants after they received either the placebo or actual medication according to some predetermined criterion, such as attention, speeches, and the like.

As long as there is random assignment of when the samples occur and each of the observations or measurements is indeed independent, then this design can accurately assess the impact of the critical program variable.

This design has no control group other than that some group members may be receiving a placebo rather than the key program element (actual medication). If random selection from some specified target population was followed, valid generalizations might be possible. But the generalizations would have to be carefully framed so as to capture the pattern in which the key program element was offered and not offered—the timing sequence. Finally, the design is subject to difficulties if there is a carry-over effect from one period to another—if the key program element continues to have an effect even at the point where the measurement is examining the absence of the key program variable.

Nonequivalent Control-Group Design

This design has a pre- and posttest feature that is applied to both the experimental group and the control group. However, assignment to the groups is not random, and therefore selection factors could threaten internal validity. An example of this design is a program comparing a group of third grade children who receive a "special" curriculum with another group of third grade children who do not receive that curriculum. Tests are administered to each group prior to and after the onset of the program.

This design has certain advantages. It can use existing or natural groups. The selection of groups is crucial, especially in terms of group characteristics. Assuming that the two groups examined are very similar, this design is more reliable than the one-group, pretest–posttest test design because it strengthens the interpretation of findings. From the evaluation, generalizations can be made. However, this can only occur if the experiences and processes between times of testing are essentially the same or similar. In our example of two groups of similar third graders, this would be difficult to ensure because they were in different schools, perhaps had different forces operating in their lives, and so on. Even if the third grade groups came from the same school, many of these possibilities could still exist—certainly the evaluation would not clearly show that they were not present and influential. Sometimes it is difficult to use this design within the same school or within the same grade level because of issues associated with which class will get the program, which class will not and why not.

If we use the language of our prior discussions, the maturation or development of the two groups can vary, and therefore it would be difficult to pinpoint the role of the program in producing results. Likewise, if the group members receiving the "special" intervention are aware that they are receiving something different or unusual, they may change simply because of their differential treatment and/or testing. Finally, the possibility of a reaction by members of either group to the process of testing is strong enough that the evaluation findings concerning the program really could be contaminated by the process of testing.

Posttest Only Control-Group Design

In this design, the evaluation focuses on two groups after some program intervention has occurred with one of the groups. There is no pretest. If random assignment does occur and if the number of participants is sufficient, tests of significance can be applied in the analysis of the program intervention. But that is precisely the issue. In the human service field, the assigning of cases by the statistical principle of randomness might very well ensure some level of unethical behavior on the part of professional staff. Why might this ensure unethical behavior? Professional behavior is always driven by the imperative to meet client needs and to meet, as a priority, those most in need. To assign people to a program or to a control group that does not receive the program may ensure "good" research represent but grossly inappropriate practice. The net result is that posttest designs often have great difficulty in demonstrating that the two groups are equivalent. This, of course, weakens the validity of results attributing differences to a program intervention. However, this design precludes any interaction and/or pretesting influences on the program and subsequent scores. Although this can greatly increase the logic for generalizations, such generalizations are ultimately tied to whether true randomness was present in the initial assignment to groups.

Pretest-Posttest Control-Group Design

On the face of it, this design approaches the ideal of experimental design. There is a control as well as a group receiving the program, and there is a Time 1 and Time 2 measurement. Unlike the nonequivalent control-group design, the principle of random assignment is present. However, as discussed above, human service agencies cannot easily, if at all, assign members, and therefore interventions, on a random basis.

Random assignment would, of course, strengthen internal validity. In fact, this design even can allow for pretesting before random assignment. In other words, pretests can facilitate identifying equivalents, and the equivalents can then be randomly assigned to groups. Yet the reality in the helping fields is that the imperatives of organizational and client functioning will diminish randomness and the more esoteric process of randomly assigning matched/equivalent members to groups. Clients will undergo crises; their functioning can and often will change; funding requirements can change; and staff preferences and experiences with certain kinds of people are just a few examples of specific factors that can influence the assignment processes.

Besides the critical concern of achieving randomness, this design also may be contaminated by the effects of the pretest itself. Such effects can occur in both groups, and this may make it nearly impossible to sort out the effects of the pretest. In a related way, the program group may respond to the simple fact of special attention that is conveyed by the program, and this may in turn affect the so-called results measured after the program intervention.

Four-Group Design

This design, which is the most complex and difficult to carry out in the human service field, combines several designs. It uses the pretest-posttest control-group design and the posttest-only control-group design. This combination recognizes the advantages as well as the limitations of each design.

This design uses four groups and tests at six points. Two groups participate in the program and two do not. Only one of the two groups participating is tested at both points—before and after the program. Similarly, only one of the two groups that do not participate is tested both before and after. All four groups are tested after the program, but only two of the groups (one participating and one not participating) are tested before the program. This will allow for comparisons within and across the groups. Thus the effects of programs can be more precisely identified.

This design accounts for the possible effects of pretesting affecting receptivity to the program, and it also addresses the possible issue of programming affecting the measurement at the time of the follow-up measurement.

Although this design may be considered the "best" because it addresses internal/external validity concerns, it is totally dependent on the principle of random assignment to different groups. As discussed previously, randomization in social services is difficult to achieve and perhaps should not be achieved in many need and risk situations confronting agencies, staff, communities and client groups.

CONCLUSION

This chapter has focused on the evolution and development of program evaluation in social work. Initially a major impetus was the recognition that consumers and community groups were entitled to receive relevant responses from agencies. Over time, the stress on accountability of programs to communities and clients was eclipsed by a stress on methodologically correct evaluative research in the context of efficiency and cost effectiveness.

As social work entered into this process, especially in the context of substantial changes in the political climate, social work came to be associated with program evaluation just at the time when the focus had moved away from political accountability and relevance to communities to that of cost efficiency and effectiveness.

Even with the concern with effectiveness, the unit of attention often was individuals and groups rather than the rich, complex political and social climate within which both agencies and people operated. The net result of this, to be developed further in the next chapter, is that groups truly at risk were often quite different from target groups (those receiving services) from which samples were drawn and to whom programs were delivered, and in some cases formally evaluated.

This chapter reviewed several program evaluation designs and examined some difficulties with them. First, there is the difficulty of achieving groups that are really comparable. There also are difficulties in assignment and achieving randomness. It can be difficult to ascertain that over time groups differ only in terms of participation or nonparticipation in the program. It is possible that pre-testing can affect programs and their results. Similarly, programs themselves can affect posttesting.

In anticipation of the next chapter, we have some comments of a different kind. There is a haunting, though often intuitive sense, that many elaborate designs presuppose what works and what does not. To the degree that this is questionable, perhaps the ultimate methodological issue has to do with the degree of fit between validated knowledge of specific interventions and the legitimacy of selecting and implementing very fixed programs which may be evaluated. The fact is that many program interventions in the human service field are not buttressed by substantial knowledge and information relative to specific populations, conditions and inter-ventions. This being the case, the securing of more information—including that about those most at risk—might be more logical, if not more politically acceptable, than so-called rigorous evaluation designs. Finally, the nexus between program evaluation and experimental design implies a level of control and rational manage-ment in the social world that may ultimately cloud the complexity and political nature of that social world.

NOTES

1. Many works were produced in the 1970s that focused on consumers and community action as a method. See F. M. Cox, J. L. Erlich, J. Rothman, and J. E. Tropman, eds., *Strategies of Community Organizations* (Itasca, IL: Peacock, 1974); R. Kramer and H. Specht, eds., *Readings in Community Organization* (Englewood Cliffs, NJ: Prentice-Hall, 1976).
2. See J. B. Turner, ed. *Neighborhood Organization for Community Action* (Washington, DC: N.A.S.W., 1968).
3. T. M. Meenaghan, R. O. Washington, and R. Ryan, *Macro Practice* (New York: Free Press, 1982), 4–5.
4. *Ibid.* 4.
5. *Ibid.* 4.
6. *Ibid.* 5.
7. Summers, "Democratic Governance," in Johnson et al, eds., *Needs Assessment.*
8. T. M. Meenaghan and R. O. Washington, *Social Policy and Social Welfare: Structured and Applications* (New York: Free Press, 1980).
9. Meenaghan, Washington, and Ryan, 34.
10. E. Suchman, *Evaluation Research: Principles and Practice in Public Service and Social Action Programs* (New York: Russel Sage Foundation, 1967).
11. *Ibid.*
12. *Ibid.*
13. *Ibid.*
14. P. Rossi, H. E. Freeman and S. R. Wright, *Evaluation: A Systematic Approach* (New York: Sage Foundation, 1979), 6.
15. R. O. Washington, *Program Evaluation in the Human Services* (Columbus: Ohio State University College of Social Work, 1979), 1.

16. E. Thomas, *Designing Interventions for the Helping Professions* (Sage, Beverly Hills, CA: 1984), 74–84.
17. For a brief review of sound reasons for research in social work, see R. M. Grinnell, Jr., and M. Williams, *Research in Social Work: A Primer* (Itasca, IL: Peacock, 1990), 12–15.
18. There are many fine works that explain the logic and technology of evaluation. Among them are A. Rubin and E. Babbie, *Research Methods for Social Work* (Belmont, CA: Wadsworth, 1989), 481–507; E. Posavec and R. G. Carey, *Program Evaluation: Methods and Case Studies* (Englewood Cliffs, NJ: Prentice-Hall, 1980); M. G. Kusher and W. S. Davidson, "Using Experimental Designs to Evaluate Social Programs," *Social Work Research and Abstracts* 15 (January 1979): 27–32; Grinnel and Williams, especially 232–264; and R. M. Grinnel, Jr., ed., *Social Work and Evaluation* (Itasca, IL: Peacock, 1988.)
19. Rubin and Babbie, 249–250.
20. Winer, *Statistical Principles in Experimental Design.*
21. M. E. Spencer, "The Imperfect Empiricism of the Social Sciences," *Sociological Forum* 2 (1987): 331–372.
22. E. Babbie, *The Practice of Social Research* 5th edition (Belmont, CA.: Wadsworth, 1989).
23. D. T. Campbell, "Factors Relevant to the Validity of Experiments in Social Settings," in H. C. Schubberg, ed., *Program Evaluation in the Health Fields* (New York: Behavioral Publications, 1969).
24. *Ibid.*
25. Our discussion is directly related to Campbell and Stanly's classic discussion of types of designs relative valid inferences. See D. T. Campbell and J. Stanly, *Experimental and Quasi-Experimental Designs for Research* (Chicago: Rand McNally, 1966). See also Washington, 73–82.

CHAPTER 11

Crucial Issues in Program Evaluation

INTRODUCTION

The preceding chapter gave an overview of program evaluation that focused on the social and political elements that promoted both the consumer and evaluation movements and the technology of "pure" program evaluation. The chapter also discussed the logic of program evaluation, which revolved around pursuit of a central question—Did/does the social intervention work? We hypothesized that over time this question was framed by a pervasive political attitude that allocations for social interventions should be curtailed.

Nonetheless, the movement for program evaluation developed a kind of life of its own, and a set of norms for "good" or "sound" program evaluation. The helping professions participated in this norm development. The "right" way to do program evaluation suggested that experimental design should be ideal for critiquing and examining the effectiveness of social intervention programs.

Although the classic experimental design was clearly the ideal way to evaluate programs, program evaluators recognized that its full employment was very difficult in the real world. Further, the more feasible and pragmatic alternatives to the classic experimental design tended to have problems in terms of internal and/or external validity issues.

This chapter focuses on nine crucial issues to be considered in program evaluation. These issues were selected because they reflect (1) the importance of the context in which program evaluation occurs; (2) the significance of key audiences and interests in influencing evaluation; and (3) the need to identify what is not seen or addressed in either programs or program evaluation. These considerations, although they affect the design and technology of program evaluation, are not inherently or exclusively technical.

BALANCING CONSUMER NEEDS AND PROFESSIONAL JUDGMENTS

A central issue in achieving valid test and comparison groups is the process used to sort people into the respective groups.[1] In Chapter 10 this was referred to as randomness, that is, the assignment by chance, without systematic bias.

As discussed earlier, true randomness can be very difficult to achieve. People come to an agency because they need or want help from the agency that might require programmatic responses. The imperative pushing the group or individual seeking help is: respond to me/us as soon as possible.

Similarly, the professional staff are guided, at least in part, by professional service norms that mandate quick responses. Although the appropriateness and effectiveness of programmatic responses (that is, that the responses produce desired results) are becoming increasingly important, the timeliness of responses, especially to those in clear need, remains a priority for both consumers and professionals. Because of this, there is a not-so-subtle nexus, at times partial, between consumers and professionals for the need for quick programmatic responses.

Professionals, as well as would-be consumers, must prioritize and make judgments. Consumers and consumer groups make judgments about what they want/need, what they feel entitled to. Professionals decide which consumer situations are more pressing or urgent than others. Professionals in certain settings even have to make triage-like decisions about consumers who may be very needy or at great risk and yet are not likely to benefit from programmatic intervention and thus should not receive top-priority treatment.

Because randomness means assignment by chance, the above discussion of influences on professionals and consumers can easily work against achieving randomness. Professionals must make judgments, and consumers typically act and expect action, in their interests. Further, the very political issues of limited allocation of resources leads professionals and consumers to eschew the concept of "pure" chance, or randomness. In the last analysis, both groups would rather affirm their own interests and responsibilities by asserting the "rightness" of certain program responses to certain types of people and situations. Admittedly, under some circumstances the experimental or test group that is receiving some intervention can be examined relative to a quasi-control group—those on a waiting list for the intervention. But the fact of the matter is that the members of the two groups—test and control—often are not and cannot be randomly assigned. Because of this, not only is the principle of randomness not affirmed or achieved, but the evaluation process often lacks a true comparison.

When one raises the topic of randomness, one should not assume that the only issue is the sorting of people into experimental/test and control groups. In fact, one can almost routinely assume that there are significant differences between program groups and the larger community. Thus, it is very difficult to generalize from any evaluated programmatic intervention to the larger community. This is especially germane for programs that plan to base subsequent prevention interventions with a larger target community on their limited service interventions with select people currently in need.

In short, balancing the needs of consumers for programmatic responses and the judgments of professionals, who feel ethically obliged to respond, and the inextricable connection between urgent need and quick response, the professional imperative for responding seems to override imperatives for testing.

THE ROLE OF BEHAVIORISM

Another key issue in program evaluation is the role of behaviorism. A central requirement in behaviorism is that the behavior being examined be measurable.[2] In fact, behaviorism by definition denotes that the only valid data are observed behaviors, and such behaviors must be measurable. In the helping fields, what is observable typically is some program and/or client goal that is achieved by the program intervention.

On a case level, this quest for measurability has fueled strong and continuous debates among many disciplines and professionals. There is controversy over such issues as: (1) the need to measure attitudes and feelings; (2) whether it is possible to measure attitudes and feelings; (3) how to select specific, structured goals and interventions for clients; and (4) whether treatment interventions and clients are too complex to be assessed by focusing on specific goals (observable) and interventions (specific and describable).

The quest for precision, scientific credibility, and respectability sometimes has led some program evaluation efforts into assessing interventions that seemed discrete because the goals were discrete and perhaps even relatively insignificant. Further, by zeroing in on goals that are very measurable, programs sometimes fail to even consider, much less address, the overall situation facing certain groups. For example, studying separately whether a reading program does or does not work, or whether sexually active young girls in a high school do or do not use contraceptives, may be analogous to seeing, feeling, measuring, and studying separate trees but not seeing or measuring the forest.

To play out the analogy, the quest for behaviorism implicitly, if not explicitly, may encourage a reductionism, and a reductionism of a particular sort. The evaluator is led to the trees because they are discrete enough to be "studyable" according to conventional behavioral criteria. Yet the forest is complex and difficult to see without broad, multiple, and variable perspectives. Evaluators tend to study what they can readily see and easily define as a goal.

Specificity in program goals in no way ensures that what is being sought is significant or comprehensive, or applicable to how certain groups fit into society. This issue of behaviorism excessively influencing discreteness can be thought of as a possible service problem in achieving "worthwhileness."[3] That is, attention is given to studying only what can be studied directly.

The key question raised by the role of behaviorism is simple: If the program being evaluated does or does not achieve a specific, discrete goal, so what? What is more noteworthy may be what is not being addressed or even seen.

DEFINING PROBLEMS AND GOALS

Inherent in the preceding discussion of program evaluation, often leading to the study of somewhat discrete and perhaps irrelevant goals, is the issue of problem definition and its relation to intervention and evaluation. Programs can be conceived of as policy in action; they also can be conceived of as a specific way to address and solve a problem and attain certain goals.

Framing a statement of a current situation at least implicitly suggests goals and ways to implement the policy and achieve the goals.[4] The question remains whether the program being evaluated reflects an appreciation of the "big picture," that is, the complex web of social relations in the larger society, especially as they may negatively affect the person or group.

Program evaluation as a technology cannot, of course, by itself be responsible if key parties do not see the big picture. Yet certain questions must be considered when critiquing the actual use of the technology of program evaluation, including:

- Do the program and the evaluation reflect an appreciation of patterens of need and risk as they are experienced by certain groups?
- Is there a target group or target area being addressed by the program?
- Does the selected target reflect appreciation of natural geographical (neighborhood) and social distinctions (e.g., race, class) between groups?

The evaluation process and the evaluation per se do not really cause these questions to be considered. It might be argued that this is the responsibility of planners and programmers. Admittedly, evaluators are influenced by political, economic, and cultural forces that structure the range of "appropriate" purposes and strategies for policies and programs (see discussion in Chapters 4 and 5). Further, the very concepts that helping professionals use in programs and agencies often imply both an individual (discrete) focus and an emphasis upon "need" rather than risk. Both of these forces, those focusing upon purposes and strategies as well as those reflecting the influence of certain concepts, are really responsible for programs and evaluation often missing the "bigger picture."

Certainly program evaluation and evaluators cannot be held fully responsible for this. But the dominant perspective of program evaluation as a set of technical procedures certainly does not encourage any significant actors to routinely examine how the very problems are being framed prior to programs being formulated. In fact, the case might be made that the technology of program evaluation, as it is often practiced in the political context in which it is embedded, might actually contribute to the perpetuation of prevailing definitions of problems. Such definitions, of course, influence and reflect purposes of policy, and such definitions are implicit in the programs that become the objects of evaluation.

GROUPS AND TARGETS

Several years ago Akers, in assessing the critical questions at the very core of the social sciences, identified possible choices in program perspectives, including:

- Why does this person think or do this?
- Why does this group do more or less of this?

- How does this individual learn how to do something?
- How does this group transmit certain behaviors to others?
- Of all the behaviors and conditions that exist, why does society respond to some and not others?[5]

In the social sciences, each of these questions has generated much theory and research. In fact, the very questions suggest different theoretical perspectives: question 1 is associated with psychodynamic theory; question 2 is associated with social structural theory, especially socially induced stress theory; question 3 is associated with learning theory; question 4 is associated with social learning or cultural transmission theory; and question 5 is associated with interactional(ist) theory.

The point here is not to review the theories as they relate to the particular questions; rather, it is that program choices are made relative to the questions that are selected by the people who create policy and program. Programs reflect choices and emphasis upon certain questions. Put another way, programs reflect a choice to ignore or pursue certain questions. Such questions are very significant in framing problem definitions, and certainly very significant in framing groups and targets upon which to focus.

Again it may be argued that the program evaluation process and evaluators are not responsible for the selection of the questions that guide and direct program strategies. Nonetheless, a technology that merely reflects somebody's preference for certain questions to guide activity is a technology that can inadvertently lead to overlooking alternative questions and interventions.

It is safe to say that, of the major questions cited above, the first one—a classical causation question focusing on the person—is the one that dominates and influences many program interventions. Further, in the context of the previously discussed concepts of need and risk, current prevailing operationalizing of policy tends to stress need over risk. Groups already in need, such as pregnant teenagers, are the ones that usually are considered at the program level. Groups at risk, such as potentially pregnant teenagers, are seldom considered at the program level, although they receive considerable attention in literature and discussion. For this risk group, programmatic resources would have to be used at very early points and in new social contexts, such as in primary school and in and among natural social networks in the community.

The above discussion presents choices—choices in targets, individuals, and/ or groups—and it also suggests choices concerning need and/or risk.[6] To respond at the program level to individuals who are pregnant is to say, after the fact, that the target is the group (the pregnant individuals) who need service.

At the other end of the continuum, programs can choose as a target a group that shares certain characteristics associated with "early" pregnancy. This could include income, family structure, school performance, attendance at certain schools (elementary), housing location, and so on. In a particular community, these characteristics could help define those who are at risk of becoming pregnant at an "early" age. However, it should be noted, especially in light of our previous discussion of issues, that, if the group is noticed as being more at risk, the bigger picture of social structure still may not be fully appreciated. In fact, when need and/or risk is seen as higher with certain groups, there may be a tendency to see the group itself as deficient or as the major cause of its own need and risk.

Programs that stress individual case interventions can also focus on preventing subsequent problems for the individuals. Similarly, group prevention efforts will probably have to deal with some individual cases where the need has not been averted. The issue here is choice, and choice in terms of emphasis at the program level.

Once again the technology of program evaluation has limited, if any, culpability in the selecting and framing of targets. Nonetheless, program staff and evaluators should carefully and critically consider how they define and select program targets and alternatives. Without such consideration, program evaluation runs the risk of reinforcing certain program selections as the "correct" or "appropriate" ones.

In selecting and framing targets—whether they are individuals and/or groups in need and/or at risk—it is also worth examining whether program interventions also attempt to modify agencies and other structures. Chapter 5 discussed how the functioning of agencies, especially in such areas as access, utilization, and referral patterns, could be of program concern. The question here is, does the program being evaluated emphasize possible goals of organizational change? If and when the answer is no, then it can be said that the technology of program evaluation is being applied to some (individuals and groups in need) and not to others (organizations).

The case might even be made that targets are more likely to be individuals and groups in need when expert managers hire expert program evaluators. Conversely, it might be hypothesized that, when consumers and community members are significant actors, programs and program evaluation tend to focus upon the host agency's possible malfunctioning. These last two conjectures in turn indicate the importance of considering whether program evaluation is operating in the context of organizational maintenance or organizational change. Finally, it is important to consider whether some program evaluation has a latent function in deflecting attention from possible targets and goals, that is, the living situation of certain groups and the possible change of relations between groups in the society.

WHO DOES THE PROGRAM EVALUATION?

Conventional discussion of this issue typically focuses upon who does the evaluation and when. More specifically, the discussion reviews whether an outsider to an agency should be brought in to do program evaluation, and when is the appropriate time to begin such evaluation.[7]

Generally the literature on these questions suggests that program evaluation should heavily involve an agency's professional staff. That is, staff members should become, in part, the subjects and objects of the evaluation.

Similarly, recent discussion suggests that evaluation is an integral part of planning, and therefore evaluation decisions should be made in the context of problem specification and goal selection.

These thoughts about participation and timing are supported by several considerations. First, there is the acceptance of the principle that those affected by, and those who have to collect the data and information for, program evaluation should be involved in the evaluation decision-making process. Although this is related to a principle of fairness, there also is a pragmatic recognition that the raw material of evaluation often has to be collected by staff members. If staff members were not involved sufficiently, it is reasoned, they might not effectively carry out their data-gathering and thus might jeopardize the very process and working of the evaluation process. Further, if the evaluation were imposed upon staff members without their significant involvement, then they would be unlikely to ultimately utilize and incorporate evaluation results into future program efforts. In short, behind the issues of participation and timing is the recognition that, if evaluation produced a defensive reaction on the part of professional staff, their unmet needs and interests could adversely affect both evaluation and subsequent programming.

Yet, in many settings, professional staff still have little or no involvement in evaluation-related decisions. It is significant that: (1) there is recognition by human service professionals that there are people who have special skills in doing evaluation, and that these people typically are not in service program settings; (2) no one really argues, however, that normatively the "outside" expert should shape and control the evaluation process; and (3) there is a high degree of acceptance by service professionals and evaluators that evaluation should be intimately tied to the goal-setting stage of program development and design.

Despite these "insights," some very thorny problems remain. In all-too-many instances, because of some perceived or actual imperative, outside experts are hired to do a fast and "necessary" evaluation to show compliance with funder and/or board expectations. Evaluation in this context often becomes monitoring, and it is done in order to demonstrate that the program is accountable to others, especially funders. The specific evaluation format is often chosen *after* the program is in operation and is heavily dominated and controlled by the "expert" (outsider). There is little or no possibility in this context of late entry by the evaluator for any sophisticated design, i.e., experimental design or one of the appropriate alternatives discussed previously. Critical deficiencies in the areas of randomness and comparison are thus routinely produced. There will be more on this specific consideration in the discussion below of the decision context of evaluation.

Also, there remains the unresolved question of community and lay involvement in program evaluation. Although professionals have become increasingly convinced of the need for evaluation and the right of professionals to be involved in decision-making concerning evaluation, there is no such clarity on the role of "others." Perhaps there can never be, but nonetheless the role that others can or should have in evaluation does affect program evaluation.[8] If, for example, the principle of involving those who are affected by the evaluation in the evaluation is accepted, does that principle require consumers and community groups to be involved? If yes, does this mean that the framing of problems and conditions to be addressed programmatically should heavily stress community expectations? If yes, does this mean that the community expectations to be addressed in any subsequent program should become a major consideration in selecting goals for the programs being developed?

Other, related questions involve what criteria should be used to develop and evaluate programs. Specifically, what weight should be given to satisfaction when reviewing programs; what role and weight should be given to relevance, that is, how well the program works with respect to community expectations; and how should importance and energy be allocated to effort, effect, and satisfaction criteria in program evaluation?

It is conceivable that certain community groups will frame problems differently from agencies and that community groups might stress goals that include more and different program efforts. Community groups might also place a greater value on their feelings and reactions to how programs are created and delivered than do professionals and agencies. In short, if the principle of involving those who are affected is accepted, evaluators may find that the importance of effort and satisfaction measures may be more important to one constituency (community groups) than to others (experts and professionals).

Obviously, significant degrees of community involvement are difficult to achieve. Considerations of time, money, organization, and staff interests work against such involvement. Further, not all professionals are comfortable with heavy community involvement in their program decisions. The net result, however, is that evaluation efforts will occur with a particular set of actors framing problems, selecting goals, and interpreting results. It cannot be assumed that if other actors, such as community groups and interests, were involved the program evaluation would be the same, or nearly the same, as if they were not involved. This issue suggests that the technology of program evaluation is heavily contaminated by both the actors and the interests that are affirmed in the deployment of the technology.

To make this point more concrete, let us use an example involving the possible interpretation of evaluation results. Say a community was given the opportunity for involvement only in the interpretation of evaluation results. Suppose those findings indicated that a given program intervention did not produce the intended discrete results, that is, it did not achieve the specific goals selected by funders and/or the agency. Would it necessarily follow that the program being evaluated would be delegitimated by the community? From the community's standpoint, the data might suggest that the program did not work because insufficient resources were allocated in the first place. Therefore, according to the community, more resources should be allocated, and the program should be maintained and in fact expanded. Or additional programs should be added that would interact with and reinforce the original program, which would be maintained, not eliminated or modified.

Similarly, a community might be concerned with exercising enough political clout to ensure that it is seen and respected. Therefore, it might regard the program being evaluated as a symbol of community power, not merely as something that is defined as effective or ineffective in the narrower terms of the experimental design. In short, program effectiveness is eclipsed by the power and interests of the community. Obviously the downside of this issue is that, historically, many communities have been used and abused by token funding for token programs that merely perpetuate dependency and make life predictable in the larger community.

To summarize this issue, the technology of program evaluation in no way assures that there will be timely involvement of all parties that would be affected by a program and its evaluation, nor does it address the complex decisions about the division of labor among professional staff, experts, and community. And to complicate this issue further, it can be assumed that each of these three parties has its own distinctive interests and perspectives that could affect the selection of goals and the interpretation of evaluation results.

DECISION CONTEXT

Earlier in this chapter reference was made to how program evaluation design could be affected by who frames the problems and what goals are addressed by programs. It was suggested that this meta-consideration could adversely affect the range and types of program options developed and therefore ultimately affect the very object (the program) being evaluated.

To look at this issue in a slightly different way, consider the possible influences and constraints that can emanate from the decision contexts affecting programs and program evaluation. Washington has suggested that program evaluation is always affected by the interests of three interacting constituencies: the donor/funder group, the provider group, and the recipient group.[9] Specifically, he suggests that the behavior and the accountability of the provider groups is shaped in part by influences from both other groups.

Crucial to the relation between the provider group and the donor/funder group is the issue of compliance. Compliance means that the program to be offered and evaluated must meet the expectations, on a variety of levels, of the donor/funder. One expectation could be that money spent in a program be used for legitimate purposes in a nonfraudulent manner. It could mean spending the money efficiently in a fiscally appropriate way, such as comparing the relative cost of a service or intervention to the relative cost of other services or interventions. If the funder states these types of expectations, and only these types, then the program evaluation must heavily stress documentation of behaviors, costs, and comparative costs.

If the funder also expects specific results or effects, then the compliance function will be extended to determine whether the effect (i.e., a stated goal) was achieved. Obviously, the latter expectation can be fused with the former. The issue here is the expectation of the funder relative to the program to be evaluated. What is expected and along what dimensions?

Relevant to the issue of possible interplay between funder and provider are two topics discussed in Chapter 4. First, what are the consequences of the possible purposes and program strategies preferred by the funder? Does the donor really wish (propose) resources to be allocated along some dimension: burden, investment, development, social stability? Does the funder assume that program strategies will have a particular focus, such as substitution, preparation, alteration, provisions of amenities, control? Second, does the funder really wish to see the world of possible intervention as merely serving individuals in need? Does the funder specify which kinds of individuals are in need? Does the funder wish to focus on the social risks that certain groups face?

It would be nice to say that the funders can consider approach all of the above choices openly. However, conventional standards as well as clear and obvious political considerations suggest that funding for programs is often available for people who either are valued or who cannot be ignored. In both cases, often an individual focus and a priority for demonstrated need take precedence. Conversely, funders are less likely to focus heavily on certain groups who are at risk precisely because they are not valued and/or are politically impotent.

The net result of this byplay is that the programs that are created are often politically safe and are not focused upon addressing structural issues that have an adverse impact on groups at risk. Because of this, the technology of program evaluation becomes heavily involved with and shaped by the preferences and conventions of funders and their range of welfare purposes and strategies.

If we now look to the intersection between providers and recipient groups, the key concern is not necessarily compliance, especially in the fiscal sense. Rather, it focuses upon the relevance of the program to the social situation of groups. Specifically, the recipient groups and would-be recipient groups are quite interested in the key organizational issues of access and availability of programs. In short, the possible effect upon providers would be that they would frame problems and conditions to be addressed differently, and the purposes and strategies could become quite different. The proposed programs could become more concerned with changing conditions in the social structure that are associated with risk. Program evaluation in this context would then focus upon rather different goals being or not being achieved, such as changing income levels or years of education.

Just as it would have been nice to say that funders can and will consider a broad range of fundable purposes and strategies, it is equally nice to say that providers will consider, perhaps equally, the interests and situations facing groups at risk. The reality is, however, that program developers often cannot be "rewarded" by communities and groups at risk for moving towards programs that focus on different, alternative purposes and strategies. Given the absence of a countervailing inducement, the availability of funding for only certain purposes, and also the training and predispositions of many professional providers, providers often move toward subtle and not-so-subtle expectations of the funder. The possibility of "good" public relations and "community improvement" may be seen as too subtle, vague and not compelling.

Up to now we have been using the term "funder" as a key influence upon the programs created and ultimately upon the program evaluation. What about boards? If anything, in this period of management of scarce resources, many board members are valued because they bring skills and competencies that are needed by the agency. An agency needs board members who are conversant with legal issues, annual fiscal reports, and fundraising. Predictably, boards often are composed of lawyers, accountants, and wealthy or at least well-connected people.

This type of board composition often has an unanticipated consequence. The board looks, feels, and is different from both the people served and from the groups at risk in the social environment of the agency. In many instances, this can lead to boards being comfortable with only a narrow range of purposes and program strategies with individual and need-driven focuses. Further, it also can encourage board members to focus disproportionately upon the short-term fiscal efficiency of efforts in program evaluation rather than effects, or even longer-term effects, or social benefits.

The actual experience in many private agencies suggests the following scenario and discussion relative to program evaluation: let us see if what we are doing is efficient; let us see if the evaluation can help us define new goals that can enable us to reduce costs; let us see if it "makes more sense" to think about serving a different population or problem; is what we are doing just not affordable? In short, although providers in the decision context are subject to pressures and expectations from both funders and recipients, the pressures may not be equally strong. This being so, program evaluation can easily move in the direction of the interests, purposes, and questions of funder and funder-related constituencies.

KNOWLEDGE AND PROGRAMS

Years ago, Suchman suggested that programs can be classified according to their stage of development, ranging from pilot to institutionalized programming.[10] Others have suggested that practice interventions can be categorized according to level of validated knowledge associated with the practice intervention.[11] In their own ways, both suggestions acknowledge that, in many instances, actual program interventions often have been based on limited levels of validated knowledge. This insight raises a critical question—just how much emphasis should be given to the experimental design in program evaluation? Why should a sophisticated design be applied to early or preliminary stages of both knowledge and program development?

Such questions encourage another look at a very basic issue—what is known and not known by the program people? Do they know who has a problem, the consequences of the problems, who has the risk, and at what levels? Does the program staff know from research which interventions have some success and which do not, and which are successful with which groups, under which conditions? Given the very strong possibility that program staff may not know very much about the interrelation of groups, problems/conditions, and effectiveness of specific interventions, then reservations about experimental designs are in order.

Evaluation, and in fact the very design of programs and goals, should stress gathering information, learning more about needs, wants, and the distinct situations facing certain groups and populations, the actual exchanges between recipients and programs, the sequential steps and effects of different program activities, and so on. In short, the evaluation should not test in the pure sense; it should absorb, take in, be fluid—all with an eye toward eventually being able to make structured interventions that are capable of being tested in a rigorous way, i.e., by experimental design.

By moving in this direction, that is, backing away from the premature and sometimes ritualistic commitment to experimental design, evaluation efforts could affirm some very key points. First, the paucity of what we know in the helping fields could be accepted in a nondefensive way. Second, professionals would be encouraged to see that they have something to offer in evaluation—as the eyes and ears of the program, they are often the ones who can define program goals that bridge practice and research. In this way, research really could become a domain owned by the practitioner; the practitioner could be encouraged to see the interrelation among practice, research, and the generation of theory. Simple and practical ways to link knowledge and program include reviewing previous program research and the amount of validated knowledge in the professional and program literature.

Yet the reality of both profession and practice often work against purposeful and appropriate linking of stage of programming to evaluation. On the professional end, especially in those quarters dominated by academics and researchers, there is pressure to do more sophisticated research. "Sophisticated" all-too-often means precisely experimental design. The result, all too often, is that pilot programs, and programs that encourage the study of the process of a given intervention, are avoided as being "too soft," too qualitative, and not sufficiently conclusive.

On the practice end, there is a different consideration, and it, too, reflects the reality of external pressures and forces contaminating program evaluation. All too frequently, practitioners become committed to a program strategy without having some level of validated knowledge to support such commitment. In some instances, this commitment can be confronted, even challenged, by the call for an appropriate type of program evaluation. Yet the program evaluator sometimes comes into the agency after the staff has committed itself to a strategy, and thus encounters a staff who feel they are the objects of study. Staff and program evaluator come to see each other as possessing very different skills and perspectives. The net result is that practice and evaluation often remain quite separated.

If the stage of programming could be honestly identified relative to how much knowledge is justifying some intervention, then program staff might see practice and formal inquiry as being less distinct and different. In short, an excessive commitment to experimental design may actually contribute to the estrangement of practice from research. When this occurs, both practice and research are adversely affected.

WHAT HAPPENS TO EVALUATION?

As long as program evaluation remains a possible element in the accountability process, we cannot assume that decision-makers and constituencies will deal with the findings of evaluation independent of their points of view and that findings derived from program evaluation will not be used selectively or for reasons other than modifications of a given program.

Program evaluation often produces findings that are used against agencies, programs, and staff. In a period of less-than-rigorous commitment to human welfare, there remains a rigorous commitment to program evaluation. The latter is often used to justify and carry out the spirit and specifics of the former—the managing of scarce resources, the allocating of dwindling resources.

This being the case, in too many instances an adaptation, even a "game" with its own rules, evolves in agencies and programs. The "game" reflects some or all of the following: (1) the program administrator's attempts to get a reading of what such key groups as board members and funders want in terms of population, coverage, modality of interventions, and so on; (2) the scaling down of ambitious goals and the avoidance of controversial goals and even controversial problems or conditions; and (3) the selection of doable and feasible goals.

Each of these three activities impinges negatively upon the evaluation design model while still allowing for verbal commitments to the evaluation model. With respect to the first, administrators can read the political environment to determine valued populations and problems/conditions. This is important because if interventions do not work, the commitment to some valued population or acceptable problem may cushion the possible negative response. Similarly, if a specific, limited intervention is expended towards a devalued population, then the intervention may continue no matter what program effects occur, as long as the program sufficiently communicates a symbolic message to the group being served and is relatively affordable.

With respect to the second and third activities cited above, what is being suggested is that administrators and staff often perceive that because program evaluation is mandated by funding requirements and convention, fighting it is fruitless. Therefore, they sometimes develop program responses that ensure high rates of success, and that are very centrist, even conservative. For example, a mental health agency or family agency could choose goals and interventions that take them away from such structural issues as unemployment connected to a local factory or industry. Instead, the agency might focus upon counseling and support to those who become unemployed, or it might focus upon behavioral goals of x number of employment referrals, y number of resume writing sessions, etc.

Such program responses may be appropriate and functional. However, the overall problem is that with evaluation tied to accountability, agencies and their staff often find themselves moving in the direction of "safe" programming where evaluation results will be embedded in issues tied to considerations other than science.

CLIENT RIGHTS AND ETHICAL CONSIDERATIONS

Often the "human side" of evaluation is presented in the ethics of program evaluation.[12] But the human side also is present in, and even dominates in the last analysis, all of the issues raised in this chapter. In fact, a case might also be made that all of the previous issues raised are potentially riddled with ethical dimensions.

Nonetheless, showing one's human side and one's sense of professional ethics can constrain the program and program-evaluation process. If we start with a recognition that clients—be they individuals, groups, or communities—have rights, then these rights must be seen relative to any possible evaluation activity. Clients, for example, cannot be denied a program arbitrarily because of a need to test the program and to have a control group. In fact, certain clients have to receive interventions, and right now, no matter what the program evaluation imperative is. Thus, the right of a client to receive help can and will constrain the orderly sorting of clients into test and control groups.

In related fashion, clients need to be informed, and they have a right to decide to participate or not participate in test programs. Some probably will decide not to be in a test program, although their need will often remain. At a minimum, this process of informing the client, and respecting the client's right to decide not to participate, slows down the program. This can lead programs to subtly encourage clients to become involved and to stay the course of the program intervention. It might also lead some programs to be less forthcoming in the disclosure process when securing consents. This could include an implicit message that if clients do not participate in this program they may not be served in some other way.

Another aspect of client rights has to do with protecting clients' anonymity. Typically the evaluation process handles this by saying that the data on individuals will be aggregated into group data and that there will be no reporting in identifiable ways of data on individual clients. Further, programs must stipulate the manner in which data will be stored and who has access to it.

Over the years, the norms and the process of protecting the confidentiality of clients who enter the experimental process have developed greatly and served clients well. However, there are two specific instances where the quest for confidentiality is not fully successful. First, in some service areas where there is a central funding source that reimburses for or purchases interventions on a client-by-client basis, there can be a requirement that names and group identifiers be reported to sources of which the client or client system is not aware. In some instances, neither agency nor professional staff go out of the way to explain fully the labyrinth through which information may be sent out of the agency/program once clients sign consent forms. This problem can arise even when programs proceed without formal evaluation.

A second instance involves the aggregating of data, perhaps from several agencies and programs over time, and then noticing certain patterns that may not have been central to an original program evaluation. Data collected over time might show that certain geographical areas, occupations, etc., are highly associated with certain problems, such as dropping out of school, cocaine use, or HIV infection. The mere collection and assemblage of data could lead to detection of patterns and possible interpretations of patterns that could have unintended adverse effects upon certain communities, groups, and occupations. Obviously the ethical issue here is not distinct to the evaluation—rather, it is in the assemblage of data and future decisions based on such data. In logic and in the social sciences, this issue is captured in the phrase "ecological fallacy"—making incorrect, inappropriate decisions about specific members of large groups or cohorts. In this day and age, this incorrectness may very well be unethical. Although program evaluation is not the ultimate source of this fallacy, the evaluation process can provide some of the raw material for such disturbing and unethical responses; responses that are often framed, as much of evaluation is, within the dispassionate term "efficiency."

CONCLUSION

This chapter discussed some of the difficulties in carrying out program evaluation. Many of the issues raised were related to the audiences, constraints, and interests operating in the context of program evaluation. These forces suggest limited choices concerning the use of program evaluation. Such choices are clearly not just methodological and technical in nature. Rather, the choices and the issues are inherently tied to ethics and politics, and these, in turn, interact strongly with the "pure" technology of program evaluation.

NOTES

1. A. Rubin and E. Babbie, *Research Methods in Social Work* (Belmont, CA: Wadsworth, 1989), 251–253, and R. Grinnell, Jr., and M. Williams, *Research in Social Work: A Primer* (Itasca, IL: Peacock, 1980), 146–149.
2. J. Simon, *Basic Research Methods in Social Science* (New York: Random House, 1978) 195–196, 302.
3. R. O. Washington, *Program Evaluation in the Human Services* (Columbus: Ohio State University Press, 1979), 13.
4. R. Lowry, *Social Problems: A Critical Analysis of Theories and Public Policies* (Lexington, MA: D.C. Heath, 1978), 3–18.
5. R. Akers, "Problems in the Sociology of Deviance: Societal Definitions and Behavior," *Social Forces* (June, 1968): 455–465.

6. M. Bloom, *Primary Prevention: The Possible Science* (Englewood Cliffs, NJ: Prentice-Hall, 1981), 39–41 for brief discussion of sociocultural events and 175–177 for social stresses; R. H. Price, R. Ketterer, B. C. Bader, and J. Monahan, eds., *Prevention in Mental Health: Research, Policy and Practice* (Beverly Hills, CA: Sage Publications, 1980) for a discussion of the role of mediating structures rather than an emphasis upon psychological well-being of individual people.
7. Grinnell, 257–258 for a discussion of program evaluator's role.
8. T. M. Meenaghan, "M.I.S. and Organizational Relations: Politics, Values and Technology," *The Journal of Applied Social Sciences* 13 (Spring/Summer, 1989): 346–352 for discussion of role of participants in the operations of management information systems.
9. T. M. Meenaghan, R. O. Washington, and Robert Ryan, *Macro Practice* (New York: Free Press, 1982), 233.
10. E. Suchman, *Evaluative Research* (New York: Russell Sage Foundation, 1967).
11. G. T. Powers, T. M. Meenaghan, and B. Toomey, *Practice Focused Research* (Englewood Cliffs, NJ: Prentice-Hall, 1985), 10–18.
12. Grinell and Williams, 7–11.

PART FIVE

Conclusion

Part Five frames the previous discussions of scientific inquiry, reason, and politics within a broad human context. Chapter 12 discusses topics related to the very complexity of the social world wherein policy, programs, and inquiry are pursued. Philosophical issues related to the concepts of person and responsibility are also raised. The chapter suggests that inquiry is not influenced only by reason and politics, but also by some very major considerations associated with values and valuing. The book concludes with the rather nonscientific position that the helping fields should engage in and revisit identifying core values that can and should influence all derived scientific inquiry. Without this, inquiry might come attached to and reflect values that ultimately do not reflect the traditional value perspectives of the helping fields.

CHAPTER 12

Context and Choices

There are several possible ways to end a book. One is to review what has been discussed and to summarize the major points raised. A second way is to identify some of the major themes that cut across the different chapters. Finally, in a conclusion, authors can raise those questions that have become clearer to them through the process of writing the book.

To some degree, our conclusion is going to reflect all three of these, although the emphasis will be upon themes and questions. In stressing these two specific considerations, we will explicate some choices within the profession, the agencies we practice within, and even within the larger society.

IDENTIFYING BASIC THEMES

This book has really proceeded on the assumption that care, how we help people, is a social construction.[1] This means that people and institutions within the larger society simultaneously create and reflect perceptions and values concerning how care should proceed. It also means that how human service professionals operationalize help and how they identify their intervention perspectives and skills together reflect perceptions and values concerning the process of care.

In this book we have tried to show that the two domains of thinking about care, i.e., the larger society and the helping professionals, are strongly interrelated. Some of our discussion has attempted to stress that the "larger" political world has influenced the professional world and vice-versa. We have suggested that although the two orders—social and professional—interrelate, the actual ongoing relationship is skewed in the direction of the larger political world being very significant in influencing the emerging agenda of human service professionals. An agenda in recent years has greatly reflected the profession's concerns, admittedly quite legitimate, about the profession's own group interests and its struggles with the issues of allocation of scarce resources. This has been especially marked in the context of the norms and values of accountability and evaluation.

This book is an attempt to rethink the relations between the profession and scientific inquiry. It also suggests a rethinking of the relationship between the profession and the larger society. We hope that the reader does not close the book and conclude that we have argued against scientific inquiry. We have not. We have recognized that for several years the profession has been at a point where accounting, especially relative to resources, has been uppermost in people's minds. Also we have recognized that the profession must, as so many have stated in the past 20 years, develop more confidence in its interventions. Those interventions must be questioned initially, if for no other reason than that we, the human service professionals, need to develop an appreciation of critical self-inquiry. Out of this very process of inquiry and questioning can come some validated knowledge about programs and interventions. If this indeed does occur, our professional identity can only be enhanced. Our professional interests may even be served—provided we are clear about the perspectives, goals, and values we are seeking.

Inquiry in action is not the problem. The problem is placing the inquiry in a sea of complexity in the social world, a world that has many values, some of which are in conflict, and many distinct interest groups, some of which are also in conflict. In valuing inquiry as we do, we are stating two points. The first is that any value, and certainly the value of scientific inquiry, must have a behavioral reference point; the value, if it is to mean anything, must be acted upon. Professional integrity requires that human service professionals become proponents of, and actors who reflect, the value of scientific inquiry. The second point is that actual carrying out of scientific inquiry must proceed with an appreciation of the context and choices surrounding the process of scientific inquiry. In many respects, to understand only the first point and not the second is to encourage the confusion between technology and scientific inquiry. It may also, implicitly at least, encourage members of the larger society—those who reflect certain values and political and economic interests—to shape and constrain the very parameters and purposes of intervention, as well as the tools utilized to support such interventions. These tools would, of course, include needs assessment and program evaluation. For intimately associated with such tools of inquiry, perhaps the very base or foundation of these tools when they are put into action, are such important concerns as:

- Which questions (and whose questions) should be stressed?
- Which interests are served by which program designs?
- Who should participate and at what points in designing and studying interventions—creation, collection, interpretation, etc.?

These are crucial questions, and they emerge even stronger after one recalls and reviews the material in the book on the technology of specific inquiry.

We need to be clear that the questions just cited promote answers that reflect choices in terms of values and interests. Although the methodology of the inquiry may appear to be neutral, it usually is not because of the values and interests that interact with inquiry as it is pursued. Usually there is a context within which inquiry proceeds, as well as there are consequences of the inquiry. The context and the consequences of inquiry must be appreciated as much as the inquiry itself. This does not argue against scientific inquiry; rather, it affirms the wonderful complexity of the social world within which the inquiry is employed. Ultimately professionals who participates in the inquiry will have to confront the questions raised above and be aware of how their answers will influence their professional behavior.

SOCIAL CONTEXT AND INQUIRY

A specific contextual issue related to inquiry has to be stressed and appreciated: the interplay between the dominant culture and professional perspectives. For the last decade, if not longer, there has been a reemphasis upon conservative political thought. This is not necessarily good or bad. Imbedded in this development, or redevelopment, has been a heavy emphasis upon the individual. This also is not necessarily good or bad.

What is far more questionable in our minds is that conservatism and individualism have been wedded to a particular notion of government and social responsibility. This point will be elaborated upon later in the chapter. For now we would like to stress that the conservatism and the focus upon individuals has encouraged human service professionals to become more conservative and nearly exclusive in their focusing upon individuals. From a value and professional standpoint this is too narrow and unacceptable.

Obviously, this nexus between culture and profession has had serious ramifications for definitions of problems, strategies of intervention, and evaluation of selected program designs. As the society has become more conservative and less welfare-oriented, problems and programs have once again stressed malfunctioning individuals. Tools of inquiry such as needs assessment and program evaluation in action often appear to reflect this implicit approval of problem definition and program strategy.

It is very difficult to explore this issue of how the social world affects helping professionals. At one level, we do not like to put ourselves under the magnifying glass. At another level, we do not like to negate the very serious and weighty issues associated with the relationship of the larger social context and the human service professions. Embedded in this relationship are the legitimate concerns of (a) practitioners' preferences to work with individuals; and (b) practitioners' right to focus upon certain theories, perspectives and skills. But, although we respect the rights of individual practitioners who wish to see the social world through the lens of individual functioning and malfunctioning, we feel that it is useful to note that current specific professional practice preferences are almost perfectly correlated with the specific developments in the larger society that stress individualism and diminished social responsibility on the part of the government.

This interplay between the larger society and the profession has produced distinct parameters within which human service professionals operate. One parameter has been sharply defined by the profession's preoccupation with certain questions and concepts, including concepts that influence definition of need, needs assessment, programs, and program evaluation. As mentioned earlier in the book, Akers long ago suggested that the social sciences and the helping professions can structure their assessments and interventions around five questions:

- Why is a person doing something?
- Why is a group doing something more so than other groups?
- How does an individual learn to do something?
- How does the group transmit its learned behaviors?
- Why do some phenomena or groups get defined as problematical.[2]

Considerations of power and structure are most present in analysis and interventions related to the second and fifth questions. Not surprisingly, these very questions are the ones that are often pursued less seriously in our society. Similarly, these two questions all too often do not greatly shape how professionals approach, study, and intervene in the social world. Because of this interplay between society and professions, certain needs assessment techniques are stressed, and ultimately certain kinds of programs become evaluated.

Even when the society and the helping professions look at groups and group phenomena, there still may not be a structural approach, i.e., they may not see problems of groups as being intimately tied to status, role and power configurations in society. In some instances, a movement away from a purely individual focus has led to studying and modifying groups. However, groups are often seen as being somewhat apart from the larger social order. Two reasons explain this: (1) certain groups are seen as different and inferior; and (2) the larger society has limited interest in seeking possible links between itself and the "inferior" group. Scientific inquiry in this context can and does lead to an excessive preoccupation with group characteristics and resulting changes of members of the groups. Inquiry does not necessarily lead to analysis or evaluation of specific structural issues, such as income/asset distributions and power differentials relative to race, gender, and class.

The fortunate fact is that, in many ways and on many levels, the American structure works for many people. Many people for whom the structure works—and such people are disproportionately white, male, and living in households with two wage earners—have difficulty seeing, much less empathizing with, those groups for whom the structure works less well. Concomittantly, just as the culture may reinforce a limited structural perspective within the larger society, the helping professions may be constrained by their preoccupation with individual causation questions and concerns within a therapeutic perspective. In closing the book, we are suggesting that professionals and training programs should spend time identifying how the questions suggested by others influence professionals and how, in some sense, the questions reflect values and influences far away from structure.

Still another way in which the context of social work impinges upon care and inquiry is the relationship between volunteerism and how we think about social responsibility. In recent years, we not only have seen the rhetoric and the reality stress the private, local sector of welfare, we have seen the near-glorification of volunteerism. Nobody can be against volunteerism, but volunteerism that is designed to replace government responsibility is very questionable.

Volunteerism, when divorced from governmental obligations or when serving in place of governmental responsibilities, often has certain characteristics. By definition it is discretionary—it can or cannot be given, it can be directed to some and not to others, it typically means no significant changes in relationships among people, and, simply because it requires that individuals choose to volunteer, it often is directed at other individuals. In short, much of volunteerism is best understood by the term *charity* rather than the term *right*.

If charity and volunteerism exist in the context of a broad spectrum of human rights, that is one thing; if charity and volunteerism exist within contraction of the welfare state and human rights, that is something else again. More specifically, volunteerism has often emerged in the context of attempts to limit public responsibility. This being the case, needs assessment and program evaluation often operate within a context in which volunteerism is espoused and where government is assumed to be uninvolved.

Buried in this particular context is a terrible confusion in our society between responsibility and provision, a confusion that affects the perception and actual use of scientific inquiry. For all too often it is assumed, even argued, that government should not provide programs and services, because others—local agencies, maybe even voluntary groups—can and should do it. Even if this were so, it does not necessarily mean that there should not be public responsibility to address certain needs and rights of certain groups. And yet, that is precisely what happens: Provision and responsibility becomes confused, even seen as one context—choice. In the affirmation of the private and local delivery of programs, the government is often argued against by conservatives. The result is, of course, limited or no public responsibility. Even among groups that are deeply committed to families and family life—the so-called traditional conservatives—that value commitment often gets circumscribed by confusion over concepts of responsibility and provision. Whether intended or not, in this example, the value of no government often takes priority over promotion of families and family well-being.

Because of this type of confusion about responsibility, inquiry often comes to be identified in a political way with the case for or against government provision. What becomes lost in the confusion is the more basic question of social responsibility. Social responsibility, of course, is a philosophical question, not a scientific one; but, like more profound philosophical questions, it can and will interact at points with the carrying out of scientific inquiry.

Examining the particular contextual issue of responsibility and provision forces us back to making choices, to affirming some values. These choices and values cannot be handled by "better" or "more" inquiry. Better inquiry, whether it be in assessing needs or evaluating programs, can only go so far. Inquiry is never context-free. For example, if we take the increasing awareness of the apparent need for triage, we can see limits to inquiry, we can see context and choices, and we ultimately can see values. Triage requires that choices be made accordingly to some specific values: rights, pressing needs, likelihood of successful interventions, and so on. Triage has emerged as an issue, as well as a solution, in the context of scarce resources.[3] It entails judgment concerning who will be the object of intervention, given the fact that resources cannot be allocated to all, certainly not to all at the same time. Triage should involve some calculation of the use of resources relative to severity of need and likelihood of success of a given intervention.

When applied to the social world, triage could easily suggest that needs assessment and program evaluation be employed in the very determination of need and the likelihood of effective interventions relative to certain problems. Triage is affected by choices that will severely affect the manner in which needs assessment and program evaluation might be operationalized. For example, could or should the concept of risk be purposefully considered within triage, and if so, to what degree? Could or should the concept of risk be applied to groups and not just individuals? Similarly, to what degree should concepts of maintenance and prevention be explicated, in addition to remediation?

Questions such as these may or may not be applied to triage and as such could affect how needs assessments and program evaluations might be conducted. If triage decisions were to focus upon risk, groups, and prevention, then the needs assessment might heavily stress structure, e.g., the access possibilities of certain groups to certain benefits, and the derived programs might focus upon changes in organizations. Conversely, a societal and professional focus upon need, individuals, and remediation might lead to needs assessment of cohorts and evaluations of programs designed to maximize individual functioning.

In and of itself, scientific inquiry does not determine how the inquiry will be employed in the context of triage, or, for that matter, in any other related provision and allocation policy decision strategy. Values and choices within the society and within the profession will ultimately define the configuration of intervention responses, as well as the scientific support for such responses and their continuance or termination.

PHILOSOPHICAL AND PROFESSIONAL VALUES

The preceding discussion stressed the relation among inquiry, values, and choices. This section specifies the "bottom line" context that affects inquiry. Basically this means that all inquiry is affected by three values or choices:

1. What is a human being, and what are the rights of human beings?
2. How much collective responsibility is required or desirable?
3. How much redistribution should be pursued within the society?

Whether or not the society, or for that matter the helping professions, purposefully think about these questions, they are always answered in society. Typically, in a pluralistic society, they are answered within the policy arena, especially the legislative arena. As they are answered, not only are the boundaries and contexts of inquiry defined, so too is the society's concept of the social ethic created. For this reason, policy-making can be seen as an ethical enterprise that normatively defines the way of, and purposes for inquiry. The corollary to this is also worth noting—creative thought about how and why to do needs assessment and program evaluation may actually influence and shape the policy that comes to be defined and translated to different groups.

To think creatively, the helping professionals are ultimately going to have to think more about their role and their values. Karl Rahner, in looking at the future of religion, said that religion always has three choices concerning how it wishes to position itself.[4] It can be in the culture, of the culture, or against the culture. Human service professionals often find themselves facing the same choices. As long as the helping professionals do not position themselves purposefully at variance with some of the ends pursued in the dominant society, there may be some reason to infer that inquiry that is sanctioned will be somewhat predictable and not lead to significant alterations of current arrangements. On the other hand, if the helping professions, or at least some of their members, do position themselves at variance with some of the current structural arrangements that are prevalent in our society, then the profession and the professionals will have to live with not just a normative view of practice, including inquiry and its uses, but also with a tolerance of high amounts of dissonance with their own culture. Amazingly, inquiry, especially in terms of operationalizing needs assessment and program evaluation, can easily lead to acceptance by and assimilation within the larger society. But the very same technology and spirit of inquiry can be anchored to a different view of the social structure and the role of the helping professions. It is ultimately in this most basic context that values and vision always must dominate inquiry.

CONCLUSION

This chapter has reviewed some of the major themes raised in the book and has also defined some of the major contextual constraints and issues that affect the use of inquiry.

- Care, the evaluation of care responses, and the very identifying of needs requiring care responses are special constructions.

- There is an interrelation among the larger society and the helping professions through the construct of care.

- Inquiry is important and necessary, and it is a requisite for achieving professional credibility and validating knowledge about interventions.

- Inquiry by professionals must always be seen within the context in which it is initiated and used.

With respect to the social context and inquiry, specific questions and issues raised in the book focused upon:

- The influence of political conservatism upon an individual focus within the helping professions;
- How volunteerism reinforces nonstructural approaches to care and the study of such;
- The confusion between responsibility and provision; and
- The myriad of philosophical and political questions generated by the emergence of triage.

In no way do we feel that science and scientific inquiry are inappropriate. But we emphasize that volitional elements on the group and individual level can and will influence inquiry in action. If they do not recognize this, the helping professions run the risk of inadvertently pursuing science as a secular religion, which puts professionals in the midst of current social and political arrangements.

We would like to end the book with the following questions: Who is this person (individually and collectively) who receives our attention? What is our responsibility to this person (individually and collectively)? These questions, as forms of inquiry themselves, obviously affect all subsequent constructions concerning care and the evaluation of interventions.

NOTES

1. P. Berger and T. Luckman, *The Social Construction of Reality: A Treatise in the Sociology of Knowledge* (Garden City, NY: Doubleday, 1966).
2. R. Akers, "Problems in the Sociology of Deviance: Social Definitions and Behavior," *Social Forces* 4 (June 1968): 455–465.
3. C. Coulton, M. Rosenbery and J. Yankey "Scarcity and the Rationing of Services," *Public Welfare* 39 (Summer 1981): 15–21.
4. K. Rahner, "The Diaspora Church," *Theological Investigations*. In G. A. McCool ed., *A Rahner Reader* (Delft: Dartor Langman and Todd, 1971), 89–98.

Author-Name Index

Subject Index